Changing Cultures,
Changing Lives

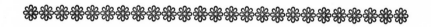

*An Ethnographic Study
of Three Generations
of Japanese Americans*

Christie W. Kiefer

❀❀❀❀❀❀❀❀❀❀❀❀❀❀❀❀❀❀❀❀❀❀❀❀❀❀❀❀❀❀❀❀❀❀❀❀

Changing Cultures

Changing Lives

 Jossey-Bass Publishers

San Francisco • Washington • London • 1974

CHANGING CULTURES, CHANGING LIVES
An Ethnographic Study of Three Generations of Japanese Americans
   by Christie W. Kiefer

Copyright © 1974 by: Jossey-Bass, Inc., Publishers
                      615 Montgomery Street
                      San Francisco, California 94111
                               &
Jossey-Bass Limited
                      3 Henrietta Street
                      London WC2E 8LU

Library of Congress Catalogue Card Number LC 74-3609

International Standard Book Number ISBN 0-87589-232-9

Manufactured in the United States of America

JACKET DESIGN BY WILLI BAUM

FIRST EDITION

Code 7423

The Jossey-Bass

Behavioral Science Series

For the issei

Preface

Changing Cultures, Changing Lives is an ethnographic study of the Japanese American community in San Francisco, aimed at showing how the cross-cultural study of personality change throughout the life cycle can enrich our understanding of man. Its contributions to behavioral science are of three kinds. First, it is the first complete ethnography of this important group since the 1930s, although there have been many studies limited to particular historical and psychological problems. Second, it is a departure from the usual approach to ethnography in its attempt to view personality as a lifelong process that dynamically interacts with cultural and historical change.

The integrating idea is not so much a theory that articulates the relationships between culture and personality as the use of examples to show the complexity and flexibility of adaptive human processes. Third, the book broadens the literature on adult development and aging by taking the methods and ideas of this interdisciplinary field beyond the confines of Western culture.

It will clarify the purpose and organization of *Changing Cultures, Changing Lives* to describe how it came about—the ideas that led to the study on which it is based, the design and execution of that study, and the guiding intellectual and moral principles that took shape during the research and writing. The Japanese American study on which this book is based was part of a cross-cultural study of intergenerational relations designed by Margaret Clark at the Human Development Program, Department of Psychiatry, University of California, San Francisco, and funded by the National Institute of Child Health and Human Development in 1967. Clark had just completed an anthropological study of the elderly in San Francisco that resulted in the publication with Barbara Anderson of *Culture and Aging* (1967). Although *Culture and Aging* was a pioneering study on the cultural background of adult personality change, Clark recognized that it suggested more than it systematically explored since it was based on a case population not originally recruited for purposes of cultural analysis. She therefore designed the new project as a comparative, in-depth study of three generations in each of three distinct subcultures: Mexican American, Japanese American, European American. This book is the final report of the entire Japanese American phase of the project.

The research plan called for a balanced mixture of hard hypothesis-testing and exploratory ethnography. Clark had found in her earlier work that a rigid belief in the values of independence and productivity was related to low morale in many elderly. She therefore chose to compare Mexican Americans and Japanese Americans with European Americans because they represent cultures in which personal autonomy of the European American kind is not highly valued; at the same time the two cultures differ widely on the ethics of productivity. The cross-cultural research design was exploratory because there existed at that time almost no ethnographic work on adult personality development in any American minority group. Little was known about the adaptive problems faced by adults in these minority communities or about typical responses to such problems. Clark realized that the study would probably throw into relief some of the attitudes and values that members of mainstream European American culture take for granted about middle and late life, and it would also bring out the relation between these givens and what happens to people as they age. The decision to sample three generations in each of the subcultures under study was based on the importance of knowing how rapid cultural change was affecting relations between community members and between family members and hence the personality development of all three generations. A working hypothesis was that rapid change, if and when it occurred, would result in conflict between generations within families, but we had little idea what specific values would be the sources of conflict.

Clark's proposal was a simple and straightforward guide to a complex research topic, and it worked extremely well. I believe in retrospect that most of the issues mentioned in the original plan turned out to be important and that the plan was flexible enough to let us discover other issues that had not been anticipated—notably the importance for personality development of simply being a member of a minority group.

I was recruited in 1968 to direct the Japanese American phase of the three-culture study. I had done research on personality and community organization in Japan and had acquired a modest competence in the language. By the fall of 1971, my assistants and I completed formal interviews with seventeen *issei,* or immigrants; fourteen *nisei,* or American-born children of immigrants; and twenty *sansei,* or grandchildren of immigrants. These fifty-one complete cases represented thirty families. The interviews averaged about nine hours in length over three or four sessions. I planned to select one member of each generation from each family in order to get reliable in-depth data on family relationships, but I had to retreat from this ideal because of the difficulty of getting everybody in a family to volunteer. I also spent a couple of days a week from 1968 to 1970 going to meetings, fairs, church services, lectures, parties, and ceremonies in the Japanese American community. I had a small number of friends in the community whom I saw in their homes and churches, on neighborhood streets, and occasionally in my office. These were my "key respondents," in the stilted language of ethnographic method. They criticized my ideas, cautioned me about some of the hidden actions and motives that made the community tick, and provided what is much of the reward of doing ethnography—friendship.

The formal interviews were open-ended. The interviewer wanted to know what the respondent thought and felt about a wide range of topics, from his relationships with his neighbors to his ideas about history. The interviewer phrased and rephrased his questions, striving first for clarity and second for comparability of results. If an answer surprised him, he would leave the interview guidelines altogether and pursue the subject of his surprise until he was satisfied that he had understood its importance. The interviews were divided into five broad sections: demography, ethnic identification, morale and attitudes toward aging, values and unconscious concerns, and intergenerational relations. The Thematic Apperception Test (TAT) was used to study unconscious concerns. We chose nine pictures to represent interpersonal relations, intending to help our subjects verbalize anxieties and needs that they could not or would not speak of in response to more direct questions. Close attention was paid in the analysis to the overt or manifest content of the TAT stories. Less emphasis was given the interpretation of latent symbolic themes or latent structural features of the stories. Since my use of TAT stories in this book is limited to illustrating attitudes expressed in the overt contents of the stories, the reader need not be familiar with TAT interpretation.

The interview as a whole was usually given in a regular order, but questions were sometimes shuffled to conform to the respondent's mood and interest. For the most part, the respondents enjoyed the affability of the interviews or found them intellectually challenging. Their early suspicions and anxieties generally, but not always, melted away after a few hours. By taking part to some extent in the community life they described, I was able to flesh out many of their references to group behavior with my own observations and get a feeling for the distribution in the wider community of the attitudes and behavior they talked about in the interviews. I worked back and forth between observing group life in the community and exploring individual experience through interviews, checking out surprises in the one arena by searching for more information in the other.

Throughout the period during which I was collecting the data and for several months afterward, I coded, scored, and compared my ethnographic notes and interview materials. In this analytic process, I treated the data in two distinct ways. On one hand, I was interested in the large, complex patterns of culture, history, and personality that allowed me to understand the community and each individual in it as comprehensible wholes. On the other, I was interested in particular institutions, events, responses, and individual acts as examples of more general human problems. The first task stressed the uniqueness of my facts; the second stressed their applicability to other times and peoples. I found that in the final analysis I had to be wary of theories and analytic procedures that oversimplified my findings because the use of such devices seemed to rob the facts of much of their sense. I am not pretending to have understood some metaphysical ultimate sense that inheres in the world I saw, but I would have had to overlook nuances of fact that seemed important to me in order to rigorously apply a psychoanalytic or a structural-functional or an interactionist model to my material. Such exercises are better left to later books in which presenting the sense of the study as a whole is not the main goal. As a result, in *Changing Cultures, Changing Lives* I have shifted theoretical focus where the shift seemed justified by the problem at hand. For the same reason I have not used numerical analyses of "variables" to support my conclusions.

Still, I did develop in the course of the research an attitude toward human behavior in general—you may call it a theory or a philosophy if you wish—which runs implicitly through the design of *Changing Cultures, Changing Lives*. I will sketch in its outlines here and refer the reader to the philosophical writings of Cassirer (1944) and Wittgenstein (1958) for further elaboration. First, man relates to his environment almost entirely through the medium of symbols. Second, symbols are arbitrarily related to the things symbolized—that is, they are invented by their users, usually according to historically based conventions about how to make and use symbols, not according to universal laws of symbol-object relations. Third, symbols are often ambiguous and malleable. They get their meaning largely from the context in which they are used, and since many symbols occur in a wide variety of contexts, they have a wide variety of possible conventional meanings. Fourth, people use the ambiguity of symbols to alter their own and each other's understandings of their environment in order to engage it in new ways. Such alteration can be clearly seen in the realms of religion, poetry, and the plastic arts, but it is no less true of science. Even the natural sciences, which present to us a world made up of apparently precise quantities of matter, energy, force, time, and space, offer us a choice between radically different experiences of the same thing, such as between wave and quantum mechanics. The ambiguity of social science as a symbol system approaches that of art or religion since it deals not only with the behavior of "things," which often can be precisely described, but also with "meanings," which never can be because they are inseparable from their vastly complex and quickly changing contexts. It is curious that social scientists study the sense of mystery and power attached to other people's symbols but forget that they are themselves engaged in symbolizing.

In order to clarify the qualities of symbols and symbolic media I am discussing, I could hardly find a better example than Joyce's *Ulysses*—the most ambitious work on the nature of symbols in this tradition. In the first chapter, Joyce portrays Buck Mulligan ascending an ancient tower that overlooks the sea, carrying "a bowl of lather on which a mirror and a razor lay crossed." Immediately Joyce begins to stretch and transfigure the symbolism of these basic elements. The cross (representing the church, man's dual nature, crucifixion, and ambiguity) is no cross at all, but a mirror (self-consciousness, introspection, art, vanity, and narcissism) and a razor (analytic thought, precision, destruction, criticism, and the hero, Stephen Dedalus). These

symbols, in a flick of the syntax, are nothing but shaving imple-
ments. The tower is a symbol of hope, the self, an ancient consciousness—and it is also a makeshift place to live. The sea represents Mother; the Greeks, with their adventure, paganism, and
poetry; snot, a saline vestige of our evolution; but it is also a
cold reality. Each of these things is a facet of the consciousness
of a people, the Dubliners, at a moment in history, 1904, as
well as a symbol common throughout the Western world. Like
musical tones, these and other symbols collide and combine to
form still more associations until the reader's mind begins in
desperation to construct its own order. The reader has become a
scientist of meaning, insisting on a hierarchy and a sequence of
symbols. Joyce eludes him, switching from intellectual to vis-
ceral preoccupations, from chord progressions to counterpoint
to a totally nonmusical, spatial organization of thought, as on a
newspaper page; finally he unlaces the structure of time altogether. Joyce tricks us into realizing that the sense of order and
stability we attribute to experience is an illusion and that almost infinite plasticity is a fundamental characteristic of all
human thought—including thought about thought.

It is interesting that Joyce followed close on the heels of
Einstein, for what one did for physics the other might have
done for Western psychology, giving convincing expression to a
superorder (the continuum of matter, energy, time, and space
for Einstein; that of human nature for Joyce) in which the old
orders appear as mere components. In Joyce's portrayal of the
mind, all anthropological philosophies including evolutionism,
functionalism, experimentalism, and romantic individualism
appear as temporary constellations in a vast and shifting galaxy
in which, given patience and the right perspective, any X equals
any Y.

The arbitrariness and elasticity of symbols is both an asset and a liability to man the symbolizer. His symbols allow him
to play creatively with his environment, but they also make it
very hard for him to feel absolutely certain about the stability
and orderliness of that environment. Mutual agreement among
men about the "real" order of the environment is therefore a
great help to every man's sanity. Culture, as a shared symbol

system, can be understood partly as a defense against the sort of perceptual disintegration whose possibility is so poignantly illustrated by Joyce. Partly for this reason, men defend their cultures vigorously against alien ways of seeing the world.

The relevance of my attitude toward symbols is this: This book is about continuity and change in human life. It is about a group of people trying to function in a complicated and rapidly changing society, beset by the extra difficulty of having to reconcile two strong and different traditions. We follow these people through a process of cultural change in which the integrity of their symbol system is seriously challenged by the Western view and through the processes of historical and personal change that strains and sometimes destroys the continuity of work, space, property, personal association, and social status.

The Japanese Americans have for the most part managed to bridge this torrent of changes with a working sense of self that looks reasonably productive and emotionally buoyant. Although there seems to be a high level of concern in the community about cultural continuity, many members have made this very concern part of the strategy by which they keep their identities intact. All in all, the amazingly diverse and supple picture of human nature that emerges from the study of change in the Japanese American community presents a challenge to many of the basic concepts of social science and offers a modest hope to mankind in the postindustrial era.

Closely related to the intellectual attitude toward human behavior that developed out of my research, and equally important for understanding *Changing Cultures, Changing Lives,* is the development of a moral attitude toward social science. I have mentioned that social science is symbolic activity. All symbolic activity has a moral aspect because symbols themselves affect the way people behave. They are an inseparable part of nearly every human act. Symbols themselves have value because they convey and create knowledge and feeling that can be used. The fact that social scientists study the process by which symbols acquire value does not exempt their science from the category of moral activity. But I disagree with social scientists who think that moral invective is the point of social science. The description of moral alternatives is a social science activity; the choosing of moral alternatives is a political activity. The difference between a political tract and a work of social science or art is that the former seeks to limit choice by assigning values, while the latter seeks to expand choice by questioning them.

Questioning values involves a decision not to act according to those values at the moment as a social scientist. But this decision usually has a very small and insignificant moral outcome for the social scientist. His work does not involve him in an attack on other people's values and it does not bar him from acting according to those values when he is not being a scientist. Great confusion exists on this point. Seeley (1963, p. 58) exemplifies one point of view with admirable clarity when he says, "Description of a vital human activity in and of itself constitutes, in my opinion, an attack upon that activity both from the viewpoint of the participants and from the viewpoint of the disinterested observer." The counterposition is elegantly expressed in a great artist's vision of his function as a social critic. Thomas Mann (quoted in Campbell, 1968, p. 328), with his concept of erotic irony, expresses his belief that the critical, intellectual, moralizing spirit, which is ordinarily aloof from life and death, mocks itself and so is able to love and idealize its own antithesis, "a loving affirmation of all that is *not* intellectuality and art, but is innocent, healthy, decently unproblematical and untouched by spirituality."

It is the self-glorifying intellect, the nihilistic irony that submerges frail and mortal life in a struggle for deathless values, that Seeley is criticizing. But this is only one of many possible levels of irony in social science. In standing back and observing his fellows, the social scientist makes them the subject of irony, but in empathizing with his subjects he is also subjecting himself to irony. There is irony in comparing the versions of truth and virtue held by different societies, but in the search for what is fundamentally human, the student throws his own gods upon the pyre. In fact, it is a lack rather than a surfeit of irony that brings out the politician in the social scientist. Politicians belong to the world of action, not intellect; they speak for many and cannot afford too much irony. The proper social scientist should wear the billowing breeches of the clown, for as he taunts he weeps. Awkwardly self-conscious, to his own torment he cannot play the game of life with innocent bravado. And with much more than mockery he tips his crumpled hat to those who can.

The study of human behavior, then, requires distance from the values that move the acts of men. But distance is not the same thing as indifference, and the student is less than human if he is truly indifferent. He must tread a line between too much compassion, which can flatten his perspective and render his speculations shortsighted and mundane, and too much narcissism, which can deprive his ideas of their human scale. The first danger is the greater when he finds his subjects' values charmingly similar to his own, while the second is the greater when his subjects disappoint him. The charge, recently popular, that the social scientist cannot understand people who do not belong to his culture and has no business studying them fails to grasp this subtle principle.

I feel compelled to say something about social engineering, or solving social problems with social science techniques, because its practice has had a great impact upon the image of the social scientist, especially in the field of ethnic studies. In either the liberal establishment style of Daniel P. Moynihan or the radical style of Charles Valentine, social engineering is not social science. When the student of behavior involves himself in "operationalizing" certain values among the members of social groups, he abandons his self-irony and his compassion for the human world as it is. He ceases to be a student of life and becomes a participant, at the beck and call of the forces and people that drive history. His activity often stands upon a narrow world view—that of the liberal postindustrial technocrat of mid-twentieth-century America. If he kept his perspective he would hesitate to join on pragmatic grounds alone, but more importantly he would see that by joining his own society and era he forfeits the artist's right to criticize, whether he is compassionate or not.

As artist-clown, the social scientist is far from disinterested in the uses of his research. However, he knows the meaning of Arendt's injunction (1967): Ethical truths must be lived or left unproven; they are not susceptible to logical demonstration. The social scientist's work cannot effectively argue a morality that its author fails to practice. If Moynihan had really studied what makes humans dignified, there would have been no need for the Valentines who followed him, because he would have seen the historical impotence of the liberal middle-class values he found lacking in the poor. If Valentine had acted on his professed values, he would have been interested in the suffering of the middle class too and found his own vision of engineered prosperity somewhere in the roots of that suffering. The real value of both Moynihan's and Valentine's work is that it demonstrates critical thinking in action, and that is a wholesome and sometimes even beautiful sight. Given the batting average of most social critics, such people as Moynihan and Valentine deserve their niche in intellectual history even if they save only themselves.

By now it should be clear that I think of social science as a branch of scholarship closely related to the arts and humanities. In writing *Changing Cultures, Changing Lives* I have tried to strengthen that relationship. These days there is subtle pressure from many government agencies and university departments concerned with research on human behavior to pursue physical science models that dissect the subject matter into measurable "variables" at the expense of the holistic, configurational approach to the understanding of complex wholes like persons and communities. While the physicalist studies undoubtedly have their uses, it is even more certain that the need for bridges between the facts of man's technically overspecialized, ethically and perceptually splintered life has never been greater. I have tried to preserve a little of the personal experience of doing the work of ethnography and to retain some sense of my respondents' individuality. Wherever it seemed to make sense to do so, I have used my respondents' own concepts and categories of thought, often their own words (but not their real names). In Chapter One, for example, I have deliberately presented the history of Japan Town in the middle of my discussion of its present appearance and functioning. That is, I have presented its history the way people who live there experience it—as part of daily life. The main organizing theme of the book is the triple process of history, acculturation, and personal development, and although the three are presented as intertwined, I have emphasized each separately. History is the organizing theme of Chapters One and Two; acculturation of Chapters Three, Four, and Five; and personal development of Chapters Six, Seven, and Eight.

Since *Changing Cultures, Changing Lives* is complex in subject and structure, different readers are bound to find different parts of it useful. Chapter One describes collective life in Japan Town against the background of its history. It tells why Japan Town is a community and how the structure and evolution of the community shape the residents' perceptions of group life. In order to understand Japanese American personality, one must know how certain historical facts—especially wartime internment—and certain contemporary institutions affect these people. Chapter Two carries the discussion of the effects of history on perception a step further. Here I turn to a detailed inspection of my respondents' perceptions of their own past, and discuss how these perceptions affect relations between the generations. I analyze the ethnic identity movement as an example of how the present structure and functioning of the community and family interact with perceptions of the past. I show how intellectual habits related to age, sex, culture, and social class affect the way people see their history and how they act toward each other. This chapter reveals how the involvement of American ethnic groups in their pasts is much more than a matter of pride, diversion, or political maneuvering. It is an activity vital to human relations both within the group and in the wider society.

Chapters Three, Four, and Five are a contribution to the concept of acculturation, as well as a discussion of how Japanese culture has changed in America and how the change has affected each generation. Chapter Three is more difficult reading than the rest of the book for the non-social scientist because it builds on a large body of literature about acculturation and personality change. This chapter introduces the theoretical discussion of the effects of acculturation on the community, family, and individual, and it briefly reviews traditional uses of the concept of acculturation. A new definition is proposed that takes into account the fact that new behaviors are often added to—not substituted for—old ones and that individuals shift back and forth between cultural idioms depending on the requirements of the immediate situation. However, acculturative changes are to some extent cumulative, and the process therefore cannot be viewed as entirely reversible. I also point out that people change roles and habits as they age and that an individual's adjustment to a bicultural environment must be constantly revised for this reason. In Chapter Four I discuss concrete changes in values and behavior that characterize the Japanese Americans, starting with the importance of generation membership in my respondents' identification of themselves and each other. I outline several categories of cultural change that have had a cumulative effect on the community, such as the loss of Japanese skills, upward mobility, and broadening intellectual perspective. My focus in this chapter is on the effects of these changes on relationships between the generations. I find that the family holds together surprisingly well in spite of change. Chapter Five turns to the effects of acculturation on the individual. After discussing several types of acculturative stress and typical reactions to them, I present seven brief case studies that illustrate ways people succeed and fail in handling acculturative stress. Chapters Four and Five are especially useful for people seeking insight into the special psychological problems faced by Japanese Americans.

Chapter Six introduces the concept of adult personality development into the study of acculturation. Here I explain why anthropologists have been slow to include the findings of the developmental literature in their theories and explain how the study of acculturation is advanced by this inclusion. I also show how including the idea of cultural variability in studies of the life cycle leads to new questions about mental health and adaptation.

Chapter Seven describes the typical life cycle in traditional Japanese culture and shows how Americanization has changed this pattern. My assumption is that there are some broad cultural norms that indicate the desirable styles of life at various stages (such as childhood, motherhood, retirement) and that these norms set up expectations and help people prepare for the next period in their lives. Cultural change disrupts this map of the lifespan and requires adjustments.

Chapter Eight reviews the main developmental problems of each generation. In general, the issei are well-equipped to handle the problems of old age as long as they remain integrated in their families and communities, but they are likely to have great difficulty if cut off from familiar social surroundings. The developmental problems of the nisei center on their impending retirement from work and on their children's growing up. The nisei have made material achievement and self-sacrifice the basis of their adjustment to society but have not developed ways of expressing themselves creatively or emotionally. They will either have to find new outlets for their achievement striving or learn some self-expressive skills. The sansei face different problems. Their individualistic middle-class values and social skills free them from many of the traditions of Japan Town and expose them to a bewildering variety of opportunities. The Japanese part of their background is sometimes in conflict with their situation, a situation that demands that they be self-assertive and decisive about their personal goals. Another conflict that affects the sansei as young adults is the differing sex role norms of Japanese and American culture. In particular, sansei women are seeking freer lives than their parents and male sansei friends have in mind for them.

Chapter Nine summarizes my view of the uses of social science and discusses some of the theoretical implications of the techniques I used in this study. I portray personality as situationally variable and emphasize the necessity of knowing both what the important social contexts in people's lives are like and how they fit together in broader cultural patterns. I find the concept of identity useful. I question survey approaches to the study of personality development because such approaches overlook the importance of the research interview as a special social context. I question the practice of forecasting personality development among large groups because this practice belittles individual variability and underestimates the importance of unpredictable historical events.

Changing Cultures, Changing Lives is one of several books on the subject of development and aging to have been produced in the last ten years by the Human Development Program under the directorship of Marjorie Fiske Lowenthal. The staff of the program, especially Joan Mello, were extremely supportive and helpful throughout each phase of the research and writing. I was ably assisted in the gathering of data by Douglas E. Sparks. Some of the data were collected by volunteer interviewers Penny Zoldbrod, Thomas Morioka, and Winifred Dahl. The interviewers greatly enlarged my appreciation of the data by contributing their unique points of view and by revealing the impact of their personalities on the interview situation. I am grateful to all of them, as I am to the many people around Japan Town who generously contributed their time to further this study—especially Clifford Uyeda, Edison Uno, Nancy Cable Yamamoto, Kenneth Miyake, and Nicholas Iyoya. Valuable criticism at various stages of writing was given by David Plath, David Reynolds, Edison Uno, Marjorie Lowenthal, Renaldo Maduro, William E. Henry, and Sharon Fujii.

Berkeley, California   Christie W. Kiefer
September 1974

Contents

xxv

Changing Cultures,
Changing Lives

An Ethnographic Study

of Three Generations

of Japanese Americans

Chapter I

The Community
as Process

If you say "Japan Town," just about everybody in San Francisco thinks of a vague geographical area centering around Post and Buchanan Streets in what is called the Western Addition district. The face of this area changes from month to month now. Aoyagi, where you used to be able to get fresh eel, has disappeared. Gone, too, is Minakin, where the old men used to sit upstairs and while away their idle hours drinking rice wine and eating Japanese delicacies. In the place of these humble

1

antiques are modern buildings that look awkward and out of scale—additions to the expanding Japan Trade Center, symbol of the prosperous Japan trade and jewel in the diadem of San Francisco tourism. It's amazing how nostalgia grips a person after a few short years of watching the change. One hears from the old-timers about the era before the Second World War, when the five-by-ten-block area bounded by Divisadero, Geary, California, and Gough Streets probably housed most of the San Francisco Japanese population. Nowadays there are still plenty of Asians in the streets—liberally mixed with local blacks and tourists—and one can still hear Japanese spoken in many of the stores. But in those days it was a real community—Nihonmachi, Japan Town, Little Osaka. Everyone the resident knew lived within those few blocks, worshiped there, went to school there, traded there, played there, often even worked there. There was no aura of dazzling fortune in the Japan trade, and no sleek commercial air about the community as a result. The world outside was much more hostile, too. Japan Town was a haven.

The dwindling population of old timers, the upward mobility of nisei, and the displacement of residential housing by commercial buildings have steadily depleted the resident Japanese population. A block or two from the new and monumental Trade Center are crumbling Victorian rooming houses inhabited by blacks, a few hippies, and a smattering of other cultural types. The streets are not safe at night, and there is pressure on City Hall from the merchants to increase the police patrols. (There was a time when the police were the last people a resident wanted to see on the streets of Japan Town.) Walk around on Sunday morning and you hear voices raised in a black spiritual from a storefront church, not even a block from the sound of Buddhist hymns. Although there are plenty of Japanese materials at the new branch of the San Francisco Public Library in the area, nearly all the kids on the playground outside are black.

Most families have moved out to the middle-class residential districts to the west—Richmond and Sunset. There the neighborhoods are quieter, the homes are newer, and the schools are better. Tebbets (1974) estimates that only 25 to 30 percent of San Francisco's 12,000 Japanese Americans still live in Japan Town. Since each family has at least one car, occasional trips to Japan Town for church services and imported Japanese foods can be arranged without much inconvenience. Some ethnic functions are located outside Japan Town. There are several Japanese churches in the Richmond District. Wedding receptions, funerals, sports events, and meetings often occur in facilities outside the community. Japanese-owned restaurants and stores which cater to a largely non-Japanese clientele are found throughout the city. The curious name of the nightclub Ribeltad Vorden in a predominantly Latin district, for instance, results from the Japanization of *Libertad y Orden*.

Sense of Community

Because Japanese Americans have dispersed so much, they as well as non-Japanese Americans often doubt that a community exists at all, whether the term is used to describe Japan Town itself or the San Francisco Japanese American population or both. Mr. Chikai, a thirty-two-year-old sansei artist, typifies a viewpoint common among the younger and more politically aware members in my study:

Interviewer: *Do you think there's a real Japanese community here in San Francisco?*

Mr. Chikai: *Superficially, yes. A real one? It's probably based more on economics than anything else. Maybe there's one culturally. We're trying to strengthen that.*

I: *What's your relationship with it?*

C: *Just street work [that is, volunteer work with community groups].*

I: *What should the community do for the people in it?*

C: *I don't think people should rip off each other. They should become more attuned to the real problems they face. They should feel more compassion for older people. They should try and get away from the profit motive. The whole Japanese Center is a rip-off. Also they should take care of the younger kids. They should stress the experiences in the cultural heritage—don't let them forget about the internment. The com-*

*munity should be a network whereby these things should be im-
plemented. When it ceases to do this, it has to be reevaluated.*

When such advocates of community are in a self-critical
mood, they tend to see their own ethnic group as factionalized
and indifferent to its own solidarity and collective effectiveness,
and getting more so. When challenged from the outside, they
are likely to take a different view. At a seminar on Asian community health problems sponsored by medical students of Asian
ancestry at the University of California, San Francisco, a white
doctor questioned the idea of trying to plan community health
services for a group as scattered and diverse as the Japanese
Americans. He was quickly answered by a nisei activist: "There
is a sense of consciousness of our own common culture. Whatever is needed, whether it's medical help or just social entertainment, we feel more comfortable if we do it ourselves."

It is difficult to say what proportion of the population is
actively concerned about the degree of community solidarity or
whether it is growing or declining. Of the fourteen nisei intensively interviewed, all but two had lived in the Bay Area for
some time before the war and clearly remembered the compact
ghettolike quality of the prewar community. My casual contact
with many other nisei confirms that this familiarity with the
community is a widespread pattern, and that even those nisei
who arrived in San Francisco only after the war have developed
a sense of the history of Japan Town through their associations
with friends who grew up there. Most nisei in San Francisco,
regardless of their present place of residence in the city, probably take the presence of longstanding formal and informal ethnic institutions for granted (and sometimes proudly exercise
their ability to transcend them). In the following interview excerpt, a forty-seven-year-old successful nisei architect, Mr. Uchida, (hereafter called junior to distinguish him from his father,
whom I also interviewed) discusses his boyhood prewar community in Oakland:

Interviewer: *You used the phrase* ghetto mentality.
Mr. Uchida: *Well, when I say a ghetto, it's probably not
what we mean by a ghetto nowadays. But let's call it a ghetto*

because you're all in this little area, this very tight-knit neigh-borhood. It wasn't like San Francisco. San Francisco Japan Town had a ghetto, I'd say. And I would say—wouldn't you say Chinatown is a ghetto?

I: *Yeah, I guess I'd say the hard core of Chinatown is a ghetto.*

U: *Of course we didn't have anything like that in Oak-land. But I don't think we could get beyond Seventh Street or the other side of Harrison Street. I don't think our horizon was beyond that.*

I: *Discrimination in housing and so on?*

U: *Right. There wasn't any place to live but right in that area. Oh, there are exceptions of course. Some of our people lived all over Oakland. But when I say ghetto mentality, I mean just that. The Japanese community centered around that area. Maybe it was the Japanese school at the center and the churches. The Buddhist churches were very active. The religious circles were social circles. All the social functions took place right in the church. You had a wedding, well, all the receptions took place right in the church. Nowadays people have a wed-ding, well, they have the reception anywhere—in Strawberry Canyon, at the U.C. Alumni House, even at the Claremont Ho-tel. It was available to us in those days, but we couldn't think beyond; the white world was completely beyond our under-standing.*

With the exception of some unusually public-spirited in-dividuals, most of the nisei and issei whom I interviewed did not apply the word *community* to a geographical area or to their ethnic group. The important human groupings in their world are kin, friends, church members, and club members. These group-ings tend to overlap but by no means coincide. Among the forty issei women who regularly attend the weekly activities at Japan Town Senior Center, for example, there are two large, informal friendship groups. When asked to explain the basis of these groups, most of the women simply say that they have been friends for a long time. Members of various churches are present in both groups.

The word *community* is sometimes associated with the

largest and most politically visible Japanese American organization in the country, the Japanese American Citizens' League
(JACL). I examine the role of this and other organizations when
I discuss community social relations, but let us note here that a
full 10 percent of the local population belong to the JACL, although many nonmembers—especially young liberals—consider
it merely a social club, serving a small and politically conservative segment of the population. Supporters see it as a reliable
advocate of the local Japanese American population as a whole
to the world outside and also as a setting within which members
can keep up acquaintances with old friends, thus providing ce-
ment for wide and amicable relations within the ethnic group.
Mrs. Kayano, a fifty-four-year-old nisei mother, represents this
viewpoint: "The only reason we belong is that we want to keep
ties among the Japanese. We don't want to lose track. We don't
take an active part. Just members."

The foregoing are the most frequent perceptions of the
term *community* expressed by my respondents. Some individuals find social relations within the ethnic group stultifying, the
gossip vicious, and the morals backward, and they would prefer
to see the disappearance of any kind of Japanese American
community, but they are a small minority. Most people are willingly involved in formal and informal ethnic associations and at
least pay lip service, like Mrs. Kayano, to the desirability of
wide-ranging mutual support among Japanese Americans.

Part of the sense of cohesiveness I am calling community,
then, is historical; it springs from a perception of continuity
from a period when Japan Town really was a ghetto. Another
part of the definition, however, is what I will call the intensity
and generality of social relations. These are comparative concepts referring to the ratio of intracommunity to intercommunity behavior. By *intensity* I mean that people within the boundaries of a defined community interact with each other more than
with those outside and that they know more about each other
than about outsiders. By *generality* I mean that they do a wider
variety of things with and for each other than with and for outsiders (see Wilson and Wilson, 1945). Naturally, one often finds
that a group of people functions as a community for some pur-

poses and that another group, which may overlap the first, functions as a community for other purposes. This simply underlines the functional and comparative meaning of the term *community*. The San Francisco Japanese American community is distinguished from the non-Japanese population of San Francisco on the bases of *intensity, generality,* and *history,* and it is distinguished from Japanese American communities outside San Francisco on the bases of *intensity, history,* and *geography.*

Although ties of kinship, religion, business, friendship, and membership in formal institutions frequently unite Japanese American individuals in different cities and different geographical areas of the country, residents in a single city or town in the Bay Area tend to form local voluntary associations and to compete with similar associations in nearby cities. Accompanying this tendency is an identification with the local groups an individual belongs to and through them an identification with the locale they represent. For example, a Japanese American church of long standing in the area recently had to find new quarters because the old church building was in an area scheduled for demolition and redevelopment by local planning authorities. Since the congregation was small, it seemed impractical to build a new church structure elsewhere. The pastor and board of deacons therefore presented the congregation with three alternatives: merge with a rather poor Japanese American church of the same denomination in a nearby town; merge with a richer Japanese American church in a slightly more distant town; or merge with a comparatively elegant all-Caucasian church in the same town—an action that would have been unprecedented in this area and that was only half-seriously proposed. After much debate, the congregation finally settled on the Caucasian church, even though many members had great misgivings about the desirability and feasibility of integration. The decision was made largely because decades of competition with the other Japanese American churches—competition in sports events, fund drives, and the general strain toward prestige—made it impossible for most parishioners to regard themselves as the potential coworshipers and colleagues of "those people."

Longstanding organizations like churches are not the only associations subject to such parochialism. In 1970, a group of sansei in Oakland formed a voluntary society for community improvement, taking the establishment of closer contacts between issei and sansei and the improvement of recreational opportunities for the issei as their first goals. About a year later, an interdenominational youth group in San Francisco established an independent program with similar goals. When I talked to members of both groups early in 1972, neither group had a clear idea of what the other was doing. A participant in one group was skeptical about the ultimate success of the other. However, the two groups did occasionally cooperate to plan areawide activities for the issei.

The sense of territorial solidarity is keenly felt by those who move to the community from other areas of the country, especially if they have no close friends or relatives here. Mr. Suzuki, a nisei professional in his early forties, came to San Francisco from Southern California about ten years ago. He found the local nisei very standoffish, in spite of family connections that helped to break the ice. "It's hard for any newcomer to be accepted here, I think. The nisei here are so status-conscious, nobody will go out on a limb by inviting you to join the group. I had it relatively easy, too, because people knew my father-in-law." Newcomers from Japan are often derisively referred to as "F.O.B." (fresh off the boat) and find it difficult to establish more than superficial contact with long-time residents. These new immigrants (many of them wives of non-Japanese Americans) and Japanese citizens residing in San Francisco on temporary visas tend to form a distinct subcommunity with many economic links to the Japanese American mainstream. Newcomers from Hawaii (called "pineapple heads") tend to form their own subcommunity.

Members of these subcommunities, as well as visitors and newcomers from other well-known Japanese communities in the mainland United States, are subject to stereotyping by locals and have reciprocal stereotypes of their hosts. "The kids say [my brother-in-law] looks more like an F.O.B. every time we see him," says Mrs. Kindaichi, a forty-six-year-old nisei housewife. "He becomes more stoop-shouldered; his head is forever nodding. You know how they do. He's become so Japanese, if you saw him, you'd think he just came here from Japan. You'd never know he'd been born and raised here, really. Yeah. It's the influence of the [Japanese] bank where he works."

In spite of the strong territorial aspect to the sense of community, mere residence within its bounds—even lifelong residence—does not guarantee full membership. Participation in certain local activities is necessary to validate the individual's membership in such a vaguely defined territorial society. Mr. Yamabe is a thirty-eight-year-old nisei with a background in social work and is a familiar figure wherever issues of Japanese American community welfare bring people together. Discussing the problem of juvenile delinquency in Japan Town, he brought up the case of a sansei boy who had a record of petty arrests. The boy had grown up in San Francisco, said Mr. Yamabe, but "I don't think he was a member of this community. I never saw him at any of the basketball games." Puzzled, the interviewer asked, "But he grew up around here?" "Yeah," Yamabe replied, "I'm pretty sure about that." "Did his family live here, too?" "Oh yeah. They still do."

As someone with wide associations in the local population and a finger on the pulse of the Japanese American community, Mr. Yamabe is probably more concerned than the average person about who is considered *in* the community and who isn't, and he probably can muster more information in a hurry in order to make that evaluation. However, both the need for such evaluations and the possibility of making them underline the presence of a vague but real shared sense of local community among the Japanese Americans of San Francisco.

Background of the Community

In keeping with my interest in human life as a process of growth and adaptation, I have drawn heavily on the past for my understanding of the way the Japan Town community functions today. The present institutions and customs of the community are evolving stages in a unique history. I have chosen the most important historical events and processes according to their impact on the way my respondents live. Although it is a convention of Western culture to separate past processes from present structures in such accounts, to view the present as history happening can be at least as enlightening.

A casual look at the growing list of books, newspaper and magazine articles, radio and television programs, and college courses on the Japanese and their descendents in the continental United States indicates the overwhelming importance of the terrible years 1942 to 1947—the years of evacuation, internment and return. The curiously small amount of documentation on the effects of the relocation experience on the organization of the community might be partly explained by the lack of detailed material on prewar continental communities. The only study published in English of an urban Japanese American community before the war that approaches a complete ethnography is that of Miyamoto (1939), and even this short monograph, while extremely useful as the only one of its kind, deals mainly with formal organization. A few more details of urban Japanese American life on the West Coast can be culled from biographical materials (Kitagawa, 1967; Kitano, 1968; Sone, 1953) and from some histories dealing with the prewar period (Broom and Kituse, 1956; Broom and Rimer, 1949; Hosokawa, 1969; Modell, 1968, 1970). Although my main goal in this study was not "salvage ethnography"—reconstructing the history of the subjects' culture—there is enough biographical material in my ethnographic and intensive interview notes to piece together, with the help of the published material mentioned above, a partial picture of the prewar San Francisco community.

The social organization of any ethnic community, including the Japanese American, has always been powerfully influenced by the place of the community and its residents in the fabric of local, contemporary American culture. Both the work of other writers (for example, Bosworth, 1967; Girdner and Loftis, 1969; Grodzins, 1949; McWilliams, 1964; B. Smith, 1948; tenBroek and others, 1954; Thomas and Nishimoto, 1946) and the reports of my respondents show that the general social atmosphere on the West Coast between 1900 and 1942 was hostile to Japanese immigrants and their children, and that social relations within the ethnic group were greatly influenced by this hostility and the discriminatory treatment which resulted from it. Further, anti-Japanese sentiment was on the whole more articulate and had more severe consequences in San Francisco during much of this period than in other major West Coast cities. The San Francisco school board tried to set a precedent in 1906 by segregating Orientals in separate schools, and San Francisco Mayor Angelo Rossi publicly denounced the Japanese, over five thousand of whom lived in the city at the time, at the 1942 Congressional inquiry into the removal of the West Coast Japanese and their American citizen children (the infamous Tolan Hearings). San Francisco labor organizations and other groups had developed a strong anti-Oriental voice in local politics perhaps earlier than those of most other towns, owing to the presence of large numbers of Chinese in their midst since the 1850s. For the casual as well as the organized xenophobe, the physical similarities of the two ethnic groups usually seemed to override cultural differences, and both were seen as equally disturbing representatives of the teeming masses of Asia. Vandalism to Japanese property; boycotting of Japanese businesses; discrimination in housing, employment, legal protection, and public and commercial services; and physical assaults on Japanese residents were all familiar parts of the discriminatory pattern. Mrs. Sakamori, a nisei, age seventy-four, recalls the treatment received from whites by her father, a Christian evangelist and leader of his community in the early decades of this century: "When I was a little girl, he used to take me with him when he drove his wagon. If he was alone, the police would arrest him for mistreating his horse. But when they saw a little girl on the seat next to him, they would leave him alone."

As time went on, discrimination seems to have gradually focused on economic activity. Discriminatory legislation prevented Japanese from enjoying the legal protection of citizenship, deprived them of the right to own land, and forced them out of certain industries such as the steam laundry business (Simpson and Yinger, 1965, pp. 420-421). During the Great Depression, many nisei graduated from secondary schools and col-

leges but were unable to get jobs commensurate with their qualifications and had to take up menial occupations or work for
other Japanese. The discrimination against Asians added to the
general economic crisis, and together these two conditions kept
the Japanese severely isolated from the larger society (Broom
and Kituse, 1956, p. 7).

Isolation and self-reliance were further encouraged in the
San Francisco community by housing discrimination and by the
segregationist policies of Caucasian-dominated voluntary organizations. Both kinds of discrimination are hard to quantify, but
we might use the Christian churches as an example of the quality and effects of segregation.

All-Japanese missions were established in California by
the Presbyterians and the Methodists as early as the 1880s. Says
Bradford Smith (1948, p. 228): "The Methodists soon had a
whole string of missions on the West Coast separately admin-
istered almost as if they were foreign missions. Other sects followed suit. So Christianity, which began by directing its adherents toward America, ended by keeping them in segregated
churches and helping to calcify the shell which surrounded
them." But the Japanese Christian churches in San Francisco
and elsewhere did provide a sanctuary from racist attacks on
their members. They helped the immigrant cope with his new
environment by allowing him his native traditions while providing information about American language, law, ethics, education, and even about simple skills which he could use to make a
living. Like many American institutions, the churches let the
immigrant on the bus but required him to sit in the back and
often told him politely where to get off.

We know little about the peculiarities of locale and social
class the immigrants brought with them (though few seem to
have been of the lower classes), but we know a good deal about
the country they came from—Japan in the Meiji Era. It was a
country that had recently emerged from a long period of political suppression, peace, and relative isolation from foreign contact. It was an intensely nationalistic country, but at the same
time gripped by Western fever: a burning desire to learn from
and compete with the advanced Western countries—particularly

the United States. It was a poor country with basically agrarian values. That is, it was patriarchal and hierarchical, family- and community-centered, and devoted to many elaborate rituals and traditions. At the same time, it was witnessing a wave of vigorous reform in politics and religion and had not yet established a modern political, economic, and religious identity.

For the purposes of this study, the most important feature of Japanese culture is its ancient and highly developed emphasis on intense cooperation among the members of any common enterprise. Most cooperative groups are organized along kinship or quasi-kinship lines and are ruled by full consensus. This feature, termed "corporate emphasis" by Befu (1962), has been indispensable to the economic and military success of the Japanese in this century and is indispensable to understanding the history of the Japanese in America.

The second most important feature of Japanese culture is its "ethical particularism" (Parsons, 1951), or situational ethics. Many writers have noted the tendency of the Japanese to evaluate acts more in terms of their appropriateness to the situation than on abstract moral principles. This particularism enables the Japanese to change easily from one set of moral principles to another. It gives an adaptive advantage to the individual who can quickly and accurately read the attitudes and feelings of his counterparts in social intercourse, but it also creates considerable anxiety for the individual who is unable to do so for some reason (for example, a totally unfamiliar milieu). It also leads to a pragmatic selection of moral principles—religious, political, or otherwise. Ethics tend to be syncretistic and malleable in Japan and among the issei in America. In other words, ethical principles from a new culture can easily be combined with or transformed into those of the old.

The third most important feature of the parental culture, for our purposes, is its so-called shame orientation. For the Japanese, social control resides in collectivities such as family, community, or even society. Fear of ridicule and ostracism is often cited as the motive for conformist behavior, and child-rearing patterns stress this mode of control. An important corollary of particularism and shame-orientation is a great sensitivity for the feelings of others. Japanese avoid directly confronting emotionally loaded issues in their relations with others. They make great use of nuance and nonverbal cues to transmit emotional messages, and they value the ability to read such cues.

With this cultural background, the immigrants arrived. The first issei to come to San Francisco were mostly men. They came for a variety of reasons: to learn Western techniques and culture, to make money, to escape conscription, to find greater religious tolerance. Most of them expected to return to Japan eventually, and this expectation profoundly shaped their adaptation to America. They were, I believe, an uncommon collection of men: unusually proud, independent, and often inquisitive. Many had broken with their families in order to come here or were later to do so in order to stay, and many stayed in the face of odds that would have discouraged less determined men. Of the seven issei men we interviewed, two were from urban areas, two from small towns, and three from rural areas. All the nonrural issei came from petty merchant families. All three rural men came from farm families, although only one can be clearly classified as peasant. Of the other two, one was of the samurai class and the other was from a wealthy farm family.

Most issei women were brought to America by their husbands or came here alone to meet them. Few expected a life of ease and fewer still found it. Most expected to live a reasonably normal Japanese wife's life, with the added blessing of freedom from tyrannical relatives—especially in-laws. Their lives involved housekeeping and bearing and raising children for the most part. For the Japanese wife, raising children does not mean simply looking after their needs. It means giving them every possible opportunity to excel, even at the cost of considerable self-denial. Women are in theory subordinate to their husbands in all things, yet they bear the main responsibility for the children's development and character. Thus, although the direct participation of issei women in noteworthy historical events is limited to a handful of incidents, as a group they had a profound effect on their ethnic history, both as shapers of their children's morals and as determined advocates for the hopes and futures of those children. Of ten issei women interviewed, five were of rural origin, two from urban areas, and three from small towns. Three of the rural women came from ordinary farm families, two from rural samurai families. The two urban women were daughters of petty businessmen, while the small-town women were daughters of a priest, a scholar, and an engineer.

Nationalism—pride in one's political identity—and ethnocentrism—pride in one's cultural identity—probably played some part in the isolation of the prewar Japanese community from the American mainstream, but my impression is that the role of these attitudes was not great in the beginning. Admiration for American technology and American government was widespread in the higher levels of Japanese society, and this attitude was also reflected in our subjects' willingness to view their American adventure at least as a way of improving themselves, though few desired to transcend their Japanese identity. Had American society been inclined to reciprocate this attitude, the history of the Japanese American community would have been different.

Early in its history, the Japanese community in San Francisco developed social characteristics that set the pattern until the relocation in 1942. By the early 1900s, it was a close-knit and remarkably self-sufficient community with many voluntary mutual-aid associations which presented a unified face to the outside world: the Japanese Association, associations representing Japanese prefectures, or districts, merchant associations, study groups, Christian and Buddhist churches, and at least one Japanese-language newspaper. These institutions in San Francisco were not very different from their counterparts in Seattle, Los Angeles, and elsewhere, as described in Miyamoto (1939), Modell (1968), Kitano (1968, pp. 81-97), and Girdner and Loftis (1969, p. 51).

Throughout the prewar period voluntary groups were mostly organized and run by issei men. Nisei-organized and nisei-dominated organizations, such as the JACL, began to appear in the 1920s but were not actively supported by the issei and had little political power in the community until the relocation crisis. These organizations tended to be "functionally diffuse" (term taken from Levy, 1952, p. 281); that is, they tended to provide a variety of services to their members, to make a variety of demands on them, and to adapt gradually to changing community needs rather than to dissolve and regroup. Studies of other communities in the United States and voluntary associations in Japan and Hawaii (Embree, 1939, pp. 112-153, and 1941; R. Smith, 1956, pp. 9-18; Dore, 1958, pp. 269-287) reinforce my belief that each religious, economic, and recreational group in the prewar community played some part in each of four main areas of community function: economic and legal; recreational and therapeutic; educational; integrative.

The pooling of resources for economic survival and legal protection in an oppressed minority community needs little explanation. Capital was raised for economic ventures through such institutions as *tanomoshi-ko*—a primitive banking venture (see, for example, Miyamoto, 1939). Commercial associations served as channels for economic knowledge and provided collective defense against discriminatory moves. Girdner and Loftis (1969, p. 51) record, for instance, that in 1906 the San Francisco Japanese Restaurant Union broke a boycott against its members by bribing the leaders of the Caucasian group who had organized the boycott. Protests directed to American and Japanese government officials through community groups were often ineffective (Kitano, 1968, pp. 81-82) but occasionally paid off, as in the case of school segregation (Girdner and Loftis, 1969, pp. 51-52). Organizations such as the churches and prefectural associations sometimes played an important role in helping individuals or whole neighborhoods in times of crisis. Says a nisei doctor: "During the influenza epidemic of 1917, I was one of those most active in helping the Japanese community. It was discovered that many Japanese were dying in their homes, and their death would not be discovered for days. Children were found in homes next to their dead parents. It was really terrible. The old Reform Church on Post Street—you know, the one they're planning to tear down for some urban renewal project—that was converted into a dispensary for flu victims. The ones who were the most effective in helping the people, though, were the Buddhist priests."

The time-honored Japanese practice of gift exchange also

helped to distribute the burden of financial stress throughout the community, as well as serving as a mechanism of social control. In this practice, gifts are given to families at weddings and funerals and to nonprofit organizations like churches and social clubs as a means of showing gratitude and keeping up appearances (see Dore's excellent exposition of obligatory gift exchange, 1963, pp. 253-268). Some of these organizations in turn provided charitable services to the community.

Puritanical European Americans easily underestimate the importance of the recreational role of voluntary associations in the Japanese American community. Because Japanese culture—like many non-Western industrial cultures—stresses the integration of pleasure and sociability (see Caudill, 1962), leisure time is often spent in organized, collective recreation. Most of the important organizations in prewar Japan Town—churches, prefectural associations, trade associations, and the Japanese Association—sponsored periodic picnics, bazaars, banquets, and artistic performances which provided casual sociability, feasting, drinking (for the men), and general relaxation among friends. Although these gatherings served many functions other than recreation, they clearly were an economical source of diversion, excitement, and color in the otherwise plain and laborious lives of typical community residents.

The recreational activities of Japanese American community groups gradually developed certain characteristics that are not typical of such activities in Japan but reflect expressive needs peculiar to the minority communities. I refer especially to the emergence of overt competition among community members. Such competition is a result of living in a social environment where upward mobility is severely limited by discriminatory barriers, as in the Caucasian-dominated world of the issei. Needs for status recognition must be satisfied within the ethnic group. Competition for status, however, can easily threaten group cooperation and therefore must somehow be limited—in this case, by ritualizing it.

Voluntary associations served as settings for this limited or ritual competition in two ways. First, recognition was given to members in the form of election to leadership positions.

Elections were usually conducted with great decorum and little overt hostility, but behind the mask of propriety offices were highly coveted. I asked Dr. Hino, an issei physician, what the issei find nowadays to occupy their spare time. Smiling, he said, "Well, everything boils down to politics doesn't it?" Many issei organizations, especially churches, published yearly reports called *nenkan,* memorializing the group's activities and its officers. These reports were serious business to the issei, and the compilers had to be extremely careful of inadvertent slights.

Second, with the gradual growth of the nisei population, games and sports became an important avenue for status competition not only among the nisei participants but among the spectators—their issei parents. Kitano (1968, p. 92) describes a community picnic: "During the races and competitive games that take place throughout the afternoon, much store is set on winning. It is important that a man's son be better than other men's sons, and the spirit of the games is more serious than one might find at an Iowa sack race."

As the nisei grew, organized leagues for team sports became a salient feature of the community and in fact one of the major group activities. Competition between nisei teams—especially basketball teams—became a way of life for many boys. Earlier I referred to the importance of sports in defining the boundaries of the community today, and evidently its importance was even greater in the past. Mr. Kimura, a fifty-one-year-old nisei, reminisces about the old days: "Well, sports is an all-year-round deal with the nisei. Some places used to have baseball and football teams, but there weren't too many to compete with. Basketball—everybody used to play, so it was pretty competitive. We used to have the A and the B and the C teams. They used to have seven or eight A teams. Now, in A league, if you have four teams in the Bay Area, you're pretty lucky."

Sports is a major setting in American culture for the ritual dramatization of national values such as brotherhood, fair play, equality, health, youth, beauty, energy, and individualism. Minority groups who accept these values along with competitiveness but are handicapped by discriminatory practices in their attempts to actualize such values in their serious everyday lives may find sports a symbolic solution to the bind society has put them in. The sports event scales down the field of activity to manageable proportions. The values of the wider society are reinforced because ideally nobody breaks the rules, losers are respected too, and the chance to win is comparatively real.

Associations

Voluntary associations played a large role in practical education. I have already mentioned that the Christian churches served as agencies for the transmission of information about American culture to their Japanese parishioners. In view of the keen interest shown by many immigrants in American education and the fact that voluntary associations had many different functions, there was considerable interest in educational activities within many of these associations. Of our seven issei male respondents, two had been "school boys"—that is, they had come here for the purpose of studying at their own expense, another graduated from a theological seminary after having been converted to Christianity, and another reports that he intended to go to school in America but found his goal economically unattainable.

Only one of our ten formally interviewed issei women had had any formal schooling in this country, although seven had had about the equivalent of a junior high school education in Japan and three had gone even further. The general low level of knowledge about American culture and the lack of English fluency among the issei women we interviewed leads me to believe that issei women in general participated very little if at all in organized educational activity dealing with these subjects prior to the war. Mrs. Oka, who speaks no English, expresses a typical lament:

Interviewer: *Are you satisfied with your life so far, or not?*

Mrs. O: *I didn't experience any unhappiness that was mine in particular—only the same things that happened to other people. So, I don't bother about it. Therefore I'm happy.*

I: *Is this because of your own efforts, or due to things over which you had no control?*

Mrs. O: *It was due to my education and background. On the other hand, if I had studied English and learned a little more about American society, I would have been very happy indeed.*

When I refer to the integrative function of community organizations I mean the transmission and support of community norms, the definition of community boundaries, and the control of deviance. In a broad sense, of course, almost everything that took place in the community and was not on balance somehow *dis*integrating had the integrative function of affirming relationships between people in the Japanese American community and serving as a channel for the expression of common values. But I am particularly interested in the socializing influences of community activities on the young and on immigrants, in the exclusion of alien values and their agents, and in the extrusion or reform of deviants.

Most salient but not alone among socializing agencies of the community were the Buddhist churches, the Japanese schools, and the ethnic newspapers. Buddhism in general, especially the sects most popular in Japan and among the Japanese in America, underwent a sea change on its importation to America from the most morally and politically tolerant of religions to something of a bastion of ethnic and national pride. Prior to World War II, a majority of mainland United States Japanese were Buddhists (Simpson and Yinger, 1965, p. 602), but another large proportion either had converted to Christianity or were from Christian families in Japan. The competition from proselytizing Christian churches probably stimulated the militant conservatism of the Buddhists. At any rate, the Buddhist churches were a symbolic center for the prewar San Francisco community. Buddhist sermons regularly extolled such values as filial piety and spiritual ties with Japan and its institutions.

There were two large Japanese schools in San Francisco before the war, and there may have been a number of smaller ones as well. These were attended, usually five days a week, by Japanese American children after their regular public-school day was over, for the purpose of learning Japanese language and other subjects not taught in San Francisco public schools but deemed important by the issei—principally what was called moral education. The unity of scholarship and morality is an idea as old as formal education itself, especially in East Asia, where education for two thousand years centered on the study of Confucius and his disciples. The idea was given fresh impetus in Japan in 1890, when the Japanese government set down the guidelines for a new system of public schools (Tsurumi, 1970, p. 99), stressing the schools' role in building character and inspiring nationalism. The issei apparently seized on the idea of moral education as a way of countering what they saw as the adverse effects of acculturation on their children.

Most of my nisei respondents had gone to Japanese school for at least a few years. For the most part, they remembered it as an unpleasant and not very educational experience. It took them away from leisure activities enjoyed by their non-Japanese peers, and the atmosphere of the Japanese school was usually stiff and stuffy to their way of thinking. They were taught proper etiquette, such as bowing and polite forms of speech; respect for authority, especially of parents and teachers; personal qualities of thrift, honesty, diligence, punctuality, neatness; and some Japanese government and history. Many students, especially the boys, seem to have spent the better part of their class time plotting escape. Mr. Kimura (nisei, age fifty-one) is typical:

Interviewer: *Did you go to Japanese school yourself?*
Mr. K: *Yeah, I had to go. And I was a good student—good at cutting classes more than anything else [laughs]. The younger kids were always passing me up.*

In a small, close-knit society where public reputation is of paramount importance, the power of the news media tends to be great. Japanese-language newspapers were widely circulated in San Francisco before the war and served as effective channels of social control. Few important achievements or community services performed by local residents or groups went unnoticed, and the same was true of scandal. The opinions of community leaders on contemporary issues were aired in these tabloids for the edification of the community. There is some evidence that the newspapers were not above playing favorites (as they often do today) and that their editors had considerable hand in shaping community morality itself. Mrs. Oka talks about her husband's business before the war:

> Interviewer: *I've heard some people went broke because they gave too much credit and couldn't collect from their customers.*
> Mrs. O: *At our store, there were some people who didn't pay their bills, but not many.*
> I: *Was it difficult for a Japanese to get credit from a Japanese business?*
> Mrs. O: *It was easy enough to ask the shopman to bill on a monthly basis. Sometimes it was difficult to get newspaper people to pay.*
> I: *Newspaper people?*
> Mrs. O: *I've heard that some stores folded because they were afraid to ask the newspaper people to pay their bills.*

The issei became increasingly concerned with the problem of social control as their children began to grow in number and maturity and increasingly confronted their parents with American idioms and American ideas in their own homes. One solution to Americanization was the Japanese school; another was the widespread practice of sending children to Japan to be educated. By 1942, the number of American citizens of Japanese ancestry educated in Japan was estimated at twenty-five thousand (Brown and Roucek, 1945, p. 333). A subtler and perhaps in the long run more effective means of passing on traditional values and defining community limits, however, was collective recreation. I have mentioned the symbolic quality of community outings in their emphasis of the cohesiveness and inclusiveness of the community. Such recreational events were usually marked as well by forms of entertainment—Japanese folk dancing, swordsmanship, judo, poetry recitation, toasts and prizes for the oldest participant or the one with the most children or group benefactors (Kitano, 1968, p. 92)—which reinforced community norms. Newcomers and youngsters were thereby encouraged to perceive the local Japanese American population, or at least that segment of it which happened to be reveling at the moment, as a united group with a distinct set of ideals—a sobering spectacle for the potential deviant.

Here we arrive at what appears at first to be a paradox. To the casual observer, the Japanese community picnic or banquet probably appeared relatively disorderly compared with the circumspect and stylized forms of relationship that characterized ordinary community life. Drunkenness was tolerated—even encouraged—on the part of adult males (who, remember, monopolized formal authority in the community). Ribald joking was expected, and humorous speeches often referred to the less admirable characteristics of community notables, to the great glee of the participants. Normally controlled appetites—for noise, riotous play, and sweets on the part of children; food, drink, and ribaldry on the part of adults; flirtation on the part of youth—were indulged. How could such a spectacle contribute to the maintenance of social order?

One answer, what might be called the safety valve hypothesis, would be that these events provided an opportunity for the safe release of instinctual drives whose expression was denied in daily life and that this release was necessary to the continued repression of these drives. Much as one might want to shrug off the wet blanket of this psychoanalytic argument, there is probably some validity to it. The individual who has been nursing a hurt inflicted by his superiors may expend his hostility with a few half-joking insults at a festival or resurrect his pride by defeating his enemies in a ritual competition.

Festivals can be seen as socially integrative, however, even if we dispense with the idea of suppressed antisocial drives. For one thing, festivals like the community picnic usually contain rituals that dramatize the social order by either mocking or repeating in miniature the values and activities of serious life. For another, they emphasize, by contrast, the orderliness of everyday life—they are metaphors for the chaos that would occur in a life without rules (Turner, 1969). Perhaps most important of all, though, is the opportunity which festivals provide for experimentation with social rules. They create an atmosphere of playfulness in which mistakes are taken lightly. The celebrants, like children who mock the serious activity of their elders, may try out new behaviors to see what happens and how it feels without the customary sense of dread or shame. Finally, the mere sharing of exciting activity tends to strengthen bonds between people. Participants are moved closer together by carrying away with them an important shared memory. This form of activity, so common in Japan Town, can thus be understood as both a cause and an expression of the sense of community solidarity.

There is yet another sense in which one must grasp the integrative role of voluntary groups in the lives of their members. Here I refer to that often conjured but rarely clarified anthropological concept, *pattern*: the notion that the entire way of life of a people in small, relatively isolated, close-knit, slowly changing communities—what Redfield calls "little communities"—makes sense as a whole to community denizens and that no part of it can be appreciated without reference to the other parts. "The unity and distinctness of the little community is felt by everyone who is brought up in it and as a part of it. The people of a band or a village or a small town know each of the other members of that community as parts of one another; each is strongly aware of just that group of people, as belonging together; the 'we' that each inhabitant uses recognizes the separateness of that band or village from all others. Moreover, to the member of the . . . isolated band or village the community is a round of life, a small cosmos; the activities and institutions lead from one into all the others, so that to the native himself the community is not a list of tools and customs; it is an integrated whole" (1956, p. 10). This view of the wholeness of life in little communities is often contrasted with the less unified, less patterned life of men in more complex societies. Murray and Kluckhohn summarize the influence of cultural patterns upon individuals in simple and complex societies by saying that in the former "the emphasis is upon patterns as binding individuals and upon the satisfactions individuals find in the *fulfillment of intricately involuted patterns,*" whereas in the latter "the emphasis must be placed more upon pattern conflict and upon the relationship this bears to personality disorganization" (1962, p. 42, emphasis mine).

Through such a conception of the relatedness of institutions and acts in the life of the little community, the need for conservatism becomes apparent: any major alteration in any part of the pattern alters the pattern as a whole and disturbs the member's sense of the meaningfulness of each aspect of his social life. Patternedness is a quality of life in Japan Town that has exerted a powerful conservative force on history. Within the circle of the functionally diffuse voluntary association, the sense of fitness of all parts of Japan Town life is affirmed. Religion, recreation, education, economics, morality, etiquette—these are abstractions that the rules of group life do not make, as each partakes of the other. The innovator is likely to be seen as an unwelcome deviant unless his ideas are cast in terms that do not threaten the overall pattern of life.

Japan Town during the prewar years was a tight-knit, cooperative, conservative community dominated by the issei men who were leaders of voluntary associations. There was apparently a remarkable degree of tolerance, equality, and mutual respect among the leading group. Most issei men appear to have been jealous of their freedom from the feudalistic institutions of Japan; they were on their guard against demagogues among them, and they were alert to personal leadership qualities, regardless of birth or socioeconomic status. Ambition and status-climbing in their overt forms were frowned upon, and the potential leader had to be careful to affect the right degree of humility. Reverend Oda, a retired but still highly respected Christian minister, began as a humble laborer, but was characteristically chosen for leadership because of his dedication and humility:

Reverend Oda: *I came here to work, and I intended to go to school. But when I got here, I didn't know how to do anything at all. I didn't know what work to do or anything. So for four or five years, together with some of my friends, I worked at this thing and that. I would try one thing and think to my-self, "This is not my sort of work," so I would leave off. At the same time I was studying English, and I began to study the Bible. Then I entered the church and went East.*

Interviewer: *East?*

Rev. O: *Yes, I went to Ohio. But before that, for a cou-ple of years, I joined the church in Bakersfield. At that time there was no Japanese church in Bakersfield, but there was a mission for the Chinese. I thought it would be a good idea to learn English and, as far as the church goes, to study the Bible as well. So I rented a house and made some little tables and benches, and I called my friends there and suggested we study English. Then there was a man named Mr. Moody who taught in the church, and we asked him to come and teach us English. So we did that for four or five years, and the number of friends gradually increased, and people became more and more inter-ested in having a church. When they were through with their work, in the evening, they would come and study and learn hymns and English. One time I said to my friends that I thought it would be good if someone became a minister for our church, and they said that I was the one, I was the one. And it came about that I was picked.*

Personal charisma and technical skill were important at-tributes of leaders in the prewar community. Reverend Toshiba, pastor of a small Buddhist congregation and active in issei af-fairs, came to San Francisco with nothing but a priest's robes and a knowledge of the folk medical technique known as *kyu,* or moxa. "I came to the United States in 1930. I had no inten-tion of staying—I just came to study. However, I traveled here and there around the country. I found that there were many kinds of faiths and churches, and none of them seemed to be doing a lot of good. I came back to San Francisco and began to talk about establishing a temple [of my sect]. There were five families that were interested from the first. That was in Novem-ber of 1930. There was no money for the temple, but I decided to treat people [using moxa] who could not get relief from doc-tors. Pretty soon there were hundreds of patients, and we built a temple."

Leadership within voluntary associations tended to rotate among issei men who had special competence that fit them for the task at hand. In dealing with the outside world, knowledge of the English language and of American laws and customs was important. For community organizing, a gift for rhetoric in Japanese was sometimes more useful. Of course many men rarely or never took up positions of leadership in these groups, and, given Japanese cultural taboos on speaking ill of members of one's own group, it would be difficult to discover whether or to what extent these individuals felt oppressed by the community power structure. However, the Japanese emphasis on rule by consensus made it relatively easy for even a minority in any given group to depose unpopular leaders or to influence the course of important decisions. Authority was held collectively by the issei males as a group and was allotted by them to individuals on the basis of talent and personal magnetism. It was a strong and resilient form of leadership, one that was difficult to break except by means of the extraordinary process which actually occurred.

We have seen that the structure of the prewar community derived from a blend of Japanese tradition, discrimination on the part of American society, and personality characteristics of the issei as a group. The issei were attracted to many aspects of American culture but found typically Japanese patterns of social organization useful in fending off discriminatory and disintegrative pressures. Many issei were eager to learn from Americans but extremely reluctant to test their learning and their ability to manage in the wider American culture because of their culturally conditioned fear of ridicule and their emphasis on accurate and detailed knowledge of norms and rituals as a guide to successful social performance. They were greatly encouraged in their reticence by the segregationism of Caucasian society. Immigration seemed to select competitive, independent personalities who favored an egalitarian, almost communelike voluntary cooperation among the adult males but insisted on the subordination of women and children. The result of this reticence and solidarity, in San Francisco, was an ingrown, conservative ghetto—as mysterious, clannish, and foreign to the outsider's eye as it was protective, comfortable, and morally sound to the eye of the typical resident.

The Relocation

The experience of Japanese American communities following the Japanese bombing of Pearl Harbor in December 1941—the sudden, forced removal of the Japanese Americans from their homes and the living conditions in wartime relocation camps—had a profound effect on the history of the community. The initial shock and confusion following Pearl Harbor drew people in the community together, but it also created a massive sense of futility and opened the eyes of many community members to the backwardness and powerlessness of community institutions. As if to emphasize this effect, United States authorities immediately began to arrest the most conspicuous members of the Japanese communities as "potential troublemakers." This action both removed much of the effective leadership from the community, making it difficult for people to act cooperatively, and created an atmosphere of fear that split relationships within it (Sone, 1953, p. 151). Many people began to fear that their associations with others might be considered suspicious by the FBI, and much cooperative activity came to a halt. One prominent nisei now goes as far as to say, "If the evacuation order hadn't come when it did, the people left in the community would have been begging for evacuation in two months. All the able-bodied ones had been removed. The people who went to camp were the failures, the women, the children, the elderly, and the sick. At the time, lots of people considered it a loss of face *not* to be arrested as a potential troublemaker."

Although I am inclined to disagree with the letter of this last statement, there is little doubt that, in one sharp blow after another, the issei men were deprived of their power and leadership. As aliens (Asians were at the time racially ineligible for naturalization), they had their bank accounts frozen and could conduct business only through their citizen children. Their organizations were not recognized as legitimate representatives of the Japanese community by United States authorities, who turned to nisei organizations such as the JACL for official business concerning the status of the whole Japanese population.

Many issei organizations were suspected as dens of subversive activity, and their leaders had to disband or risk arrest.

During the internment in relocation camps, a number of factors further eroded the power and prestige of the issei men. Authority flowed from the Caucasian caretakers in charge of the camps. Fluency in English and familiarity with American customs became primary prerequisites for leadership in many important new areas, such as ensuring measures for health, education, and other necessities previously handled within the traditional community. This delegated authority gave the nisei an advantage. Citizenship became an important new criterion for leadership in many areas for the same reasons. Issei were barred by race from citizenship. New forms of self-government were instituted, including such practices as creating political entities (for example, "blocks" or "neighborhoods") by fiat, holding elections by decree, and suppressing dissent against elected representatives. These processes encouraged leadership by individuals who were deviant by community standards (Leighton, 1945). Jobless, the issei were deprived of much of the economic basis of their authority. They could no longer use economic pressure to enforce their decisions, either in the community or within their own families. Barracks life disrupted family authority in many ways. Shame-oriented issei parents were reluctant to discipline children in the crowded barracks where neighbors could easily hear them. Common dining facilities virtually destroyed one of the most important of all Japanese rituals—the family meal. Increased leisure and decreased community authority led to the formation of strong peer groups among the nisei, which often countered family values. In sharp contrast to the old communal festivals, which doubled as rituals of group solidarity and outlets for self-expression, recreation in the centers was almost entirely segregated along age and sex lines (Broom and Kituse, 1956, p. 38).

Individuals were affected in different ways by the relocation, some finding it an opportunity to exercise their particular skills for the benefit of the group, others withdrawing from public life, and a few—exempted from internment to pursue their education—striking out on a solitary path in another part of the country.

Following the relocation, the issei struggled to rebuild the Japan Town they had known before the war, but against great odds. During their absence, the site of the community had been occupied by others—mainly working-class blacks and other minorities who had come to San Francisco to fill jobs opened by the wartime economy. Many issei had lost their businesses and were to spend the rest of their working lives in menial service positions. Though defeated, Japan was still America's enemy, and American patriotism still discouraged Japanese customs. Moreover, Japan lay in ruins and was in no position to export either the material support or the moral encouragement necessary for a flourishing Japanese culture in the United States. The ingrown institutions of the old community, such as the Buddhist church, had little material benefit to offer, although they undoubtedly provided badly needed moral direction. The community services most urgently needed by the San Francisco Japanese American population were jobs, housing, and legal and legislative support, which had to come from the Caucasian society.

For these reasons leadership patterns changed. The individuals and the groups that knew the Caucasian world well were in demand, and this often meant the older nisei, the more acculturated issei, bicultural institutions like the Christian churches, and groups such as the JACL who advocated American ways. Buddhism and other Japanese religions lost members, although many of them still retained large and devoted followings. Many of the old self-help institutions, such as the Japanese Association and the prefectural associations, became mere ghosts of their former selves. The scattering of the Japanese community and its lack of financial resources also presented barriers to reconstruction. Friends and fellow group participants lost track of each other for years at a time. Without funds, it was difficult for groups to publicize meetings or pay their operating expenses.

In spite of these difficulties, the rebuilding of a viable community went on. In retrospect it appears that the emphasis had changed from one of self-containment and preservation of tradition to one of symbiosis with the dominant white society.

But the basic pattern of life—the meaningful whole organized around Japanese principles of belief and action—was not lost. The almost heroic efforts of those returning to Japan Town to resurrect their way of life can only be understood, I believe, as evidence of the spiritual vitality of that way of life.

Reverend Toshiba reminisces: "From the relocation camps, some people went east, others returned to San Francisco but could not go back to their homes because many black people had moved into the area. No one knew where anyone else was, and it was very difficult for people to find each other again. My congregation was completely scattered. I began to work as a gardener, but after a few months I became ill since I didn't know how to do it properly. Then I got a job as a salesman for a local soy sauce maker. I traveled all over the area. When I found a Japanese family, I would ask where the other Japanese in that area lived, and they would tell me, 'Well, there's another family three miles in this direction.' In this way, I gradually found where people were living. I traveled as far as Monterey. When I went to people's homes to sell them soy sauce, they would ask me to perform Buddhist services, such as memorials for the departed and so on. They also asked me to practice moxa. Eventually, there were enough families to start the temple again."

Japan Town Today

Looking at Japan Town in the 1970s, one gradually becomes aware of a serious paradox. There is a great deal of collective life, as there was in prewar days (an ethnic directory lists 111 organizations serving the twelve thousand members of the community), and there is also a great deal of diversity and conflict. The observer first perceives the community steadily disintegrating, only to discover on closer scrutiny the constant renewal of collective life. He also experiences the sociability of the community as a congeries of forces in dynamic equilibrium. Social bonds are now strong, now weak; groups pull apart only to regroup in stronger combinations; ideas now create antagonisms between people, now mediate their differences. In the description that follows, I identify those cultural and historical features of community life and thought that contribute to centripetal, bonding tendencies and to centrifugal, freeing tendencies in social behavior. My heuristic metaphor is that of an equilibrium between collectivism and individuality.

Japan Town was never very close to the hypothetical little community—the isolated, homogeneous, self-sufficient, unchanging small group proposed by Redfield as the antithesis of complex urban society. It has always been open to influence from the larger society around it, and it has always been differentiated in terms of the religions, occupations, classes, and geographic backgrounds of its inhabitants. Its history, especially since the war, can be seen as a process of increasing internal differentiation similar to the urbanization of folk society with strong folk elements. The rise of the nisei to leadership added to the generational differentiation of community institutions—a process that has been carried further by the recent arrival of the sansei at the threshhold of social maturity. The return of the Japan-educated nisei, or *kibei,* added a cultural dimension to this process, as did the arrival of the postwar Japanese as students, war brides, and visiting businessmen. Probably the most important factor in the differentiation of the community population, however, has been its economic and social progress within American society. Although discriminatory barriers to upward mobility have by no means disappeared, discrimination in employment, housing, and education has abated since the war, and Japanese Americans have had a much wider choice of where and how to live than they had before the war. The result has been an increasing diversity of life styles accompanied by an increasing diversity of social outlooks and codes. For example, a large number of nisei are now in the health, welfare, and education professions in San Francisco. Many of these doctors, teachers, social workers, and public health officials share the perceptions and values of their non-Japanese coworkers regarding social issues that affect the community; these professional perceptions and values often conflict clearly with those of other Japanese Americans. Likewise, the decline in housing discrimination has led to the geographic dispersal mentioned earlier in this chapter, and this dispersal in turn has led to the development of diverse neighborhood-specific concerns and outlooks on public issues among some nisei. But even under the impact of this differentiating process, some forms of collective life have survived.

A great deal of the average Japanese individual's life—waking or sleeping, working or playing—is spent in groups larger than two persons. Seen from the viewpoint of Euro-American culture, this is a collective way of life. Anglo Americans tend to prefer pairs, with a corresponding emphasis on the personal qualities of the actors and an internalized sense of social responsibility. Social life in Japan Town, as one would expect, falls between the Japanese and the Anglo American styles.

The most important collectivity in terms of its ubiquity in the community and its influence on the individual is the family. Each individual is seen and ideally sees himself as a representative of his family in community relations. In response to a question about another individual, a person is likely to say, "Yes, I know the Takahashis—a good family," or, "I never knew Frank too well, but I knew his Uncle Edward a long time." There is much concern about the accomplishments and failures of one's own kin, especially those in succeeding generations. The importance of kinship to status can be seen in the following remark from Reverend Oda, which he offered with great personal pride: "My daughter Helen married Okubo—George Okubo, he's a doctor. They are really a fine family. There are four doctors in that family, all brothers." Familism tends to decline in strength with succeeding generations, although there is a good deal of variability within each generation.

Miss Mita is a twenty-two-year-old sansei whose relationships with her family and with the ethnic community are currently distant and strained because she is living with a Caucasian boyfriend. From this vantage point she speaks almost wistfully of her friends' families:

Interviewer: *Describe the typical nisei-sansei relationship.*
Miss M: *I'd say variable degrees of relationship. There are the very close. I've seen feuds, but a basic family loyalty that binds the family despite the feud. And I've seen out-and-out*

feuds, where they really split. All in all, despite the closeness of
relationships there's a loyalty that binds them. I don't know if
it's characteristic of nisei-sansei. I'd say there's a greater loyalty
between sansei-issei—sort of revered, you know.

The theme of her remark—cohesiveness in spite of conflict—might describe family relations in any rapidly changing
society, but it indicates that open conflict of opinion and interest has become a fixed feature of life in many families. As long
as the family stays together, symbolically if not in the same
household, few young people see anything scandalous about frequent family arguments. The quality of family solidarity is important because the family is a model of cooperative social life
in general in the Japanese American community.

Outside the family, the most influential collectivity is the
ethnic churches. Exactly two-thirds of our interview subjects
were at least occasional churchgoers, and another 10 percent
were inactive adherents of a local church. Here again generational comparisons reveal striking change. There is a geometric
decline in church participation with generation. Sixteen of our
seventeen issei subjects were active in church groups but only
eleven out of fourteen nisei and seven out of twenty sansei. The
sample was not unbiased since many respondents were contacted through churches; however, the generational trend is supported by observation of the larger community. One would
think that such a lack of participation by the young would indicate not only spiritual traditionalism—that is, religiousness characteristic of a past era—but also the general social and political
conservatism associated with middle and old age. However, the
picture is much more complex than this. Some of the ethnic
churches, typically the small Buddhist and Shinto sects that attract almost exclusively the elderly and foreign-born, are ideo-
logically conservative. They are not active in social change, at
least visibly, although they contribute members to some change-
oriented interchurch agencies. The most progressive in terms of
community activity are the large Christian churches, the Methodist and the Presbyterian.

The largest Buddhist church, Jodo Shinshu, is in a special

position. Until very recently, it has been under the control of
conservative Japanese clergy and lay leaders, and some of the
younger ministers and parishioners feel it has failed to attract
the more socially conscious youth. Bishop Tsuji of the Buddhist
Churches of America wrote in 1971: "We encourage the individual to become involved [in social causes], based on the
man's own feelings according to his study of Buddha. The standards of Buddhism discourage division. It is our feeling that the
church itself doesn't have to write letters or protest. All of the
answers for us are in our philosophy" (*Hokubei Mainichi,* June
21, 1971). However, there are some signs that Jodo Shinshu
churches are rising to the challenge of adapting to new community forces. A few young sansei from the Bay Area have elected
to enter the Buddhist ministry, and I know of two who are active in community reform. Some nisei members of the Buddhist
church are also concerned about the lack of youth-conscious-
ness on the part of their ministers and are seeking to change it.

The congregations of all the major Buddhist and Christian
churches include people of different ages, occupations, and income levels, and therefore the church leaders face the difficulty
of providing a variety of services if they are to keep their congregations. The fact that there is only one all-Japanese American church of any single denomination in San Francisco does
not contribute much to the loyalty of members because there is
little stigma attached to changing churches and many people do
for a variety of reasons. Mrs. Morita, a sixty-nine-year-old issei,
was an adherent of a local Shinto church for many years, although her parents had been Nichiren Buddhists in Japan, and
her children and grandchildren are Presbyterians. A few years
ago, she joined the Presbyterian congregation. "Once I took my
grandson, Jimmy, to the Shinto church, and he got scared. He
clung to me and cried, and he said, 'This is not God! I don't like
this god!' I felt very badly, and after I got home I talked it over
with my husband and we decided to go to the Christian church.
We felt badly because the children's hearts were different from
ours." Other respondents told us that they changed denomination because they moved to a new neighborhood closer to a different church. One sansei changed from Christian to Buddhist

because his friends were on the Buddhist church basketball team.

Ideological conflict also exists within the various churches. One Buddhist congregation in the Bay Area split in two over a controversy about whether or not to spend large sums on the church school—a departure from traditional ideas. The issei elders in some churches are seen by the more progressive members as an impediment to needed change. Mrs. Kofuku (nisei, age forty-three) discusses the problem: "I feel I have a real responsibility to the church, and I want to support it, not only financially, but with my presence too. I think it's important. And because I feel so close to the minister—I think he's great—I think he needs the support of people like us who, you know, think as he does, who aren't willing to go along with the old people in their demand for a certain kind of worship."

The larger church congregations are divided into a number of specialized groups, usually by age. The issei generally attend Japanese-language services, which are separate from the English services attended by most nisei and sansei. Each of the large churches also has a woman's association composed mainly of elderly issei and a few nisei. The issei regard their churches mainly as a source of contact with other issei and as a source of profound spiritual experience. Says Mr. Daibutsu (nisei, age fifty-six): "The issei in our church really seem to get something out of the services. There is such a look of serenity on their faces during the sermon. Half of them, you know they can't really hear what the minister is saying, but they seem to get such peace of mind from being there." The emphasis on spiritual values in many of my issei interviews confirms this observation.

Mrs. Kindaichi (nisei, age forty-six) discusses another aspect of the church's role in the lives of the issei:

Interviewer: *How do the issei feel about the Japanese community here?*
Mrs. K: *I think the church is their community. They feel very strongly about it.*
I: *Why do you suppose that is?*

Mrs. K: *I think they need it because of the language. They need it. This Buddhist priest was saying he wanted to change the service to the morning, but if the issei don't have something to do all Sunday afternoon, they're lost. That's their whole life. It's the concern for each other that keeps them on their toes.*

For the issei there are also classes in traditional Japanese arts, picnics and outings, potluck suppers, and occasional entertainments sponsored by the church.

For the sansei, there are the church youth groups—both interethnic, such as the Young People's Christian Conference, and intraethnic, such as the Japanese Community Youth Council—and the church-sponsored sports teams. These youth organizations pose no threat to the nisei-dominated church leadership but are ways to interest the youth in church affairs and to assure some continuity in church and community institutions by training young leaders. There has been a serious decline in the size and number of church socials throughout the Bay Area, reflecting the attrition in sansei membership. Many of my sansei respondents dropped out of regular church activity in their early teens and turned to sports as a focus of ethnic social activity. Some sansei, however, remain active in church-centered groups well into college. One such group has recently taken a visible and vocal role in pressing for community reform, especially for better public services for the issei and for young people. Leaders of this group have been active in liberal politics in general, sometimes to the embarrassment of community conservatives.

It is the nisei and, in the case of the Buddhist church, kibei (Japan-educated nisei) who dominate the leadership of the churches. Although there is a full spectrum of outlook, some trends can be seen in my niesei respondents' attitudes toward religion and religious institutions. First, they tend to have little concern about religious doctrine per se and to show a general tolerance for differences of belief. I have not recorded a single instance of a nisei respondent quoting religious doctrine to support a personal belief, although many issei are inclined to do so.

Second, most nisei think the churches exert a stabilizing and integrating influence on the ethnic community as a whole and on young people in particular. For the churchgoing nisei, the church is the community counterpart of the family—it exposes the young to a value system which is broadly cooperative and tolerant, avoids extremes, and emphasizes social responsibility rather than individual choice. Mr. Morita, a forty-seven-year-old nisei, is more enthusiastic than most nisei men about the benefits of church membership, but his reasons are fairly typical:

Interviewer: *What does your religion mean to you?*

Mr. M: *I just feel that there is something better than this in the life hereafter. It also gives me a better understanding of others and the feeling that I am doing something for others. It helps me get along with others. Most of my close contacts are through the church.*

The socially integrative function of the churches is symbolized by their central role in the ceremonial life of the community. In addition to regular Sunday services there are weddings, funerals, and special services on religious holidays. The Buddhist church conducts monthly ceremonies memorializing members whose death anniversary falls in the current month. Church-sponsored sports events and socials continue to fulfill some of the needs for recreation described earlier. In recent years, there has been a widespread revival of interest in ethnic traditions and with it a resurgence of two Buddhist festivals: the birthday of Buddha, celebrated on or near April 8; and the Buddhist All Souls' Day, or *O-bon*, celebrated early in August. Both are happy occasions, involving the wearing of kimonos and the performance of Japanese music and dance. *O-bon* in particular has begun to attract non-Buddhists as well as Buddhists so that one ethnic newspaper reported three hundred dancers and many thousands of onlookers at the San Francisco *O-bon* festival in 1969 (*Hokubei Mainichi,* August 11, 1969).

A brief description of *O-bon* illustrates the way community institutions protect many traditions by adapting them to changed circumstances. Several weeks before the *O-bon* festival,

members of the Buddhist church begin to hold classes of instructions in the traditional *O-bon* dance. Most of the dancers
are young Japanese American women, by no means all Buddhists. There is a smattering of middle-aged men and women
and one or two Caucasians. Dancers wear either formal kimonos
or much simpler cotton *yukatas* for the dance, and there is considerable excitement over the planning of the costumes of the
younger women. On the appointed day a bandstand is set up in
the street in front of the Buddhist church, and the street is cor-
doned off to traffic. Beginning around seven o'clock in the
evening, a Buddhist prayer is read in Japanese over the public
address system. Immediately following the prayer, recorded
Japanese music is piped over the loudspeaker, accompanied by a
live traditional drummer. By this time the dancers have assem-
bled in the street and form a long line, two or three abreast,
around the platform. A master of ceremonies is also present on
the platform, and he occasionally announces in English the
names of the Japanese tunes and exhorts the dancers. The
dancers are ringed by a large crowd, mostly in street dress, but a
few are wearing kimonos. Prominent in the crowd are family
groups who appear to be relatives of the dancers and small
knots of sansei boys who have come to watch—and be watched
by—the young girl dancers. The boys are boisterous, calling
wisecracks to each other and to the dancers and jostling each
other and their sedate neighbors in order to get a better view. A
fair number of non-Japanese are present as well; perhaps 5 or 10
percent of the crowd. The gymnasium of the Buddhist church is
equipped with tables and chairs, and in booths around the pe-
riphery Japanese delicacies are sold along with coffee, dough-
nuts, hot dogs, and Coke. The gymnasium is crowded and the
trade is brisk. After about an hour of the traditional *O-bon*
dancing, the master of ceremonies introduces a Japanese American jazz combo who mount the outdoor bandstand and begin to
play. There is no dancing, however. Sansei boys and girls stand
around the platform in groups of three or more, talking and
laughing. By about nine-thirty the show is over and the crowd
drifts away. A cleanup committee quickly appears and begins to
tidy up the street and the gymnasium.

The revival of interest in the *O-bon* festival is symptomatic of the renewal of widespread pride on the part of the San
Francisco Japanese American community in its cultural origins.
The secularism, the mixing of cultural elements, the emphasis
on youth, and the interdenominational participation are all
symptomatic of the functional diffuseness and flexibility of the
churches as focuses of community social life. Looking at the activities of the churches, one sometimes gets the feeling that the
ideological divisions in Japan Town are after all few and insignificant.

Another group of formal organizations which contribute
to the sense of community unity are the various secular philan-
thropic organizations. The Japanese Benevolent Society owns
and operates a Japanese cemetery and also contributes funds to
worthy community organizations. The nisei Optimist, Lion, and
Rotary clubs sponsor sports teams and Boy Scout troops and
also contribute generously to community groups. The YMCA is
devoted to the needs of community youth. Merchants' associations, like the Japanese Chamber of Commerce, have charitable
functions as well as that of looking after the well-being of the
ethnic business community. These groups are much more restricted in their membership than the churches, some being
made up mostly of nisei men (such as the Lions and Optimists),
others including women and issei as well (such as the Japanese
Benevolent Society), and still others including mainly younger
and more progressive nisei and sansei (such as the YMCA). As a
result, these groups tend to have a political character; the
YMCA is a liberal force in the community while the nisei service
and merchants' groups are more conservative. Ordinarily these
political divisions lie in the background of community affairs.
Only when controversial issues arise do they move to the fore-
front.

Political debate and reform, as well as social action, are
more explicit functions of yet another group of formal associations, of which the JACL is the oldest and largest example. New
groups of this sort often form around specific political issues
and sometimes fade rapidly into obscurity. A left-wing pan-
Asian student organization, for example, appeared in mid-1968

and disappeared from public prominence after about two years of popularity. With the exception of the JACL, which I discuss below, these organizations contrast neatly with the churches as forms of collective life. At one extreme are organizations that are highly diffuse and flexible in function and include members of both sexes, of many ages and backgrounds, and with different values and attitudes; at the other are those that are specific in function and whose members have homogeneous values and interests. The churches are close to the first extreme, and the political groups are close to the second. The service clubs fall somewhere between the two. The two extremes do not encompass all the formal organizations in Japan Town since some, like the prefectural associations, are both diffuse in function *and* homogeneous in membership. But by illustrating the interrelation of structure and function in voluntary associations, they point up the paradox of increasing diversity within a community based on a collective way of life. Groups at the specific and homogeneous extreme, limiting their membership to advocates of a particular cause, underline the growing heterogeneity of the community. Groups at the diffuse and differentiated extreme soften and smooth over divisions by including many different elements of the community in many diverse activities.

The JACL is a unique political organization for Japan Town and illustrates an equilibrium between collectivist and individualist forces in the community that leads to orderly change. It has a large scholarship fund. For older members, it organizes many recreation events and travel tours and offers such benefits as group insurance and credit. The membership of the San Francisco chapter of the JACL averages a little over a thousand, or about 10 percent of the Japanese American population in the city. It is the largest single chapter in the nationwide organization and is the national headquarters. Although the main purpose of the JACL is to look out for the legal and political interests of the Japanese in America, it has become diversified in function and has sought to form its members into a broad political coalition. Until recently, the local chapter as well as the national organization seem to have been successful in steering clear of heated political issues that might split the organization, but it appears to be getting increasingly difficult to do so. In spite of the officers' efforts to compromise with civil rights activists within the organization, for instance, many activists have split from the San Francisco chapter and formed their own chapter of the national organization. The fact that this group stayed within the association attests to the vitality of the JACL form of organization, which allows considerable autonomy to local chapters and, in typical Japanese fashion, strives for consensus through compromise.

The JACL has some detractors in the community at large. Some sansei have begun to see the junior branch as an exercise in sandbox politics, where members are given grown-up-sounding titles but no voice in political affairs, or as a social club, where "nice Japanese girls" are encouraged to mix with "nice Japanese boys." These same sansei find the organization as a whole wishy-washy in its politics and apathetic to needed community reforms. They have forced a reorganization to give youth complete autonomy.

Ordinarily the political and ideological divisions within the community are of little concern to the average resident. A small group of people who are always active in public affairs tend to line up on different sides of issues without expecting to sway community opinion much one way or the other. Such activists often complain about the apathy and inertia of the average Japanese American. Mr. Suzuki expresses it well in his wry, rhetorical style, referring to a news item potentially of great significance to Japanese Americans: "You read about Spiro Agnew calling that nisei reporter a 'fat Jap?' If he had said 'fat nigger,' or 'fat wop,' or 'fat kike,' all hell would have broken loose. But in the Japanese American community, it will be just as if I dropped this coffee cup off the table. A small noise, then somebody will come along and sweep the pieces under the rug. I try to get people to write letters to their representatives and to the newspapers, but they won't do it."

Occasionally, however, certain events arouse widespread interest, if not action, in the community; sometimes even changing the complexion of community affairs. One such occurrence was the student strike at San Francisco State College in

the fall of 1968 and the concurrent appointment of well-known
semantics professor S. I. Hayakawa to the presidency of the college. The student strike centered on demands by minority students, chiefly blacks, for reinstatement of black staff members
who had been fired, for amnesty for black students involved in
the controversy, and for adding more minority staff and more
courses tailored to minority needs. The struggle reached the level of mass rallies, disruption of classes, and the presence on campus of the Tactical Squad of the San Francisco Police. As violence on the campus escalated, the dispute became a struggle
between civil rights activists and conservative college administra-
tors backed by the police and the governor's office. At the
height of the difficulty, Hayakawa, a strong law and order advocate, was appointed acting president by the governor. Meanwhile many Japanese American students had joined the strike.
In the following months, Hayakawa announced a program that
included negotiations with the striking students, but repressive
measures against staff and students who disrupted normal campus activity. Many of Hayakawa's remarks were thought anti-
liberal and oppressive by the striking Japanese American students and their sympathizers in the community, who branded
Hayakawa a "banana"—yellow on the outside, white on the inside—someone who had betrayed his ethnic group in return for
white recognition.

Meanwhile, conservative elements in the Japanese community, including parents of some of the striking students, saw
Hayakawa's actions as highly courageous, and felt that his as-
cent to national prominence was a signal victory for the whole
ethnic group. Although Hayakawa had been only a marginal
member of the Japanese community all along—married to a
Caucasian, living in a white suburb, and occasionally openly
critical of organizations like the JACL—his Japanese American
supporters began to claim him as one of themselves. One ethnic
newspaper was outspokenly critical of Hayakawa at first, then
changed its outlook and began publishing his articles.

A high point in the controversy was reached when the
local JACL invited Hayakawa to speak at a meeting. The anti-
Hayakawa faction, both within and outside the JACL, de-

manded the cancellation of the invitation. The JACL officers refused. A picket of the meeting was organized and carried out; it was the first major public display of dissent within the community since the war, and however sincere and well founded the motives involved, the community was profoundly shocked. Rumors had it that some prominent people among the pickets were subsequently boycoted. Church groups and public service groups held community meetings to discuss the difficulty and the wider ideological divisions within the community that led to it. Many of these meetings cast the crisis in terms of a growing generation gap between the sansei and their nisei parents. Although these meetings seemed to fill a need on the part of distraught nisei, in fact the sansei were most active in organizing such sessions. The content of the sessions leads me to believe that the organizers were motivated partly by a sincere desire to open up communication with their parents' generation and partly by their perception that the time was ripe to politicize the community. This perception was apparently wrong. The young activists had not been around Japan Town long enough or studied its history carefully enough to realize that cooperative group action in response to crisis is anything but the sign of a new order there. It is a habit, a useful one for preserving the traditions that hold the community together. The events surrounding Hayakawa have made him a concrete symbol of deep value cleavages among Japan Town residents but also a symbol of the resilience of community culture. This resilience profoundly effects the relationship of the individual to his group and thereby the course of his development.

The Hayakawa incident illustrates how new points of view gain popularity in the community, how new organizations form to carry them forward, and how the competition between organizations sometimes becomes intense. However, all the formal voluntary associations in Japan Town, I believe, operate according to a group of assumptions about communal life that has come down unbroken from premodern Japan and that has a broadly conservative, integrative effect on the community as a whole. For one thing, leadership is diffuse, and action is seldom taken without the consensus of the whole group. Both Anglo observers and activist participants in group meetings often complain about the great reluctance of leaders to take a stand on any issue until group consensus is clear and about the enormous expenditure of group time on the process of feeling out the mood of all present. After such a process, few people leave angry, and those who do tend to be the extremists and the impatient. Closely related to the emphasis on consensus is a willingness to shift points of view in order to avoid disrupting group processes. Open hostility in public groups is strongly disapproved, expressions of concern for one another's feelings are frequent, and nonverbal forms of communication are extensively used in order to avoid raising embarrassing issues. Said one Caucasian minister of an ethnic church, "The nisei are the only people I've ever seen who can sit down at a meeting and arrive at a decision without anyone having *said* anything!" Since such attitudes are less popular among European Americans, those members of the ethnic community who are most critical of them tend to be those who adhere to other European American ideals as well.

Friendship

Friendship is another kind of behavior that has a distinctive cultural pattern. But since informal relationships between friends leave no historical record outside of an occasional biography, it is extremely difficult to assess changes in friendship patterns or to measure the effects of such patterns on the course of community change. A great deal of the average Japan Town resident's life, however, is spent in casual associations with non-kin of his own sex and general age group. These associations have had a profound effect on social attitudes. Like the formal associations in contemporary Japan Town, informal associations tend to be comparatively stable over time and to include a wider range of activities and values than the typical middle-class European-American friendship. Friendships form in churches, neighborhoods, schools, or, often in the case of the nisei, relocation camps and persist throughout life where conditions permit. Groups tend to be small, rarely including more than a dozen, and tend to comprise a narrow age range. Among the nisei, close personal friendship between individuals of the opposite sex is rare. Although an individual of either sex might consider a heterosexual couple his or her close friends, he or she is likely to interact much more intensively with the member of the couple who is of the same sex. This pattern appears to be breaking down to some extent among the sansei, however. Casual friendship groups often include both sexes but seldom couples—a situation that will undoubtedly change when the sansei acquire spouses and children. These friendship groups will probably be less segregated by sex than in the nisei pattern.

The functional diffuseness of friendship patterns, especially among the issei and nisei, can be seen in the tendency of friends to do each other economic favors, to join the same formal organizations, and to spend leisure time together. Nisei businessmen and professionals often give special rates to their friends or procure goods for them at cost. Nisei prefer to patronize their friends' businesses. Gift exchange is an important feature of friendship as well. Not only are gifts required from friends on special occasions, such as weddings and funerals, but small gifts are usually brought when friends visit each other. Friends are also often employed in the traditional Japanese role of the broker, intermediary, or go-between. If A wants to discuss something with B that would be embarrassing to himself, to B, or to both of them, A will ask C to act in his behalf either to secure the agreement of B to a discussion or to settle the matter without direct contact between A and B. Likewise, if A wishes to discuss something with B but is a stranger to B, he will ask his friend C, who is known to B, to introduce them and arrange a meeting or to carry out the transaction with B himself.

Together with stability and functional diffuseness goes a personal commitment to friendships that requires a high degree of loyalty to members of the group, makes entrance into new groups difficult, and makes it possible for the group to exert relatively tight control over members' behavior. The individual sometimes feels that he has a choice only between going along with the group and dropping out of social activity altogether. After discussing at some length the limitations of the friendship clique, Miss Suzuki (sansei, age eighteen) says: "It's a trap, you know? Sometimes I wonder what I'm doing, going around with the same old people, even though I don't agree with a lot of what they think. But then I'll say to myself, 'But it's better than sitting home doing nothing, right?' "

Communitywide and intercommunity events—sports events, church bazaars, dances, picnics, club meetings—are opportunities for small friendship groups to mingle with other groups. For the nisei, these occasions often mean renewing old acquaintances; for the sansei, the emphasis is on making new ones. For the member of a small, tight-knit peer group within a small, tight-knit community, the possibility of seeing new faces is appealing and attracts many young people to community events. Until recently, according to one respondent, there were many intercommunity church socials which served such a purpose. Now, however, the participation of teenage sansei in church groups has greatly declined, and young people go to Japanese American college dances and public bazaars instead. Bowling tournaments and basketball games continue to attract a large number of sansei. Such events also are stages in the negotiation of a member's status within his peer group. By choosing carefully the friends with whom he attends a public function and how he behaves there, a person can gain in the esteem of his age-mates. The friendship group forms a link between the individual and the community at large, much the way the family does. Within the limited social world of the peer group, a person learns many non-kinship roles, acquires status, and takes on attitudinal and behavioral traits by which he is known to others in the community. We can now appreciate the significance of Mr. Yamabe's remark earlier in this chapter: "I don't think he was a member of this community. I never saw him at any of the basketball games." If the person in question had been a member of the community, he would have been a member of a friendship group. If he had been a member of such a group, the group would probably have gone to at least an occasional basketball game since basketball is often the only event in town where other groups might be found. If the group had gone to a basketball game, the youth in question almost certainly would have gone

too since his only alternative would be to do nothing. Therefore, he must not have been a member of the community.

The intermediary, or linking, function of the friendship
group is clarified if we apply the equilibrium metaphor to the
role of the group in the community. At times, friendship groups
may align themselves with major community institutions, values, or opinions, thereby contributing to overall communality
in the equation. At other times, the friendship groups may serve
as the propagating grounds for deviant opinion—as when the
group rallies around a member who has been defined by some
large sector of the community as deviant—thereby contributing
to heterogeneity.

More important for the personal adjustment of the individual to historical and cultural change, however, is the fact that
the friendship group is the main social setting wherein the
meaning of public events and private actions is discussed and individual perceptions and interpretations are put to the test of
group reaction. The attitudes and values that are thus the products of this primary group process play a major role in wider
public exchanges and strongly affect the course of community
life. In the next chapter, I explore this facet of the historical
process—that is, defining and reacting to portentous events.

Chapter II

History and
the Individual

History is not a set of symbolically neutral facts in fixed relationship to the present. Each generation must understand its history in the light of its own current experience—and vice versa. How a member of the Japan Town community regards himself, how he regards his fellow Japanese Americans, and how he regards the world outside his community and his ethnic group are perceptions that guide much of his behavior and interact dynamically with his understanding of the past. Moreover,

49

as Lyman (1973) shows, the past has a peculiar significance for many of my subjects *because* they are Japanese Americans. As members of a small, homogeneous, recently arrived, racially distinct, and frequently oppressed minority group, they are likely to consider their history close, unique, and emotionally vivid.

The intensity of their feelings about the past is expressed in a variety of ways. In their language, the very terms *issei, nisei, sansei, kibei,* and their variants point to historical statuses. In their politics, one finds major conflicts between different schools of historical interpretation and between those who advocate greater public consciousness of history and those who, for one reason or another, regard their history as a private matter. Advocates of historical consciousness have been highly active in the movement for establishing ethnic curricula in the California schools, along with black, Chicano, and Chinese American civil-rights leaders; so far, however, they appear to be a minority in Japan Town.

An understanding of the personal interpretation of history is crucial to two of the major focuses of this study, relations between generations and personal development. Generational difference in personal views of history might reveal previously hidden causes of the generation gap, at least among middle-class populations, where the gap tends to be most severe. Putting one's parents' generation in historical perspective, as middle-class youth often do, can be like looking at them through the big end of a telescope; they appear less as purposeful, effective, autonomous persons and more as the products of forces greater than the individual. This process requires children to reject their parents' self-definitions. Parents often reciprocate by attributing the behavior of young people to current child-rearing practices, educational methods, and the influence of television and movies.

In the field of personality studies, some theoretical attention has been paid to the effects of historical perceptions on identity (for example, Strauss, 1959); psychoanalysis and gestalt psychology have been concerned with the relationship of autobiographical distortions to personality functioning. However, aside from the psychoanalytic treatment of the lives of

great men (for example, Erikson, 1969), little research has been
directed at the interaction of historical perception and personality development. That such research might be rewarding is suggested by the following excerpt from the autobiographical essay
of Daisuke Kitagawa, a humble issei priest caught up in the
holocaust of relocation. During that taxing and confusing time,
Kitagawa happened upon an article by Paul Tillich which interpreted contemporary history from a vantage point above cultural biases. Says Kitagawa (1967, p. 153): "Tillich's thesis transformed me from one of the victims of misfortune . . . to one of
the participants in contemporary history, moving toward a universal society. What better orientation to life in American society could I have than that which Tillich had offered me?" Few
if any of my respondents were as articulate and as introspective
as Kitagawa, but many had clearly given considerable thought
to their history. In fact, this chapter was suggested by the importance of personal history in Japan Town conversation.

A serious methodological problem bears on my study of
historical perception. Because prejudice and discrimination on
the part of whites plays such an important role in Japanese
American history and because the investigators were mostly
white, two possibilities exist: that respondents concealed or
soft-pedaled their perceptions of discrimination in the interest
of politeness and amity and that those who volunteered for the
study were less resentful of non-Japanese than the norm and
less perceptive of discrimination in their views of history.

These problems cannot be completely laid to rest. The
concept of personal history set forward here is that of a set of
perceptions that change constantly as the individual's grasp of
himself and his social setting changes. Since I couldn't possibly
look at perceptions of history in important settings such as private interactions between Japanese American friends, relatives,
or lovers, I cannot claim firsthand knowledge of some contextual effects on perception. I did, however, check the effects of
my methods on the data in several ways. For one thing, I con-
tinually monitored public communications channels in the community throughout the research period and recorded the major
accounts of history that were exchanged there. The ethnic

newspapers, for example, had much to say about history. Ethnic studies classes, social service and church groups, and ad-hoc meetings on issues of community concern—situations where Japanese Americans were communicating primarily to Japanese Americans—were frequent scenes of discussion and debate about history. Presumably the accounts presented in such contexts were similar to those exchanged in settings closed to me. For another thing, because I was in regular contact with a number of socially alert community residents with a wide range of personal contacts, I was able to test my understanding of the main attitudes toward and interpretations of history found in the community by discussing the subject with them. These encounters were often extremely helpful.

As another control, three of the in-depth interviews were conducted by a volunteer sansei. Comparison of this material with the rest of the interviews suggests an interesting pattern: Whereas the two nisei interviews conducted by the sansei volunteer support the suspicion that some respondents are more outspokenly resentful of Caucasians when interacting with an interviewer from the same ethnic group, the other interview, of a sansei, does not support this suspicion. In other words, the control interviews taken together support the ethnographic observation that personality, education, and generation influence both the perception and communication of hostility between ethnic groups. Furthermore, individuals tend to stereotype the way they believe their acquaintances perceive history, reducing the complex and idiosyncratic to easily manageable oversimplification. For example, some sansei, raised in a comparatively egalitarian atmosphere, resent what they perceive as the racism of earlier times, attribute neutral attitudes toward this racism to the nisei, and then assume that the nisei are trying to be more acceptable to whites by denying their real feelings. This characteristic may be true of individual nisei, but the stereotype glosses over some important variations in the way nisei perceive their own history.

Still another complexity bedevils the student of historical perceptions, whatever his background. Some subjects give at different times contradictory interpretations of historical events. One gets the impression that certain subjects are using the interviewer as a mirror while they try on views of their own history to see which one suits best. Others apparently shift their historical interpretations to correspond with the contexts and emphases of the questions, indicating that historical accuracy is less important to them than, say, an interesting conversation. Probably the most important check I have on the validity of my data is the wealth of other information about attitudes and personality gained from the intensive interviews. This information permits the evaluation of styles of self-perception and self-presentation peculiar to particular respondents. For example, because some individuals are quite outspoken in their resentment of certain Caucasian traits but show little hostility toward major discriminatory events of the past, different weight can be given to their statements.

In the process of presenting things systematically, some distortion is unavoidable. The separation of history, culture, and self is mine, not the subjects'. I have inferred historical processes where the subjects have spoken in personal terms, and vice versa. Furthermore, in trying to explain variations in personal views of history, I have had to assume the existence of some historical facts and events from which to evaluate my respondents' perceptions. I have taken the license of reifying historical perceptions that represent common denominators among the more articulate members of the community. I believe this activity of generalizing from concrete personal experience is what Mills (1959) refers to as the task of social science, the "union of history and biography." But before this union can be achieved, we must first make the distinction between history and biography. This first step usually sets aside the individual's own experience of his past. The complexity of eliciting genuine perceptions of history involves, then, more than the ethnic background of the researcher. While I do not deny that being non-Japanese was a liability in many ways, I think that the thoroughness of this analysis is rarely matched in community folklore.

Styles of Perceiving History

When I began the analysis of historical perceptions, I expected to find clear-cut perceptual styles peculiar to each generation—issei, nisei, and sansei. Japanese Americans tend to see things according to these distinctions themselves. As one sansei man, age twenty-two, said: "The nisei had the worst in the struggle for survival here. They understand the old ways, and [they understand] the Americanisms in their kids. The issei were discriminated against, but they didn't understand it. The nisei understood, and they were still discriminated against." Of course the broad historical experience of the three generations *was* different, and there are systematic generational differences in perception. Having lived the whole span of the period of history that interests us, the issei tend to view it as a string of personal events, without the objectivity that characterizes the nisei and sansei. Having grown up after the war and evacuation, most sansei are bound by neither guilt nor stoic values to minimize the tragedy of those years, unlike the issei and the nisei. The issei picture tends to dim as time goes forward, the sansei picture as time stretches back.

Gross overall differences in historical perception cut across generations, however, and have implications for understanding the personal development process as important as generational differences. For the purposes of this discussion, I found that by rating each interview as a whole I could divide the subjects into four general types: *historians, personalizers, old ahistoricals,* and *young ahistoricals.* Their distinguishing characteristics are as follows:

Historians (five issei, ten nisei, thirteen sansei). Historians see the past from a supraindividual perspective. That is, individual life for them is imbedded in a larger historical reality which goes on independently. They may or may not derive causal statements or laws of change from this reality. They are more likely to see the past as stressful than as neutral or rewarding. The following excerpts from historians' interviews illustrate the way they think of history as a worldwide process independent of their own lives. Here are two examples: "When I travel here and there over the world, I find out nowadays all the young children, their ideas are coming closer and closer. It is because air travel is bringing them all much closer" (Mr. Uchida, senior, issei, age eighty-one). "I just finished reading *The Great Betray-*

al [Girdner and Loftis, 1969]. There was a lot of soul-searching when those leaders decided to do that [the decision to voluntarily cooperate with internment officials]. For that time in history, it had to be. The sansei criticize that decision, and some nisei did too; but the more I read about it, I think they did what had to be done. The blame isn't theirs, the torch shouldn't have been given to them. We were very young and ignorant in those days—we didn't know anything about legal procedures" (Mrs. Kofuku, nisei, age forty-three).

Personalizers (six issei, four nisei, four sansei). Personalizers are aware of historical events both closely and distantly related to their own lives, but they subordinate those events to overtly subjective perceptions and feelings. The important thing to them is the interior or subjective state associated with a historical event or process, and they are relatively unconcerned with the meaning of that event for others, or for a generalized other. They are not likely to search for causal principles, at least not consistently. When they do offer an historical interpretation, one often gets the feeling that the interpretation has an emotional validity for them independent of its fit with the "objective" facts. For example:

Interviewer: *Do you think the Japanese are treated equally in this country nowadays?*

Mrs. Kindaichi *(nisei, age forty-six): I think we've made it economically, but I don't think we're accepted.*

I: *Can you be more specific?*

Mrs. K: *Mostly feelings that you get. Or, maybe, maybe it's the other way around. Maybe it's [that] I don't feel I'm being accepted. Maybe* they *think I am. Maybe people do accept me, but I don't feel it.*

And another example:

Interviewer: *How do you feel about the nisei's decision to go to camp without resisting?*

Miss Kobayashi *(sansei, age twenty-five): Well, under the circumstances, I feel... I guess that was the only thing they could do. I keep on speaking in terms of nowadays. Under those circumstances there was nothing they could do. Since there was such hatred against the Japanese, and the Japanese Americans were really paranoid, too. What . . . the United States did was really unbelievable. I guess I wouldn't have such bad feelings about the United States if they were more honest about their history.*

Old Ahistoricals (six issei). This classification consists of a group of issei women who show almost no knowledge of and no interest in history beyond the limits of their own families and close social networks. For them there is no history that is not peopled by familiar faces in familiar surroundings. The fact that they are more inclined to dwell on the pleasant aspects of the past than are the historians is an intriguing finding I do not fully understand. I expect there are three main reasons: the unpleasant things in their historical consciousness are too close to be faced comfortably; they are not intellectually motivated enough to get things historically accurate; and they are more traditional than others in their values and therefore constrained to avoid complaining. Attempts to get these people to talk about history generally failed. I will not bore the reader with long excerpts from the interviews wherein repeated probing about historical detail is answered by only vaguely relevant personal memories or by a complete change of topic.

Young Ahistoricals (three sansei). There are really two subtypes in this group: those sansei who are too young to have learned anything about history to speak of and those who may know something about history but are profoundly uninterested in it. The latter (in my sample, two men, ages twenty-five and nineteen) are of special interest because, as we shall see, their attitude is probably much more widespread than my sample indicates. Again, examples are impractical since the group is characterized by a lack of historical material.

We can see some overlap of styles of historical perception among the generations. This overlap can be partly explained when we look at the characteristics of personalizers and ahistoricals. All the old ahistoricals are issei women, reflecting the cultural ideal that Japanese women of the issei's era should be non-intellectual, self-effacing, deferent to men, and dedicated to family and home. None of these women speaks more than a few words of English (though one has been a domestic in a Caucasian home for forty years!), although all are literate in Japanese. They all seem to have dedicated themselves to their families and to have left worldly affairs to their husbands. Of the issei personalizers, two are women. These women differ from the ahistoricals in being unusually well-educated (at least two years of college) and have high social background. They are hard to distinguish socially from the historians, except that the latter seem to have more upward mobile families. The four issei men who are personalizers are distinguished from the male historians by advanced age, ill health, poor education, or some combination. Thus the three oldest men (all in their eighties) and the one most ill fall into the personalizer group; the three youngest, two of whom are among the three best educated, fall in the historian group.

Turning to the nisei, we see the continued influence of education and socioeconomic status on style of historical perception. Of the four personalizers none had more than a high school education and only one had clearly upward mobile children (one child at the University of California, one in medical school). Nine out of the ten nisei historians were either college educated or had children in universities or with university (not trade school) degrees. Neither sex nor age appears to be a factor in nisei perceptions of history.

The sansei picture is more complex. I have already mentioned that one of the young ahistoricals was too young (fourteen) to have much sense of history. The other two, both men, appear to be examples of what is sometimes referred to as the "bluing of America." Bright, energetic, and of blue-collar parents, they seem to consider history a waste of time. They are extremely future-oriented and economically practical. They probably resemble a great many nisei of thirty years earlier, and their type is probably much more widespread among the sansei than this study indicates. We would expect such young men to see little relevance in my research and to be too committed to too many practical things to take part in it anyway. Remarks from our more historically minded sansei subjects support this supposition in that they feel most sansei are not like themselves. One of the sansei historians has a set of values almost identical to that of the ahistoricals but differs from them in that his father is a university graduate.

Both sex and socioeconomic status also appear to separate the personalizers from the historians among the sansei. All four personalizers in this generation are women. Although three have some university education, none have college-educated parents. Two are originally from rural backgrounds. Sex, education, and socioeconomic status do not, however, account for the whole difference between these two styles of perception. Apparently other factors are involved as well since three of the eight women historians are also from working-class backgrounds.

To condense the results of this analysis into a few words, we might say that people's perceptions of their history are clearly influenced by their social background, status, and age. Schatzman and Strauss (1955) conducted a similar analysis of reports of a tornado in the southern United States, and found the same differences in perception between social classes. Social roles influence the kind, number, and diversity of social contacts people have, which in turn effect the breadth and flexibility of their perceptions. In many cultures the lower classes, women, and the elderly are more restricted in their social contacts than are the upper classes, men, and young people and have corresponding differences in their patterns of thought and communication. In later chapters I discuss the possible effects of internal development on these perceptual patterns.

This analysis may have important implications for any group seeking to establish an identity in a multicultural milieu (and nowadays, this seems to include most of the world's people). If cultural background or national origin is to be the basis for a strong group identity, history must be interpreted broadly. The interpretation must be compatible with the variety of lifestyles within the group and their corresponding experiences of the past.

Issei

We now turn from the styles of historical perception to the content. It has become almost a cliche among observers of Japanese American society that the third generation wants to remember what the first and second generations want to forget, especially with respect to anti-Japanese discrimination. The discussion of perceptual styles indicated major variations on this theme, but one cannot deny its accuracy as a description of a trend. My main purpose in the following pages is to discuss how accurate this description is and to inquire into the psychological and cultural reasons for it. I hope this exercise will serve as a model (not a standard) for similar studies of the relationship between persons and their environments. I also hope it raises some questions for the nisei and the sansei themselves, such as, "How does one choose a view of history?"

Almost universally, the issei divide the past into two distinct periods—prewar and postwar—and see the latter as a great improvement over the former. Among difficulties frequently mentioned as characteristic of the prewar era are getting by in the United States with no understanding of the language or culture, prejudice and discrimination directed against the Japanese, and bad economic conditions, especially during the Great Depression. But despite this view of the prewar environment as harsh and often hostile, almost all issei believe that success or failure is a matter of personal ability in the long run. Rarely do they excuse themselves for setbacks on the grounds of persecution or misfortune. They see themselves as active agents in the construction of their own history. Says Mr. Daigen, age eighty-two: "If two people have the same qualifications and one is Japanese and the other is a Caucasian, naturally the Caucasian will get the job. Before, it was even worse. You can't help it if they think of the Caucasian first. But the main thing is ability. If you can deliver the goods, there's always an opening somewhere."

Although most issei recognize the racism of the prewar and wartime eras, they show remarkably little bitterness or resentment about it. Often they seem more concerned with affirming their own innocence than with laying blame on anyone.

Often they excuse their oppressors on the grounds of ignorance, as in a typical remark from Mrs. Honda, age sixty-five: "The most frightening thing was when we had to go to camp during the war. We didn't know what was going to happen. It was very frightening. Of course I feel American because I have been here for forty-seven years, and I was in Japan for only eighteen years. We all feel American and obey the United States laws. But people don't know that."

Flagrant incidents of discrimination are clearly remembered, but the issei tend to regard such incidents as exceptions to the normal course of events. In the following incident, Mr. Daigen is careful to note, for instance, that his persecutors had not been real Americans:

> Interviewer: *What sort of thing makes you angry?*
> Mr. D: *Oh, it depends on the situation. There are various ones. For example, I was an institution gardener. The assistant gardener was a German-type person, and the doctor that came was German. The assistant and the doctor were always using German. He'd sometimes say bad things about me in German. And the doctor of course would take the assistant's side and accuse me. I'd hear about it, and it would be things that never happened, or stuff I knew nothing about. In that situation I was really shocked.*

The evacuation and relocation are viewed by the issei with mixed feelings. Most say that they were shocked and afraid at first, then relieved at finding that the government did not intend to torment or exterminate them in reprisal for the acts of Japan. Some, like Mr. Uchida (age eighty-one) have come to see life in the camps in a generally positive light.

> Mr. Uchida, senior: *We had much better treatment than we expected in the camp, We didn't know what was going to happen.*
> Interviewer: *As an issei with an American education, did you get involved in self-government in the relocation camp?*
> Mr. U: *Yes, at every camp they had self-government.*
> I: *Did you take part in it?*

Mr. U: *Oh yes. I was a block councilman and was discussing with the administration about the children's education, food, and all kinds of things. There were many problems. Smuggling of the administration's stuff and all that kind of thing.*

I: *Smuggling?*

Mr. U: *They got lots of beef for the people in the camps, but the people in the warehouses stole the meat, so the people didn't get any of it. We brought it to the attention of the camp management. Especially the education was very, very poor. Finally, we found out that the government doesn't want a very good education system there because then the people wouldn't want to fly away from the camp. Same thing with the hospital.*

I: *How did you feel about it?*

Mr. U: *Of course it was not good from the Japanese people's point of view, but, from the administration's point of view, of course they couldn't help it. And, from the long point of view, maybe it was very beneficial for the nisei because they were able to establish a new way of life.*

Mr. Uchida's ability to take an active part in camp affairs has a great deal to do with his positive perception of the episode. Other issei express ambivalence. Mrs. Tani (age seventy-six), for instance, tells of her anxiety and the terrible economic consequences of the evacuation and adds that her husband took to drink at the time. Her response to a later question contradicts the feelings we would expect to find, and so may be a poignant sign of a deep inner conflict: ⸚

Interviewer: *How do you feel about the nisei's decision to go to camp without resisting?*

Mrs. T: *At that time, we had to go come what may. It just couldn't be helped. I think it was good. We entered camp and we felt safe. If we lived outside, there were various bad— there were people who would persecute us. I enjoyed it in camp. I was able to do the things I wanted to do. Before that, I was too busy.*

There are a few issei who see the evacuation with straight-forward resentment. In response to the above question Mr.

Daigen says: "The issei were branded as enemy aliens. In such a short time—twenty-four hours, or [at most] a week—we had to go out and go to camp. Had to dispose of our property or our enterprise, even household furniture. The biggest blow was to the farmers, who had to leave with the crop growing. They had to give up the whole thing. Of course it was wartime, but I think there was an economic motive behind the evacuation. Caucasian farmers cleaned up what was left, with a big profit."

The postwar period is viewed by the issei as a vast improvement over the prewar era in almost every respect. They tend to feel that their children have done well, that discrimination has all but disappeared, and that they themselves can be thankful for such things as social security. The one big regret that remains widespread among the issei has little to do with the toil and suffering of their lives: They know that their native culture is fast passing from the face of the earth: "In the old days," says Mr. Fujii (age eighty-five), "it was true of Japanese character to be devoted to education. Nowadays it is not so, not since the war. The Japanese used to have this spirit of exerting themselves on behalf of their country and standing together. But nowadays they are not taught to be that way. This is the case even in Japan these days. In the old days we had what we call moral education. Then, one was taught things like loyalty to one's master and to honor the emperor. Japanese democracy is the wrong way. Nowadays they have all sorts of trouble there. That's because the communist ideology has come in." The following excerpt is from an interview with Mrs. Oka (age seventy-nine):

> Interviewer: *How do you feel about the younger generation in general and the difficulty between them and their parents?*
> Mrs. O: *Since the world is changing, there is nothing that can be done about it. I would like the children to respect their teachers more. When I was young, I was always told not to disrespect my teachers. But now even in Japan, they don't adhere to that, I think.*

Both cultural and psychological factors influence the issei's perceptions of history. In some ways their perceptions are clearly the result of their being Japanese and in other ways are the result of universal or nearly universal psychological traits. Cultural factors include the famous Japanese principles of endurance, patience, and self-restraint, which issei subjects often cite as guides to happiness and success. As Mrs. Tani puts it: "[When I get angry at somebody], I get the Bible and through it I learn. Then I endure whatever it is. I think that's best. I endure it." In response to another question: "In the old days, I couldn't endure very well. But through these instructions, this enduring becomes more comfortable. When you age, your feelings become more even. Well, when you get mad sometimes, it's easier to endure."

Closely related to endurance is the concept of gratitude. The main tradition espoused by Buddhist issei (and recall the issei are deeply religious as a group) stresses the indebtedness of the individual to his ancestors and to the world. The Japanese Christian churches naturally emphasize God as the source of bounty, but like the Buddhists, teach that one must receive humbly and with pleasure whatever rewards life holds. Grumbling and negativity are strongly disapproved.

Foremost among the principles brought from the Japan of the issei's youth is respect for authority. A peaceful and productive life is felt by them to result from a well-ordered human society; order in turn is seen as the product of respect for rules and those who legitimately make them. During the evacuation, most issei probably did not fully understand the Western concept of constitutional rights and therefore believed United States leaders acted within their authority, however unfairly and harshly.

These traditions would naturally discourage the issei from expressing resentment or self-pity in connection with their past, but do they feel such resentment and self-pity? Is there a discrepancy between their reported and their inner feelings? This question leads to another important ethical principle of the issei, harmony. Harmony between man and man, between man and nature, and within the individual is among the highest goals of Asian culture. Confucianism and Zen are based on the pursuit of different sorts of harmony—Confucianism emphasizes the social world, Zen the natural and spiritual world. Although our subjects do not often verbalize this value, their life styles indicate that it is important to them.

Harmony has two implications for the issei perception of history. First, the issei tend to repress feelings which are out of harmony with social demands. For example, Matsumoto, Meredith, and Masuda (1970) predicted that issei would describe themselves as more inclined to hide their feelings than would nisei or sansei, but the opposite turned out to be the case. This finding may show that the issei have learned to suppress inner conflict to such a point that they are unaware of feelings which are not socially acceptable. In this sense, I believe they usually "really feel" what they tell us. Second, the issei interpret historical events to preserve harmonious interpersonal relations here and now and to minimize inner turmoil and anxiety.

What is the major threat of the evacuation experience to the tranquility of the issei mind? To answer this question, we need not invoke their cultural background. Anyone who undergoes such an experience and interprets it as tragic, avoidable, and unpardonable is susceptible to overwhelming feelings of guilt. Under the circumstances that greeted the issei during and after the war, guilt could be expected to arise from three different sources. In order of their likely occurrence, they are: identification with the aggressor, the suffering of one's fellow oppressed, and the betrayal of oneself.

Observers of the parallel and contemporary experience of the Jews in Germany (for example, Bettelheim, 1943; Cohen, 1953) note that the survivors in the Nazi concentration camps tended to be those who took the attitude of their oppressors, the SS guards, toward themselves and their fellow inmates. As I note elsewhere (Kiefer, 1970) this behavior is widespread and helps account for the effectiveness of physical and psychological torture in producing behavior change. Under conditions of extreme and prolonged stress during which normal sources of social support and comfort are removed or diminished, most people experience a loss of self-esteem. This is a painful experience, and people generally look for some way to escape it. If they cannot avoid this painful experience, they seek within themselves a cause for the loss of self-esteem. If they find a specific internal cause for this loss and can remove the cause, there is hope of restoring some of their lost pride. Thus persons who have been tormented for some supposed error or deficiency often end up agreeing with the definition of themselves offered by their tormentors and trying to atone for the error.

Dependency on one's parents as a child is universal, and it is an easy experience to remember when one is placed in an unfamiliar position of enforced dependence. A child can often regain his parents' love by accepting blame, and a similar desire to atone accounts for identification with the aggressor. Many issei could scarcely escape it during the relocation. They felt that they had been deficient in feeling and expressing loyalty to their host country. The fact that the United States had denied them citizenship and violated its own laws in persecuting them had little bearing on their feelings under the circumstances. Man is a fundamentally social creature; his psychological well-being depends on others' evaluations of his acts, however prejudiced or ill-informed. Thus the issei are not inclined to judge the relocation as unfair even when they recall the suffering and loss it brought them.

Having accepted some responsibility for the evacuation, the issei were at once vulnerable to another kind of guilt. Others less to blame were suffering for the imagined transgressions of the issei. Their children—the whole nisei generation—were the victims of their mistakes. I have never heard of a nisei publicly making such an accusation of the issei, and those who say it even to themselves are probably few (as we shall see, the nisei have their own guilt feelings to deal with). But the issei had for decades upheld the traditions of their homeland against nisei protests and suddenly had to curse themselves for their pride. It is a tribute to their strength of character that most issei were able to hold onto that pride and avoid the same vicious circle of passivity and self-hatred that often visits the victim of rape. For many issei, the price of pride was having to minimize in their own minds the losses that they and their fellow Japanese Americans had sustained.

The issei also had to contend with the guilt of self-betrayal. Many issei had chosen to come to this country in the first place—sometimes against the protests and warnings of kin—and they had chosen to remain here after others left in disgust. They had staked their livelihood and that of their families on the promise of their new environment. Could they now admit the possibility that their gamble was a serious mistake, that American society was basically and irreparably faulty? As long as they could see the evacuation as a natural disaster like the typhoons and earthquakes of their homeland, impersonal and therefore blameless, accidental and therefore unavoidable, they would not have to feel the guilt of self-betrayal. Their present perceptions tend to agree with this picture. The evacuation was "all a mistake," a result of that impersonal cataclysm, "the war."

History is thus an environmental stimulus to which the issei have had to respond in order to function effectively in the present. For any individual, according to the breadth and detail of his historical consciousness, history not only offers a guide to the solution of new problems, but also requires an interpretation that preserves self-esteem. The uses and dangers of history are intertwined in the business of living, and for that reason cultural tradition provides a guide for historical interpretation. The typical issei is required by his culture to accept responsibility for himself, his family, and his ethnic group; he is aided by traditions that place personal and social harmony above self-consciousness and which accept tragedy as a normal ingredient of human life. If the issei were responsible for their own losses and failures, they were also to some extent responsible for the success of the nisei.

Nisei

For the nisei, these traditions have survived, but they have been weakened by exposure to American individuality, optimism, and self-expressiveness, and history has also treated the issei and the nisei differently. In their perceptions of history, the nisei are more outspoken than the issei about prewar discrimination, but they also seem to vacillate on the subject, indicating strong ambivalence. As our discussion of styles of historical perception indicates, the nisei regard discrimination as a general social condition affecting the whole ethnic group rather than as specific incidents affecting only themselves. Some nisei see themselves as exceptions to the rule for their ethnic group, feeling lucky that they have escaped serious personal insult on the grounds of race or culture. Says Mrs. Minamoto (age fifty): "I was the one of the first Japanese to enter East Grove Elementary School. It was in two rooms and had about ten students per class. I was about six at the time. I had two wonderful white teachers: Mrs. Davis for the first, second, and third grades, and Mrs. Martin for the sixth through eighth. I was one of the first Orientals there. I recall it was really wonderful. I think I was very fortunate because there was lots of prejudice then. During Christmas there were wonderful programs, all the kids exchanging gifts. I remember having so much fun." Mr. Kimura (age fifty-one) offers another example, talking with a sansei interviewer about his first job after the war.

Mr. Kimura: *Well, the coworkers weren't too bad. At that time there was another Japanese in Bakersfield working in the same union, and the reaction up there was much worse to Japanese working in [that industry]. I went to a meeting where the trouble in Bakersfield was brought up, and they pointed out to me that I had been accepted and there hadn't been any trouble. They said it wasn't my fault that the war had started, and that we should work together, and the membership concurred about that, and I think they got it straightened out in Bakersfield about that time too.*

Interviewer: *That must have put you under a lot of pressure.*

Mr. K: *No, it didn't. At first, the first job I had, I was kind of skeptical about whether these fellows would accept me, but they were very nice about it.*

Both of these subjects are outspoken, as are most of the nisei, about discriminatory incidents that did not involve them directly.

In many interviews, subjects express feelings of deprivation that stem from their exclusion from mainstream American society, but they are reluctant to lay the blame squarely on any particular characteristic of that society. As one would expect, the women emphasize their isolation from white social circles and the personal rewards they saw there. Mrs. Minamoto implicitly blames her parents for much of this isolation: "When I was going to high school in that era, there was a lot of prejudice to minority groups. We were left to ourselves. We had few American—I mean Caucasian—friends. During that time, many people from Japan felt girls going out with boys wasn't proper, at least not until they were engaged. We grew up under Western education and saw our friends going out, and boys would ask us—Japanese boys—and we'd ask [our parents] and they'd say no. It was a big hassle, the struggle between the older and the younger generation. It started about the time we entered high school, and Junior Prom was the first time any of us broke that barrier. A group of us went. It was the first time that we went to a school social like that."

The nisei men emphasize the lack of economic opportunity, although they also mention social isolation. Again, economic difficulty is sometimes seen as a direct result of discrimination, a result of the Depression, a result of issei interference with their education, or a combination of these. A chracteristic ambivalence is shown by Mr. Fujii, a fifty-six-year-old nisei dissatisfied with his career. At one point he refers to the Depression as the reason for the failure of a family business that derailed his hopes. At another point he says that the evacuation was the specific cause. At still another point he offers the following explanation:

Interviewer: *Would you say you're basically satisfied or dissatisfied with your life so far?*

Mr. F: *Well, I don't like to say "dissatisfied," because I figure it's my own doing, what I got or what I failed to get. So I'd say I'm satisfied, although I suppose everyone would like to have a little more.*

The ambivalence of the nisei about the best way of interpreting their past is closely related to their profoundly divided ideals and images of who they are and what their relationship to American society is (see Chapter Six). The nisei have had to separate the Japanese and the American sides of themselves, and they have learned to switch back and forth with the same agility that they switch languages. As Japanese, they see history through the eyes of a cohesive minority group. As Americans, they see it through those of an individual who happens quite accidentally to be of a different race. It is inconsistent with their identity as loyal Americans to perceive discrimination as an American character trait. It is equally inconsistent with their Japanese identity to perceive history any other way.

Regarding the evacuation, this ambivalence is complicated by many other things. In a sense, many nisei were liberated by the evacuation from the strict control of their parents. About half of my nisei respondents believe the evacuation was in the long run beneficial in this respect. Their social horizons were broadened, restrictions on their individual development were relaxed, and, in many cases, new economic opportunities were opened to them. Says Mr. Morita: "Well, I can't say I really felt liberated by the experience, but it opened up new experiences. It depended on things like what your parents' plans were, too. Many issei wanted to go back to Japan, but my parents gave up that idea as a result of the relocation. It's true that many of the issei thought about us as kids, and their eyes were opened by the relocation experience." And Mrs. Minamoto: "Well, in the beginning I suppose there was bitterness [about the evacuation]. It was something that happened and you had to go through with it. Gains were with it too. Loneliness. We missed my father and husband. We made the best of what we could do in camp. We felt we were deprived of those years, losing our property and personal belongings. We had to start from scratch. We'd only been married ten months. But the issei lives were thrown out the window. A lot lost friends that they thought they'd entrusted property to. When they came back they found that they weren't as good friends as they thought. Probably some bitterness about that, but they salvaged what they could and started over. There was prejudice before the war, and many had the desire to go back to Japan, especially wives. They were cut off from their families, had no security. But things were changed. Maybe this country was the place. Their children were schooled here, and their feelings changed. Then things weren't so bad after all. Maybe some good came out of it after all."

The nisei say, probably correctly, that it was the issei who really suffered during the evacuation. This perception is dangerous to their self-esteem. The nisei had often been advocates of Americanism against their parents' protests; now America had betrayed them all. Then too, the evacuation handed the nisei an easy victory in their struggle for recognition and independence. Focusing on the harshness and injustice of the incident might therefore be difficult for many of them. One hears instead of the good effect the hardship had on nisei character and of the respect the Japanese Americans gained in the eyes of the United States for their dignity and courage in the face of outrage. Although the nisei are much less inclined than the issei to invoke the ethic of patience, it also has been an important motive in shaping their perceptions of history.

Most nisei also believe that they were not to blame for their decision not to resist internment and that their generation was responsible, largely through the heroism of nisei soldiers in World War II, for the reversal of earlier anti-Japanese prejudice. Earlier in this chapter I quoted a nisei respondent on the first point. Regarding the second point, Mr. Hibana's remarks are fairly typical:

Interviewer: *Has anyone in your family or community ever done anything to make you ashamed you were a Japanese American?*

Mr. H: *No, I don't think so. I think there are a lot of things to be proud of.*

I: *Can you give me an example?*

Mr. H: *I'd lots of friends in the Four-Forty-Two. [The all-nisei 442nd Regimental Combat Team, operating in the European Theater, was the most decorated U.S. unit of its size in World War II.] A lot of fellows died. We can point with pride to that, all of us.*

The most common nisei perceptions about the postwar period focus on the decline (but not disappearance) of anti-Japanese prejudice, on the growth of economic prosperity, on the atrophy of prewar community institutions, and on the moral effects of all of these processes on their children, the sansei. While nisei have mixed emotions about the decline of ethnic solidarity and community life—some taking a good-riddance attitude, others showing disappointment or anxiety—there is more agreement on the effects of postwar prosperity and assimilation on the sansei. Mrs. Minamoto says: "I always feel the nisei people, because they couldn't have much when they were young, are overindulging their children too much. I feel that sometimes. I tried not to do it with my son, but undoubtedly I did it some." Mrs. Hata (age fifty-seven) offers a different interpretation:

Interviewer: *Did you ever disagree with your children?*
Mrs. H: *Their way of thinking and ours clashed sometimes. They are centered on now.*
    I: *Is there disagreement about anything in particular now?*
Mrs. H: *If there is, it's about money. When we were young, we had to work for money, and we were conscious of it. Now it's too easy.*

While many nisei are troubled by the moral effects of the sansei's "soft life," some are also impressed by the greater poise of their children's generation: "They're a thinking generation," says Mrs. Kofuku, "and a very bright generation." Mrs. Kindaichi (age forty-six) says: "Typical sansei? Young, free, thinking, feeling. All those adjectives come to mind for the sansei I know. Involved people. I have a great deal of respect for them as a whole." And Mrs. Minamoto agrees: "Very carefree. Very outward. Young, too—don't seem to have the golden life ambition that the nisei had. I guess they do in their own little way. They're not shy about mixing with other ethnic groups like the issei and nisei were."

Perhaps the most troublesome contemporary historical event for many nisei is the meteoric rise of Japan to world eminence. Having more or less severed and concealed what was Japanese in their self-perceptions, they are inclined to feel betrayed by this circumstance. Some, like Mr. Uchida, have recently acquired a taste for japanalia and for books about Japan in an effort to recover some of their historical ties. Most of my subjects appeared embarrassed by their lack of knowledge of the new Japan but were unlikely to do anything about it for the time being. Nisei consternation over the subject is reflected in the popularity of letters from Japan in the English-language sections of the major ethnic newspapers, lengthy reports from a mysterious land of supertechnology and descriptions of strange customs hauntingly familiar from childhood. Many representatives of the new Japan are found in the banks, shops, hotels, and temples of Japan Town, but most nisei are not intimate with them. It is a familiar sight to see a nisei matron pointing and nodding mutely in a Japan Town shop—able to understand the clerk's fluent modern Japanese but too embarrassed of her own archaic and rusty speech to answer. The image the nisei have always had of the stiff, polite F.O.B. in his voluminous blue suit and starched white collar crumbles under the onslaught of the chic, animated, and suave new Japanese.

A disturbing new historical development has begun to touch the nisei recently—the deterioration of United States-Japan relations in the 1970's, chiefly over trade disagreements, and the consequent revival of anti-Japanese sentiment in certain sectors of American society. The extent of the difficulty, and its potential effect on the nisei, can be seen from the following excerpt from an article by Norman Pearlstine in the *Wall Street Journal*, reprinted in part in the *Hokubei Mainichi* of August 12, 1972:

In Phoenix, Star Chevrolet warns the public in ads: "Remember Pearl Harbor, when they tried to take your country from you. They are back with cheap imports to take your jobs, pensions, and social security."

During a strike at the Fontana, California, plant of Kaiser Steel Corp. pickets cry: "Jap steel! Jap steel!" and curse the supervisors who drive through in Datsuns and Toyotas. They say nothing to men driving Volkswagens.

*A South Carolina congressman, Rep. James R. Mann, in-
serts a song called "The Import Blues" into the Congressional
Record. The song is critical of "Jap-made products" and the
"slant-eyed people of the Risin' Sun."*

*The American Immigration Committee of Decatur, Geor-
gia, a small right-wing group, publishes a "population report"
calling for an end to immigration of "aggressive Japanese" because they may wind up controling the federal government.*

*Newsman Robert Abernathy of KNBC-TV in Los Angeles
receives a barrage of hate calls and letters after covering "Execu-
tive Order 9066," a photographic exhibit concerning the wartime internment of Japanese Americans. "In the first ten min-
utes after the segment went off the air, we got fifty-five calls
cursing us for implying that the roundup of Japanese Americans
had been a mistake," he says. "The callers didn't see any difference between Japanese soldiers in the Western Pacific and Japanese Americans here. They thought internment was better than
they deserved, then or now."*

*In 1967, researchers at UCLA published a poll showing
that 48 percent of Californians approved the incarceration of
Japanese Americans in camps during the war. The poll also
showed a strong relation between the image Californians have of
Japan and acceptance of Japanese Americans.*

In response to this trend, a prominent Bay Area nisei was
quoted in the same article: "In the 1930s we had a similar situation. It started with bad-mouthing of the Japanese, and then the
hostility was turned on us. And I'm afraid it's happening again."

These events revive and underscore an important characteristic of the nisei perception of history. Their temporary enforced exclusion from American society reinforced the Japanese
side of their identity and encouraged them to see the evacuation
and other discriminatory actions as fitting the pattern of their
relationship with the United States. Although postwar prosperity has done much to contradict this interpretation, the nisei are
still tempted to believe that they were right after all. With this
perception come the old inner conflicts and self-accusations.
Mr. Daibutsu (age fifty-six) describes discussions with his chil-

dren about the evacuation: "I've said to them what did happen and how wrong my judgments [that it would never occur] were at the time. It goes to show, anything can happen."

Some nisei in the San Francisco community recognize the connection between collective guilt and the nisei tendency to smooth over the evacuation. Mostly professionals active in community affairs, they believe a thorough reexamination of the whole incident is the only possible road to restoring self-respect for the nisei and their children. They feel the suffering of those years must be relived and the guilt laid squarely where it belongs: with the American government and those citizens who encouraged discriminatory actions. Advocates of this point of view have been instrumental in introducing Japanese American history into the California schools and colleges, getting books on the subject published, organizing television and radio programs about the evacuation, and distributing information to communities through lectures and exhibits.

This viewpoint has its opponents. Many observers, including a nisei, misinterpret the desire to resurrect the events surrounding the relocation as an attempt to stir up resentment between races; some nisei are afraid that it will create a backlash and cancel out many of the postwar gains of their community. But to encourage dissension is not the intent of the historical activists. There may be much to gain by unloading the false guilt and venting the repressed anger behind the present nisei perception of history. Perhaps the generations will then be united by a common feel for the dignity of their culture rather than segregated by the guilt between them. Perhaps then too will the nisei meet Caucasians with the sense of brotherhood that can come only from a perception of true equality.

Sansei

The sansei in this study are probably more socially conscious than the typical sansei of their age range (fourteen to thirty-three, average age 21.8). Although there is wide divergence in their views of history, one trend which emerges clearly is the shift in outlook as one moves from high-school to post-high-school age respondents. This trend is not surprising. Five of the seven high-school sansei are thoroughly uncritical of their parents' generation, they closely reflect their parents' attitudes about most things, and they are inclined to accept the status quo of Japanese Americans in United States society. The other two—also unsurprisingly—each have at least one articulate, socially conscious parent who is a clear-cut example of the historian type (see discussion earlier in this chapter).

Nine of the thirteen post-high-school age sansei are openly critical of certain attitudes and actions that they deem typical of the nisei. The sansei's criticisms center on what they believe to be the nisei's love for status and possessions, their uncritical patriotism, their "trying to be white," and what is perceived by the sansei as their wishy-washiness in dealing with the hostility of others. Miss Kayano (age twenty-three) discusses the equality of the Japanese in America:

Miss Kayano: *I think this so-called acceptance is superficial. The nisei put on a facade. They attempt to be white Americans. Due to this, they've won acceptance by American society. They've sort of tried to minimize their Japaneseness.*

Interviewer: *How do you mean, "minimize their Japaneseness"?*

Miss K: *My parents try to hide a lot of things, like the camps and the hostility, to win acceptance. To raise their kids as* Americans.

Miss Kayano gives another example: "Yeah, I think that the nisei, all through their lives—they went through World War II and the camps and everything—have tried to make it through what is the white standard, when you make it in America—good home, good car, things like that. They've been trying, almost, to be white. And I think a lot of sansei think differently. It angers them that they might have to try and be white to make it in America."

From these remarks, it can be seen that the sansei are in a peculiar position with respect to their ethnic history. Most have not experienced the evacuation and other forms of extreme discrimination they know their parents went through, yet they are aware of other forms of discrimination today and can easily imagine what their parents suffered. But they are inclined to reject their parents' interpretation of the prewar and wartime years. They see them as more degrading, meaner, and more unjust than their parents do. The interpretation given by Miss Kobayashi (age twenty-five) is more vivid than most but conveys a common sansei theme: "You know, it's really strange because my parents never talked about [the evacuation]. Bits and pieces, but no bitterness or anything. I don't think it really hit me until high school, what had really happened. I was reading this book, and I just started crying. I didn't realize what my parents or other parents had to go through. This guy, he read this book. He's around thirty now. He said when he read it he was so full of bitterness and hate that when he saw a white guy he felt like hitting him. Because you don't *know* about it, and when you find out about it . . . The movies—*The Pride and the Shame* [a film about the evacuation]—I couldn't sit through it. It's sad, it's really sad. When you are really humiliated and degraded in camp, you have to make yourself acceptable. One way is to take on the accepted ways of society, not really looking into them."

What is the real nature of the disagreement between the nisei and sansei generations on the question of history? There is a common belief in Japan Town that the sansei assign much of the responsibility for the evacuation to the nisei because of their failure to resist, and the issei being unable to resist on account of their lack of knowledge and their alien status. My data do not support this bit of folklore. Even the angrier sansei feel that the low posture of the nisei was more a result of the evacuation than a cause. They recognize that the Japanese on the West Coast were a tiny, defenseless group in a sea of racial antagonism, that the nisei were mostly mere children at the time, living in ingrown Japan Towns or back-country lanes, and that resistance was out of the question. The disagreement appears to lie in the meaning each generation attaches to the nisei's behavior. The sansei make little distinction between wanting to be accepted and respected by others (a very Japanese as well as a very American trait), wanting to be *like* others, and having no use for one's native culture and history. Reflecting the outward appearance of others is often a condition for being liked by them but does not necessarily mean wholesale remodeling of the self or slavish conformity. Showing deference, avoiding overt conflict, and respecting others' sensibilities are at the core of the unique culture the issei brought with them to America and passed on to the nisei. The nisei have in fact retained more of both their history and their culture than many of their sansei critics have. Often at great cost to their inner harmony.

The subject of the evacuation is painful to the nisei, not only because they lived through it, but because they have had to live *with* it as a reminder of their own ambivalence and of what they see as their possible (not probable—possible is enough) guilt for causing the suffering of others. The sansei will not let the nisei take credit for their own mistakes. The nisei do not see their life styles as responses to white pressure or demand but as the fulfillment of personal obligations to their parents, their society, and, above all, their children. If they have misread their obligation or failed in fulfilling it, they want at least a little recognition for the error. Their dream has been to be free to live as they please, and the message of the critical sansei is that even their apparent success is really in disguise the reverse of that dream's fulfillment.

History presents personal problems to the sansei, too. For one thing, they are inclined to agree with their parents about their own softness and ignorance of hardship. Says Mr. Kawada (age sixteen) when asked whether his parents made any mistakes in raising him: "I guess they made a few mistakes, maybe. Maybe I've been spoiled too much. I've gotten too much of what I wanted. I've gotten away with a lot that maybe I shouldn't have. On the other hand, I guess I'm growing up all right, so they haven't made any bad mistakes." Miss Nakadai (age twenty-five) talks about the different hopes of the two generations: "Nisei women had to get married and have kids. My generation, it's not so. Maybe we're more greedy. As a woman, I want my own bag." And Mr. Chikai (age thirty-two): "A lot of nisei went through parts of the Depression. They don't want to see their kids going through that thing. The sansei have developed a dependence on the affluence of American life that makes them very vulnerable."

This style of perception looks like one of those interesting alloys that often seem to precipitate from the mixed cultural contents of the sansei's unconscious. It recalls the Puritan ethic of early America and the Japanese principle of deep gratitude for parental care. Whatever the source of the sansei's perception of history, there is certainly an element of guilt in it. If my reasoning concerning the effects of guilt on issei and nisei views of history is sound, the sansei should also want to forget about the evacuation and all that preceded it, as indeed some sansei do. I think there are two main reasons why the older and more politically active sansei want to emphasize these events. One is the need, stimulated by cultural assimilation, for ethnic solidarity and ethnic pride. The other is historical. The civil rights movement of the 1960s and 1970s challenged the supremacy of white middle-class culture, encouraging the sansei to criticize the injustices of the past.

As members of an ethnic group that is cohesive and homogeneous compared with the non-Japanese world, sansei share much of the stigma of the evacuation era, even though they were yet to be born. The civil rights movement has been animated by the principle, which appeals to the sense of self-betrayal lying ready to consciousness in all stigmatized people, that inaction is a crime and silence a blasphemy. The activist sensei are afflicted with the malaise of a stigmatized ethnic identity, vague but real guilt over their own prosperity and comfort, and dissatisfaction with their dependence on parents and community. The civil rights movement has helped them to diagnose the disease—racism—and to devise a cure—ethnic self-consciousness and self-determination. This diagnosis and cure require a definition of history with two essential features: first, the existence of extreme discrimination in the past, and, second, little difference between the past and the present in that respect. I am not trying to explain away the search via ethnic separatism toward ethnic identity, nor to belittle the activists themselves. On the contrary, the ethnic identity movement is an adaptive strategy based on a creative interpretation of history and on the common personal needs of many sansei. It may be an effective strategy for many people for a while. It would be amazing if it turned out to be a perfect solution since history must be negotiated person by person and day by day.

If ethnic activism and the historical interpretation it is based on are one adaptive response to the sansei's needs, another common response is to go in the opposite direction. Five of the thirteen post-high-school sansei respondents explicitly dissociated themselves from the sansei as a group and were openly critical of the ethnic activists. Their view of history varies considerably, although they agree that the nisei have been too economically successful. They believe however that both the nisei and the sansei have become snobbish and cliquish as a result, and that ethnic activists are no different from the rest. Says Miss Daibutsu (age twenty-one): "[The radical students] talk about Western snobs, but they are actually radical snobs. When you lose that rationality and you can't see anything else, that makes me mad. And they try to make you feel guilty, and they try to make me feel that I've been discriminated against. That's stupidity, and it makes me mad." Miss Nakadai (age twenty-five) describes the typical sansei: "Typical? Which type? In San Francisco circles, it's neat hair, perfectly dressed. The Japanese American stereotype. I can't take it myself. They've completely embraced the capitalist structure. Their values are strictly middle-class."

The nisei are not the only source of information available to the sansei about their own ethnic history. In addition to a growing number of published works, college courses, and other educational resources, a vague, confused oral history is available in the street, and much popular folklore is available in the mass media. This folklore portrays the Japanese Americans as an ideal minority, successful in mainstream American terms by virtue of hard work, thrift, patience, and loyalty. Although the average nisei accepts, with reservations, this popular view of himself—it matches the self-image of some—some nisei and many sansei do not agree with it for four main reasons: It is a stereotype that denies the autonomy and dignity of the indi-

vidual, robbing him of his right to be treated as a person instead
of an object; it implies that the Japanese Americans are now accepted by white America, which is not strictly true; it belittles
the right of Japanese Americans (and, by implication, other
minorities) to oppose the majority; and it suggests that passivity
and compliance—traits that are scarcely valued in the American
version of maturity—are characteristic of the Japanese. The sansei disagree with the "ideal minority" view of history because
they have been assimilated more into middle-class American culture and adopted many of the changes in its system of values
such as the growing respect for nonviolent protest as a vehicle
of social change, which has come about largely since the mid-
fifties. As I explained earlier in this chapter, conformity and
passivity are not linked in Japanese values the same way they
are in American. The sansei accept, on the whole, the American
belief that conformity is suspect in itself.

The changing image of Japan on the world scene, reflected in the American media, has extensive and difficult-to-
measure implications for the sansei perception of history. It
must be difficult for the postwar generation to understand why
so many nisei appear to have turned their backs on their homeland. Japan has risen from a poverty-stricken victim of its own
militarism to become not only the wealthiest nation in Asia, but
the third-ranking industrial power in the world—a moral and
technological miracle. But the sansei activists have trouble using
modern Japan as a symbol of ethnic pride because it too closely
resembles the United States. They are critical, for instance, of
the commercialism of the Japan Town shops and banks, many
of which are outposts of Japanese firms. On the whole, however, the declaration of one's Japanese ancestry no longer incurs
the risk of being associated with jingoism, totalitarianism, or
shoddy merchandise. There is often a distinct note of pride in
the sansei pronunciation of the word *Japanese*. The economic
and political fortunes of Japan are precarious, however, and
should she suffer a change of fortune the Japanese Americans
may be unpleasantly surprised to be reminded of the real
psychological importance of the homeland.

Controversy over the proper interpretation of and attitude toward history still boils in the Japanese American community. This state of affairs is natural and even commendable. History in this community is like poetry, politics, and religion rolled into one. It is a subject of common interest and great personal importance. It is a medium through which people can express their anxieties, affirm their commitments, offer their understanding. If the discussion of ethnic history is to promote growth and understanding between ethnic groups or between factions within groups, two principles must be recognized. First, perceptions of history, although they may be tentative, indistinct, and changeable, are nonetheless real and true for those who hold them. Second, universal human characteristics, such as the need for self-respect and for the approval of others, cause differences in historical perceptions, the tools with which individuals adjust their reactions to self and environment in search of a more comfortable alignment.

Chapter III

The Concept
of Acculturation

Earlier, I defined culture as a shared symbol system. However it is defined, culture is an abstract concept, ordinarily remote from daily concerns unless one is an anthropologist. Because of this abstractness, serious difficulties arise when we discuss the effects of cultural change on the individual. It is difficult to be clear and consistent about what is cultural as opposed to personal or historical and about the nature of the group whose culture we are describing. It is difficult to avoid thinking

82

about a culture as though it were a list of neat directions, like a Boy Scout manual, or a chest full of gadgets through which the human objects of our inquiry rummage in search of the correct response to a given situation. In short, it is difficult to remember that the culture concept is only a mental model and that it is used with precision only when talking about specific, regular behavior patterns that distinguish one specified group from another.

I am concerned here with the relationship between culture and personal development. My major assumption is that the individual who lives in regular contact with more than one distinctly different culture must make some sense out of the contradictory habits and beliefs of his human surroundings or he will be confused in his thought and his behavior. This assumption has a long history in anthropology. It has motivated many studies of contacts between cultural groups and resulting changes in belief and behavior, a genre of anthropological literature united by the elusive concept of acculturation, that is, the process of cultural change resulting from the continuous long-term contact of two or more groups with distinctive cultures.

If the concept of culture is tricky, the concept of acculturation is a jungle of intellectual booby-traps. As Beals (1962) points out in his review of the subject, the fact that most cultures have never been absolutely homogeneous, static, or isolated makes it difficult to measure the effects of culture contact on individuals, let alone groups. The precontact statuses of cultures are extremely difficult to reconstruct. Then there is the problem of translating behavior from one culture to another. Since cultures are generally (and I think properly) viewed as configurations, the whole of which gives meaning to each part, the exchange of behaviors, attitudes, or personality traits between cultural groups often involves a subtle change in their meaning. The lack of apparent behavioral differences cannot be a very reliable measure of cultural fusion or similarity. A good example is the tendency of the issei to perceive themselves as emotionally open (see Chapter Two). To them, emotional openness means a conscious sense of harmony between inner feelings and social demands and does not involve the middle-class American idea of introspectiveness. Moreover, group habits that appear objectively different to the social scientist might not appear that way to members of either group and may not be sources of conflict or confusion. This has been the case, for instance, with certain Christian beliefs in the Japanese American Buddhist community.

Because of this subjective quality of group differences, it makes little sense to measure acculturation by employing attitudinal or behavioral trait lists. An even stouter objection to such simple-minded techniques appears when one considers that cultural standards seldom apply rigidly to all behavior within the group; distinctions are generally made between social situations, just as conventions about the meanings of words differ from context to context. This is why the linguistic term *context* is often extended to refer to social scenes or situations—a practice I also follow. I have already spoken of the situational ("contextual" would do just as well) morality of Japanese values, but this behavior is to some extent true of any society. Even in the universalistic West, honesty is the best policy, but not when a new mother asks your opinion of her baby's looks. As journalist Charles McCabe has said, "Hypocrisy makes life endurable."

It is remarkable how human beings learn to adapt behavior to context. During eighteen months in Japan, my four-year-old daughter Katrina learned that she could control any adult who spoke Japanese because for those who used that language she enjoyed the double license of childhood and foreignness. I had to give up using Japanese with her because she was incorrigible unless spoken to in English. Although her Japanese behavior was acceptable to her Japanese acquaintances, it was not typical of Japanese children her age, who tended to be much more polite and shy. She was apparently performing a role that was native to neither her parental nor her adopted culture but grew out of the interaction between them. It complied with a set of standards peculiar to the intercultural context.

One problem illustrated by the example of my daughter—that is, situationally specific and reversible acculturation—has gotten attention in anthropological studies. Lebra (1972) gives the name "nonlinear models" to a number of studies which recognize the situational character of adaptations to bicultural environments, including those of Gluckman (1960), Mayer (1962), McFee (1968), and Berreman (1964). Green's (1971) concept of situational ethnicity derived from the study of blacks in the southern United States and the Caribbean is another example. Lebra's discussion of the difference between the older, linear model, and the nonlinear (1972, p. 6) is worth paraphrasing in part. First, the nonlinear model assumes that a new culture is added to the old one, while the linear model depicts partial replacement of the old culture by the new one. Second, in the nonlinear model acculturating people are free to choose between cultural alternatives according to the demands of the situation, while the linear model supposes that accepting one cultural standard entails all out rejection of the other and of those who prefer it. Third, the nonlinear model stresses that acculturation processes are contingent upon *context* and are therefore a function of social relationships, roles, audiences, or reference groups. The linear model, on the other hand, seems to take for granted the direct and entire embracement of the individual by a culture.

With the exception of Lebra's work, studies of Japanese American acculturation have most often employed a linear model, with all its horrors. This is true of studies by Matsumoto and others (1970), by Horinouchi (1967), and by other researchers. Earlier literature, especially the spate of articles in the 1930s that questioned whether the Japanese were even assimilable in America (for example, Strong, 1934; Yamamoto, 1938), but also including such careful research as that of Caudill (1952) and Caudill and DeVos (1956), apparently set a precedent that overwhelmed later researchers. Maykovich (1972), for instance, uses the concept of reference group in her study of Japanese American identity but implies that one reference group is always dominant for normal people and that acculturation is therefore a linear movement from one reference group to another.

I am not aware of any thorough treatment in the literature of anthropology of the problem of special intercultural contexts, or intermediate cultures, that develop around areas of contact between two cultural groups. Redfield and Singer's (1954) classic description of the role of market towns in the evolution of cultures comes close to offering a model of such an intermediate culture but falls short: "On the side of social structure, the city is the place where new and larger groups are formed that are bound by few and powerful common interests and sentiments *in place of* the complexly interrelated roles and statuses that characterize the groups of local, long-established culture" (emphasis mine). By the use of the words *in place of* and not *in addition to,* Redfield and Singer indicate, even while transcending the linear model of acculturation, that they still believe the process is substitutive.

I now must distinguish between the terms *acculturation* and *assimilation,* as the latter has been used extensively in studies of ethnic minorities. The term *assimilation* is used somewhat ambiguously to refer to two distinct processes, both of which I consider subprocesses that sometimes accompany acculturation. One is the disappearance of outward behavior traits that distinguish a minority population or an individual from the host culture. The other is the disappearance of exclusive and discriminatory behaviors on the part of the members of the host culture, which permits the minority group or individual to join the host society. Assimilation studies emphasize behavior as distinct from mental processes, and for this reason I prefer to use the term *acculturation* to mean the learning, by members of one cultural group, of skills and values native to another group. The fact that a member of an American minority group behaves, talks, dresses, and even conducts his private life just like the descendent of an early American settler and is viewed as an ordinary American by his European American acquaintances says little about deeply held feelings which might inspire him to passionate declarations of his ethnic ancestry under certain circumstances. There are many families in San Francisco whose Danish ancestry is unknown to their neighbors and business associates and who are scarcely distinguishable in their behavior from any other European American group but who read a local Danish newspaper, belong to a Danish lodge, and enjoy Danish drink, food, song, and sport on special occasions (Chrisman, 1971). Are such families assimilated or not? Are they more or less assimilated than, say, Japanese American families who live in white suburbs, speak nothing but English, belong to no ethnic organizations, and know nothing of their ancestral culture but are viewed by their neighbors and European-American acquaintances as Orientals?

Such difficulties can be avoided by steering clear of the concept of assimilation and homing in instead on changes of specific cultural traits as they occur within the context of a specific situation. Stereotypes held by ethnic groups about each other and about themselves, for example, can thus be seen as symbol systems that are shared within the group and added to their original cultures and whose meaning and function must be examined anew by the social scientist each time they are used in a different context (see Berreman, 1971). Thus the meaning of ethnic background always depends on how the participants of an interaction define the situation.

This concept will become clearer if we define more carefully what is meant by *context* and *definition of the situation.* In most initial contacts between members of different ethnic groups, participants lack information about the variability of behavior within the other group and so tend to respond to each other according to gross ethnic, age, sex, and status cues. Theoretically, such cues set up expectations in the actors regarding appropriate behavior. Under these impersonal circumstances, we can imagine the different kinds of intercultural contexts we would expect to find if we confine ourselves to, say, pairs involving males or females who are young, middle-aged adult, or elderly, in two cultural groups (*Table 1*). We might find that some of these contexts never occur, that some are functionally irrelevant (for example, the sex distinction might not be meaningful in children and the elderly, thereby reducing the number of contexts by a third), or that other status distinctions such as social class take precedence over those we have selected.

As acculturation proceeds, two things happen to our paradigm. First, more and more people in one or both groups become more and more aware of the variability of behavior in

Table 1

Intercultural Contexts (Culture A and Culture B)

AmyBmy	AmyBma	AmyBme	AmyBfy	AmyBfa	AmyBfe
AmaBmy	AmaBma	AmaBme	AmaBfy	AmaBfa	AmaBfe
AmeBmy	AmeBma	AmeBme	AmeBfy	AmeBfa	AmeBfe
AfyBmy	AfyBma	AfyBme	AfyBfy	AfyBfa	AfyBfe
AfaBmy	AfaBma	AfaBme	AfaBfy	AfaBfe	AfaBfe
AfeBmy	AfeBma	AfeBme	AfeBfy	AfeBfa	AfeBfe

m:male f:female y:young a:middle-aged adult e:elderly

the other group so that situations previously defined as the same for purposes of action are now perceived as different. Thus new contexts develop, sometimes replacing and sometimes supplementing the old ones. Second, more and more members of one or both groups become more and more intimate with members of the other group and in the process learn how to control the other participant's perception of the context so that intercultural contact yields greater and greater potential for rewards. In situations where power is held chiefly by one group at the expense of the other and intercultural contacts are consistently more punishing for the subordinate group, members of that group must and do learn a much more elaborate repertoire of techniques for managing intercultural contacts to their own advantage. In the process of learning these techniques, minority group members seldom lose their native culture or become absorbed by the majority culture. Their acculturation is highly situational under these circumstances (see Berreman, 1964).

Managing intercultural situations successfully depends largely on the ability of the minority group member to influence the definition of the situation made by the other participants. For example, most European Americans regard Japanese Americans as quiet, sensible, unaggressive, and also as noncommunicative and hence unpredictable. Suppose a Japanese American, Mr. Endo, is accused by his neighbor, Mr. Fudd, of having made a pass at Fudd's wife. In this situation it is to Endo's advantage to appeal to Fudd's readiness to define him as quiet and sensible and to discourage Fudd's use of the inscrutable stereotype. The next day, Endo learns that his boss is considering him for the position of sales manager, which calls for a certain amount of dash, verve, and thunder. In this situation Endo, who wants the job, now avoids the quiet stereotype and invokes the inscrutable one to make it difficult for anyone in the office to question his capabilities. According to the demands of the situation, Endo has influenced, probably unconsciously, the definition of each situation made by the other participants. If he gets the managership and succeeds, he may make a lasting change in the minds of many people about Japanese Americans, thereby integrating his group into American society a little. But Endo's definition of the situation might be rejected by the others, it might be accepted for the time being but later revoked in the light of new developments, or it might result in his removal from the category "Japanese American" in others' eyes with little effect on their perceptions of the whole ethnic group. The ability to successfully manage interethnic contacts is perhaps best developed among black Americans, who have a long history of discriminatory contact. The process of situation management is eloquently documented in the work of Baldwin and Malcolm X.

Accompanying situational acculturation is a linear, absolute process. As Endo becomes more and more adept at securing rewards from the dominant culture, he comes to expect more rewards from it, to spend more and more time in intercultural contexts, and to consider himself a natural participant in those contexts—that is, to identify with the roles he plays in them. He is influenced by the values and perceptions of the dominant group and loses his own ethnic habits of perceiving and behaving. Endo makes acculturative adjustments to the changes he has made and is making in his own cultural behavior; he acculturates to his acculturation, and no view of culture contact which ignores this will account for all that happens. This process can be understood easily if the relationship between man and his environment is compared to a governor and a motor or a thermostat and a furnace, in which a change in one triggers a change in the other. Changes in behavior patterns result in changes in the environment, which in turn result in further behavioral changes, and so on. When a person becomes more acculturated, he begins to spend more time in intercultural contexts or at least think about them differently, with the result that his environment is not the same. This change in turn requires further adjustments in his behavior. A person who knows, even unconsciously, how to switch behavior according to context is a different sort of person from one who has never learned this skill. Moreover, the difference is anything but trivial when we think about each person across contexts, or as a whole. When we talk about personality, it is just such behavioral sets, or skills, that we refer to.

In spite of the progress of acculturation, however, even when ethnic groups are in contact with each other over many generations members of each group still spend the bulk of their time in such culturally homogeneous settings as family, community, and ethnic peer group. As a result of the importance of ethnic background in ethnically mixed situations, ethnic self-consciousness becomes an important ingredient of many ethnically homogeneous situations as well, for instance, when ethnic group members joke about the image held of them by the outgroup or discuss how to avoid or change this image. To the extent that different ethnic groups in contact with each other maintain their own identity, two intragroup processes related to ethnic self-consciousness appear universal: the exchange of information about people outside the ethnic group, especially their behavior in intercultural contexts, and the affirmation of the superiority of some ethnic group traits over traits of outsiders, supporting the value of ethnic group membership and identity. The contemporary works of Berreman (1971), Barth and others (1969), Gans (1962), and Hannerz (1969) document this fact in today's world, and the writings of Aristophanes and Dante indicate its antiquity.

Another process related to acculturation within the Japanese American community is a result of intercultural relations changing so rapidly that stable ethnic identities cannot easily develop. This process is the collective search for a coherent, convincing, meaningful definition of one's own ethnic background and the propagation of these ethnic self-definitions. As

historical perceptions in the Japanese American community indicate, members of this group often cannot accept the ethnic
self-definitions of earlier generations. Relations between ethnic
groups have changed too much since the time when parents
were going through the same developmental stages their children now are going through. What is more, the speed of such
change creates areas of great ambiguity in relations between
groups, raising the danger of an unstable and confused self-
image for those strongly committed to such relations. Returning
to the example of Mr. Endo, we can readily imagine that he
might begin to wonder who or what he really is. Is he the sensible, unaggressive good neighbor or the untried, daring leader,
or is he both or neither? Although Endo's problem is not radically different from that of any other individual in a complex,
rapidly changing society, his command of two cultural idioms
greatly increases both the diversity of demands on him and the
diversity of choices open to him.

In the case of the Japanese Americans, the search for
identity is complicated by a shift from agrarian to urban-indus-
trial environment. Urbanization means the addition, not substi-
tution, of a whole new type of social relations, characterized by
temporariness and anonymity. Members of distinct subcultures
in industrial cities preserve much of the intimate, stable quality
of nonurban social relations but develop a specific set of skills
for handling fleeting, urban relations—skills they exercise in
periodic forays beyond the boundaries of their ethnic group or
neighborhood. Sometimes these skills are cultivated at a particular age almost as a form of entertainment, as in the case of the
young Italians in Boston whom Gans (1962) calls "action seek-
ers" and in Washington's black cabaret set, the "swingers" (Hannerz, 1969). In addition, as an ethnic group acculturates, the
distinctions between whom one is intimate with and who is
anonymous become less a matter of ethnic identification. Those
one is on close terms with are less and less likely to be members
of one's ethnic group, and vice-versa. In a group as small as the
Japanese Americans in San Francisco, all fellow Japanese Americans are at least potential intimates whether personally acquainted with each other or not. However, any member of the

community knows many people outside his ethnic group better than he knows many members of the group. The Japanese American must therefore separate his contexts into at least four types—intimate Japanese American, anonymous Japanese American, intimate non-Japanese American, and anonymous non-Japanese American. Such distinctions become delicate when contexts overlap, as for instance when a sansei walking with her Caucasian boyfriend runs into militant sansei friends who do not know the boyfriend. The resulting anxiety and confusion is not clarified by calling the encounter "cultural conflict" because there may be no real disagreement in cultural values, only in the definition of the situation. In Chapter Five I return to the relationship between acculturation and personal stress.

Studying acculturation from the viewpoint of the individual is a job complicated by age-related changes in each person's life. The relationships of a ten-year-old to other people in his environment and the psychological skills appropriate to those relationships are different from those of a twenty-year-old, which in turn are vastly different from those of a forty- or sixty-year-old. Individuals acquire new statuses; enter new groups; develop new skills; and lose habits, friends, and attachments as they age. In other words, the culture of a twenty-year-old and that of a forty-year-old at the same time and place are different, just as the cultures of the sexes are different. Anthropology is poor in concepts for discussing the process by which an individual adjusts to age-related changes in his social environment, probably because the study of this process puts a lot of strain on the concept of culture itself. The learning of a culture by a person in a reasonably stable, homogeneous social milieu is sometimes referred to as *enculturation,* and we might extend this term, as Wallace (1970) would, to cover the entire life span. But it would be stretching the concept beyond recognition, I think, to apply it to the changes in personality that accompany aging. For this process, I prefer to use the term *development.*

In a multicultural milieu the processes of acculturation and development are intertwined. Differences of behavior between persons in such a milieu at different stages of their lives can be clearly understood, I think, by keeping the distinction between these two processes in mind. For example, during the early stages of the ethnic minority group member's life, the important people for him are likely to be his parents, siblings, and playmates. His position on any hypothetical cultural continuum is likely to be strongly affected by the positions of these people on the same continuum. Later, as his social horizons broaden, he is influenced by the mass media, his teachers, schoolmates, minister, even by lofty heroes and heroines out of history or Hollywood. Spouse, in-laws, coworkers, and new friends may be added next, to be replaced later in life by children, children's friends and in-laws, and eventually grandchildren, each group making its own input to the acculturation process. Cultural change might proceed rapidly during certain stages, only to be reversed as new influences come into play. An extreme example of this change is Mrs. Kindaichi's nisei brother-in-law (Chapter One) who "became more and more Japanese" under the influence of his job.

More is involved in development than the Japaneseness and Americanness of the socialization influences on the minority group member. His age is often also a factor in determining the way he is defined by members of the majority culture and thus in determining their reaction to him. Young recent immigrants from Japan, for example, are at first meeting defined by Caucasians as equivalent to highly acculturated Asian Americans of about the same age, whereas middle-aged nisei and sansei, much more familiar with American culture, are defined as less Americanized. Because they have the advantage of a favorable definition, the young immigrants probably acquire certain United States cultural habits much more easily and rapidly than the nisei did. The same phenomenon may lead to the opposite effect with respect to other habits since the immigrant who wins quick social acceptance may not feel pressured to give up certain Japanese traits.

Still another question raised by the developmental perspective concerns the congruence, or fit, of certain traits of the cultures in contact. Cultural ideals pertaining to one age group in both cultures might be at least superficially similar; at an-

other age, vastly different standards might apply to the same behavior. For example, Americans often admire the quiet, obedient comportment of Japanese American children but regard
similar conduct in adults as a sign of timidity. Behavior that appears similar in ideal American and Japanese American children
turns out to have a different meaning in the two cultures from
the start because the Japanese children are acting grown up and
the American children are not. This hidden difference muddles
the measurement of cultural similarity and confuses intercultural relations. Adolescence and young adulthood are extremely
stressful stages for Japanese Americans because parental expectations of their offspring's behavior at this stage are vastly different in the two cultures; but the stress often abates as norms
are once again in accord during middle age.

Each culture has its own notion of the stages of normal
development, usually several for each sex, through which individuals ought to pass. Some of these developmental stages correspond at least in appearance; in other stages, the differences
are painfully obvious. If we choose to view interacting cultures
as monolithic structures with fixed norms and ignore age-
specific changes and variations, we are likely to portray the
maturing bicultural individual as though he were meandering
drunkenly back and forth across our cultural continuum.

Chapter IV

The Cultural Process: Issei, Nisei, Sansei

Any attempt to discuss the cultural role of the Japanese in America must deal with the remarkably clear-cut differences between three generations, both in behavior and in self-perception. The subject of this chapter is the substantive differences between the generations, but first I want to explore why the differences are so clear cut. Or, to be more logically careful, I want to look at some distinctive characteristics of Japanese American history and culture that seem logically related to generational distinctness and generational self-consciousnsess.

95

Generational Identity

Generational identity presents a two-part problem. First, there is the question of the circumstances that favored its original appearance. Second, there is the question of the persistence and elaboration of generational identity—what functions it has served and for whom, to account for its vitality as a device for ordering experience and behavior. Some of the answers to the first question are obvious. The original immigration of the Japanese to the West Coast was of short duration—occurring mainly between about 1885 and 1924. Most of the women arrived between 1907 and 1924. The immigrants were therefore fairly homogeneous in age or at least there was a minimum age threshhold that resulted in a gap in age between the youngest Japanese immigrants and the oldest Japanese Americans born in the United States. Little overlap in age exists between the issei and the nisei today, and little has existed in settled Japanese American communities since the 1920s. The tendency of the immigrants to have children after their arrival in the United States was another factor in establishing distinct generational identity because it resulted in the appearance of a large cohort with a very different cultural background from that of their parents. There was also an important legal impetus for the generational distinction. Immigrants from Japan were excluded by race from United States citizenship and from many other rights following upon citizenship, while their native-born children were automatically citizens. This distinction was not merely a formality; even nisei minors could hold deeds on property, for instance, where their parents could not, and I have already mentioned (Chapter One) the governmental acknowledgement of nisei authority during the evacuation and relocation.

The size, geographic distribution, occupations, and social organization of the immigrant group may also have contributed to the formation of generational identity. Ichihashi (1932) tells us that there was considerable migrancy and job changing among the Japanese in the United States prior to about 1910 but that this trend diminished rapidly in the following decades. Because they were a small group subjected to discrimination in housing and jobs and because they followed nonmigratory long term occupations, the farmers, small businessmen, and service employees who made up a large proportion of the Japanese population from about 1910 on tended to settle in small urban ghettos and rural hamlets. These circumstances were ideal for the development of close-knit, highly cooperative, and tightly controled ethnic communities. The tight organization of these communities together with the cultural and economic dominance of the issei men meant that the social organization of the community followed generational lines as well. Before the war, then, the term *issei* designated those who were in the ethnic power establishment, and *nisei* those who were out.

As the American-born generation began to grow in number and in age, the usefulness of the generational distinction grew rapidly as well. The nisei spoke English fluently and regarded the United States as their home. Although they were basically Japanese in many of their underlying attitudes, they had many American tastes, skills, and habits that their parents lacked. They were culturally different. The cultural significance of the generational distinction is underscored by a special term, *kibei*, used for nisei who were sent to Japan in an effort to preserve their competence in and identification with their parent culture. The distinction was necessary because the kibei were neither functionally issei (being younger and having American citizenship) nor culturally nisei. They were subjected to a kind of double jeopardy. Being both less skillful in American culture than the nisei and subordinate to the issei, they often held low status. They were therefore safe targets for the scorn that many nisei felt toward the "backwardness" of issei ways.

The distinction between nisei and sansei also preserves the cultural meaning of membership in a particular generation. This distinction has lost some of its legal and organizational importance and is sometimes dropped altogether, as when *nisei* is used to refer to any American-born Japanese. More age and cultural overlap exists between these two generations, so that it is sometimes necessary to distinguish young nisei and all sansei on one hand from older nisei on the other when discussing cultural and political change. However, the distinction between nisei and sansei is useful in understanding certain broad differences of habit and personality, as we shall see.

Curiously enough, some features of Japanese culture that were shared by the issei and nisei encouraged the development of generational identity. I have mentioned the cultural importance of age for prestige, but another trait might have been even more important: the extreme emphasis on proper form and etiquette. In Japanese culture, with its elaborate formal rituals governing all social interaction, great anxiety surrounds the possibility of a social gaffe. A Japanese who doesn't know exactly what is expected of him in a social situation is much more uncomfortable than an American in the same predicament. In Japan I quickly learned that no amount of pleading would make people come to a meeting or party unless they knew exactly who else was going to be there, knew what their social-rank was, and felt competent to handle interaction with the other participants. To some extent the issei had to relax their standards of form in their dealings with American culture since there was much they simply did not understand. This relaxation was permissible because the issei retained their foreign identity. But the nisei had no such out. For one thing, they knew enough about American social form to get by in many non-Japanese contexts. For another, most of them explicitly rejected the foreigner role and so could not excuse themselves for social ineptness. In terms of generational identity, this meant that the nisei, whose culture was not quite American and not quite Japanese, felt truly comfortable only in the company of other nisei. The possibility of a social gaffe greatly increased when the context was either strictly Japanese or strictly American. What is more, every nisei at some level recognized this characteristic in his fellow nisei and joined with them in a silent pact to keep things polite and superficial in each other's company. Later I have more to say about the masklike quality of nisei social relations and the sansei rebellion against it.

Words tend to become loaded with emotional imagery. Once the habit of using the words *issei, nisei,* and *sansei* became widespread, it also became habitual for the users to perceive their social universe as properly ordered by the distinctions these words implied. After the generational terms had become popular on account of their usefulness, the second step in the development of generational identity was the elevation of generational terms to prime importance in the identification of self and others and the investment of these terms with strong emotion. Once the generational term *issei,* for example, came to have positive value for an individual as a self-definition, such statements as "The issei are stubborn" and "You are not acting like an issei" were personally meaningful. Norms for evaluating the issei-ness or nisei-ness of behavior developed and were added to norms governing sex, expression of ethnic background, and so on as standards of performance. The generation became a reference group, with its own rules of status and definitions of boundaries. Members reinforced one another's generational identity and sought to enforce some degree of conformity to group norms and definitions. The dynamics of this process are essentially similar to the dynamics of relations between ethnic groups. To the extent that the generations are culturally distinct, there is a need to defend the generational culture against the slights of other generations with other values and perceptions.

Turning from the background of generational identity to the content of perceptions about one's own and others' generations, we find that some clear-cut trends emerge. The issei are the least united and least consistent group in their perceptions of the other generations. They feel that the nisei and the issei are culturally similar enough that they understand each other fairly well, but they consider the sansei too Americanized to understand them. Aside from this perception, the issei seem hesitant to generalize about the generations, and, when they do, generalizations offered by one often disagree with those given by another. Mr. Oda (age eighty-eight) talks about the generations.

Mr. Oda: *Well, the nisei are still okay. The reason is they were raised at the knee of the issei. They pay attention to what the issei have to say. They do this even though there is a difference in the way of thinking between the issei and the nisei. But when you get to the sansei, since they were raised by the nisei, they are very close to being American, and they have gone a long way from the Japanese ways. They have that tendency, when you try to straighten them out.*

Interviewer: *How do most of the nisei feel about the issei? Do they listen to what they say and respect them?*

Mr. O: *It varies according to the individual, but generally speaking, most of the nisei do not know Japan.*

Mrs. Kosen (age seventy-five) has a similar perception:

Interviewer: *Describe a typical nisei.*

Mrs. K: *Depending on the person, the feelings are different. Some are more Japanese. Some, more American, have different feelings than those of their parents. They're all different. Since they're close to the issei, they do have some Japanese points. But the sansei— [She does not go on.]*

But Mr. Fujii (age eighty-five) places a different emphasis:

Interviewer: *How well do you feel [your stepson] understands you?*

Mr. F: *I think the young people understand the issei quite well, but we have a different way of thinking, since they were brought up in this country. They have no respect for their elders and teachers. It is due to the Communist ideology.*

The lack of a widespread, common opinion among the issei about generational identities is related to a number of factors. Being less mobile than the nisei or sansei, the issei have narrower social horizons, as Chapter Two indicates. They interact intensively with a small group of people, mainly their families, close friends, and fellow church members. They seldom have the opportunity to compare their generational perceptions with other issei outside this group. Because their thinking tends to be more concrete and particular than that of the nisei, they are as a group simply less given to broad generalizations about social relations. Another probable factor is the lack of a pressing need for a distinct generational identity on the part of the issei. The issei *are* distinct, whether they like it or not, from all other groups in American society; so distinct, in fact, in language, customs, and historical experience, that they may dislike to be reminded of it by their own children. To be reminded of generational differences is to remember that their culture is dying out.

Yet another factor that contributes to the lack of a consistent view of other generations is the Japanese cultural emphasis on interpersonal harmony and filial piety referred to earlier. The issei are more motivated than the nisei or sansei to perceive intergenerational relations as close and harmonious or, put another way, to suppress perceptions of intergenerational distance and conflict. Good relations between relatives is, to them, a sign of moral strength. The parent who is rejected by his children in his old age must be guilty of some earlier moral failure. Mrs. Honda (age sixty-five) expresses this view:

Interviewer: *Do you think Japanese American older people are better off, worse off, or about the same as other older people?*

Mrs. H: *The Japanese people enjoy their children more, perhaps.*

I: *Why?*

Mrs. H: *Because the parents do as much as they can for the kids, so when the kids are grown, they naturally do the same thing for the parents. That's the old Japanese style. Many Americans don't know that.*

Added to this cultural motive is the issei's real or potential economic dependence on their children and their consequent need to perceive the children as actually or potentially supportive.

Turning to nisei perceptions of the issei, remember that my interviews were for the most part conducted with members of healthy three-generation families. The generational perceptions of nisei whose parents are ailing or dead might be quite different. The nisei's perceptions of the issei are more distinct and universal than issei perceptions of the nisei. The most frequently mentioned issei traits are strenuous devotion to work, poor command of English, and a tendency to stick together. Individual nisei also mention the issei's conservative morality, patience, and physical hardiness. In their perceptions of the issei, nisei emphasize issei industriousness and patience and seldom mention interpersonal matters. This extremely important feature of the relations between issei and nisei is discussed in detail in Chapter Eight. This emphasis stems not from a cultural difference between the generations but from a combination of historical, cultural, and developmental peculiarities in the Japanese American experience.

Talking about their own generation, the nisei are more varied in their perceptions, but they are certain there is a definite nisei style. The majority think of their own generation as a true mixture of Japanese and American cultures, somewhat closer culturally to the issei than to the sansei. Some stress the affluence or the conservatism of the nisei, and several respondents mention their competitiveness and jealousy. The interesting thing about their perceptions of their own generation—and their children's—is the great attention paid to personal qualities and corresponding lack of emphasis on goal-directed behavior. They seem less interested in what the nisei and sansei do or how well they do it than in the feelings and moral attitudes that characterize these groups. The nisei consider the sansei cheerful, extroverted, and thoroughly Americanized. The high education level, intelligence, and lack of achievement motivation of the sansei were each mentioned by one nisei respondent.

In Chapter Two I dealt at some length with sansei perceptions of the nisei. Chiefly, sansei portray their parents' generation as materialistic and conformist. With regard to the issei, the sansei focus more on their expressive qualities than do the nisei. They often describe the issei as generous, self-sacrificing, polite, happy, and close to their families. This is the description one would expect Japanese to give of their grandparents, as we shall see in Chapter Seven. References to issei endurance, toughness, and hard work are also common.

It is difficult to characterize how the sansei view their own generation except to say that they tend to be negative. I mentioned earlier (Chapter Two) that the sansei accept the "soft" definition given them by the nisei. Several respondents also described the sansei as mixed-up, feeling lost, and conformist. A majority of my sansei respondents saw their own generation as highly Americanized.

In terms of generational identity as a whole, the sansei seem significantly less willing than the nisei to stereotype either their own or other generations when asked to do so. Three of my respondents refused to describe a "typical" sansei, and two said that the sansei are no different from anybody else. Such reluctance could indicate that generational identity reached its high tide with the nisei and has already begun to recede as a feature of the Japanese American experience. But the secession of the sansei from the nisei-dominated JACL is an indication of the strength of generational identity at least among one sector of the sansei. Another likely interpretation would be that the sansei have a more complex perception of their social world than do earlier generations and therefore have less use for stereotypes. We would expect to find this cultural process accompanying the growth of an urban, West Coast, middle-class life style (Schooler, 1972).

Contexts, important to acculturation, are important also to generational identity. An old adage says, "Ask a dozen people what love is, and you'll get a dozen different answers." The adage unfortunately does not add, "Ask the same person in a dozen different contexts, and you'll get a dozen different answers, among which you will be able to distinguish certain regularities." People know what the word love means because it always occurs in a context, and the context usually gives a certain specificity to the word that is tolerably similar for all participants in the context. Consider "I love you" and "I love your hat." Confusion results when the syntactical context is interpreted differently by the participants or when the context lumps together meanings usually kept discrete ("Define 'love' ").

Japanese Americans have generational identities in the sense that they know what *issei, nisei,* and *sansei* mean in context and that they often identify themselves as belonging to a group which wears one of these labels. There are even certain regularities, as we have seen, in the general meanings given these terms. However, it is not very useful to define the nisei identity, for example, unless one gives some idea of the range of its contextual variation. When I asked twelve nisei respondents, "Do you consider yourself mostly American or mostly Japanese?" six said that they were mostly Japanese, four said mostly American, and two said half and half. The context was that of a series of questions asked by a Caucasian (in one case, a sansei) interviewer who is only superficially known to the respondent. Lengthy discussions on the subject with members of the community—both nisei and sansei—with whom I was better acquainted, however, indicated that among themselves the nisei are inclined to emphasize their Americanness. Public expressions of this emphasis are found in the objection of many nisei to the hyphen in Japanese-American (because to them it subordinates their American identity to their Japanese identity) and in the motto of the JACL: Better Americans in a Greater America.

The concepts of intracultural and intercultural contexts discussed in Chapter Three are useful for understanding both acculturation and relations between generations because a) the two types of contexts represent different kinds of input into the acculturation process, b) they often require systematically different definitions of participants and actions, c) they must therefore be kept separated in the participant's perceptions, and d) more individuals spend more time in more intercultural contexts and less time in fewer intracultural contexts with each succeeding generation. A full scale essay on the implications of this process is beyond the scope of this book, but it is important to recognize that participation in different contexts affects the Japanese American's self-perception as a member of an ethnic group and as a member of a generation.

It has been observed among many American ethnic groups that members of the third generation often seek contact with their cultural roots, reversing to some extent the process of Americanization carried forward by their parents (Hansen, 1952). This trend is marked in the Japanese American community (see Clark and Pierce, 1973; Kitano, 1968). Part of the explanation may be, as I said earlier, the historical coincidence of the civil rights movement, the rise of Japan to world eminence, and the maturing of the sansei.

But the return to cultural roots may also be explained by the greater participation of the sansei in intercultural contexts and the greater rewards secured or expected by them through these contexts. This apparent contradiction is explained by the increased exposure of the sansei to situations in which they are stereotyped by non-Japanese Americans. Most students of self-perception agree that our perception of ourselves is heavily influenced by the perceptions that others have of us. A member of a distinguishable ethnic minority group interacting with people of other groups is often perceived in terms of his ethnicity, or ethnic group membership. These perceptions are communicated to him sometimes bluntly but more often subtly. He takes them into account in his perceptions of himself to the extent that the perceptions of others are important to him. The more he participates in interethnic contexts and considers them potentially rewarding, the greater their influence on his self-perception is likely to be. Perceiving an interaction as potentially but not actually rewarding is often equivalent to perceiving it as actually depriving. The individual's ethnic group membership influences others' perceptions of him within the ethnic group as well. However, far from being congruent with stereotypes applied in intercultural contexts, these intracultural stereotypes often explicitly contradict or counterbalance them, as in the case of defense against stigma. For example, Japanese Americans are aware of the "inscrutable" stereotype held by European Americans, but among themselves often interpret caution and reticence in dealing with outsiders as signs of self-respect, loyalty to the group, and good sense.

For the minority individual who spends most of his time interacting with members of his ethnic group and expects most of his social rewards from such interaction, the discrepancy between intercultural and intracultural stereotypes does not present overwhelming difficulties (although it may be quite worrisome). He can keep his contexts clearly separated, ascribe a greater importance to his intracultural self, and withhold affect —to the extent of conscious role-playing, if necessary—in presenting his intercultural self. This process describes most nisei. In addition to the ethnographic observation that nisei spend most of their time with other nisei, my interview data also suggest this conclusion. I asked people to name their five closest friends. Out of the seven nisei responses that could be classified this way, six gave five Japanese names and one gave four Japanese names.

While I was doing research in Japan, I spent most of my time among Japanese, who quite naturally expected me to behave like their stereotype of an American. At first I resisted vigorously trying to shed my American identity and be accepted on something like equal terms. Seeing that this was futile, I gradually gave up the struggle and began to trade on certain aspects of my foreignness. I even began to feel defensive about America and Americans for the first time in my life. (At the same time, I admit, I became extremely defensive about Japan and the Japanese in the presence of critical Americans.) Although I had studied Japanese culture for years before going there and had known many Japanese as colleagues and friends, I had never had my identification with Japanese culture questioned so seriously.

I think my experience might be analogous in some ways to the experience of the sansei in San Francisco. Most of them grew up in a family and community where the value of assimilation into American culture was not seriously questioned, where group identity carried a strong mainstream-American flavor, and where, in fact, Japaneseness was considered inept and an embarrassment. But being fluent in non-Japanese language, well-versed in the local non-Japanese culture, and much closer to non-Japanese people than their parents had been (out of nine sansei listing their close friends, only two gave five Japanese names; the rest gave three or fewer), the sansei were strongly pressured to accept definitions of themselves offered by non-Japanese. In these intercultural contexts the sansei were in effect told by their non-Japanese acquaintances: "You are not like other Americans. You are Japanese, Oriental, Asian, or Third World." The discrepancy between the messages in the two contexts—a discrepancy that the nisei had been able to tolerate—became unbearable for the sansei because of the increased importance of intercultural contexts in their lives. Perhaps the only workable solution was to develop a healthy pride in their Japanese ancestry and culture.

Such a rebuilding of ethnic identity among the sansei could be accomplished only where the following minimal conditions exist: a setting that provides freedom from stereotyping by non-Japanese and by the parents' generation; a common identity problem shared by the group, with enough strong leadership or mutual trust to question the accepted norms of the ethnic community and experiment with new self-definitions for extended periods; and some means of collectively negotiating, or testing the responses to, new self-definitions of other groups that serve as important sources of identity (for example, nisei and non-Japanese).

The first two of these conditions are met tolerably well by some sansei friendship groups, but the third requires the greater focus and closer coordination of activity now provided by a number of new sansei-dominated community action groups and by sansei groups which were previously under the domination of nisei (like the Junior JACL) but which have increased their autonomy. These groups typically perform a wide variety of charitable and educational functions, but they also serve as the communication channels through which new ethnic and generational identities are negotiated with the world at large.

Negotiation is usually a slow, trial-and-error process in which self-perceptions are exchanged by members of a close-knit group. Some of these perceptions are reinforced and others are received negatively; shared perceptions are adopted and enforced (that is, deviance from them is discouraged); and, as the group gains confidence about its shared self-perceptions, they are tested on other groups. It would be extremely difficult for a neutral observer to record an example of this complex, subtle process, and it would be next to impossible for an observer who was excluded categorically from the small, close-knit peer groups in which most of the action takes place. I can offer a hypothetical example of this process, however, based on second-hand evidence. Suppose that a group of sansei growing up in Japan Town are taught by their parents and others in their community that they must ignore ethnic and racial attributions from non-Japanese. "We wish to be accepted," the parents say. "Therefore we do not acknowledge messages that attribute foreignness to us." Once these sansei enter school, they are bombarded by messages they must not respond to from non-Japanese peers and teachers, while also recognizing that the intercultural school context offers potential rewards such as friendship, status, sex, and material security. They feel uncomfortable about having to participate in a context where they cannot acknowledge the perceptions others have of them. They begin to discuss this feeling among themselves and support each other's perception of the situation: "We are not accepted, and we refuse to withdraw into ourselves, into our families, or into our ethnic community. We must face the discrimination squarely. We must accept our differentness." Members of this group begin to study Japanese American history, go to Japanese films, and eat Japanese food more often. They talk about these experiences among themselves and subtly reward each other for participating in them. If a member does not go to ethnic films or read the right books, he finds he has little to talk about that interests his friends. He is pressured into their style of life under the implicit threat of being ostracized.

Members of the group now speak openly with non-Japanese of their history and culture and of the subtle discrimination they feel. They begin to resist definitions of themselves as "no different," which they see as mainly hypocritical and patronizing. They begin to search Japanese and Japanese American history for the antecedents of their current values and attitudes, and, of course, they find them. These sansei are now able to affirm their freedom to their parents' generation. They have found a way of adjusting to the multicultural world that feels better than the one their parents offered them. They see their parents as misguided and confused because they have not adopted the sansei way of adapting. The following song, written by sansei Andy Hanami (courtesy Pacific Citizen), is a satire on their attitude:

This is the story of Tokyo Joe
Who came to this country a long time ago,
Who learned to speak English so that in the fields,
He could be gardener of Beverly Hills.
And he couldn't untangle his head.
    Then Joe got married and nisei appeared.
They grew up together near San Pedro Pier,
But during the war they were all sent away.
And inside the camps you could hear nisei say:
And we better untangle our heads.
    After the nisei, the sansei appeared.
We grew up together around Crenshaw Square,
We're smart and we're groovey, we're gentle and kind.
And we know where we're going—
Cause we read the signs.
And we better untangle our heads.

Members of our hypothetical sansei group begin to rate the acceptability of other groups according to whether their life style and self-perception are similar. When members of like-minded groups come into contact, mutual borrowing is likely to take place, with the result of broadening and leveling sansei identity. Ethnic studies courses, sansei underground publications, and even touring musical groups help to sow the successful new self-definitions in the minds of the whole generation. Because most new self-definitions arise out of daily behavior by a process of trial and error, the chance that any given perception spawned within the friendship group will be permanently adopted by the whole generation is thus extremely small. The perceptions with the widest currency tell us a great deal about the common experiences peculiar to the sansei generation. The fact that many sansei describe their own generation as confused probably stems from the great proliferation of new self-perceptions caused by their participation in a variety of contexts. Many factors bear on any particular sansei's choice of friends or ethnic identity styles. A complete discussion of the subject would require a much larger sample than the one I used. I recommend Maykovich's (1972) study of sansei identity, which suggests some ways the sansei's choice of life styles and beliefs is affected by the life styles and beliefs of their parents.

In this discussion of generational identity, I have been setting the stage for viewing broad changes in culture characteristic of each generation. These cultural changes are psychologically complex and nonreversible. The special characteristics of each generation, in particular its styles of self-perception and the behaviors that result from them, are very much the products of previous acculturative change. I have said earlier in this chapter that the main significance of generational identity lies in the behavior and value differences between generations. A discussion of these differences requires a new perspective. So far, I have been discussing acculturation as a process involving individuals in contexts. Now I am interested in the broad values and behaviors that are the cumulative results of this process as it involves the whole Japanese American community. In the following discussion I investigate a single type of context, interaction between generations within the family.

Process of Acculturation

I am not so much interested in cataloguing the whole spectrum of acculturational changes and the reasons for them as I am in identifying the changes that have a major effect on the way the generations behave toward each other. This limitation greatly simplifies the task, but one still must be careful in attributing a causal relationship between acculturation and intergenerational relations. When one is talking about groups, intergenerational relations refers to a category of cultural phenomena that can be both a cause and an effect of change. It must be excluded from the causal side of the equation before one can speak of it as a category of dependent phenomena. Although I am taking license with the complexity of relationships between intergenerational relations and other cultural processes, such license is permissible when it helps to make sense of the data. Behavior does not change independently according to separate processes any more than spring comes independently to frogs, flies, and lily pads. But one can study frogs with only passing reference to lily pads and flies in order to simplify things.

In this spirit, I have dissected out of the system of cultural change the following dominant processes, which clarify intergenerational relations. Processes that begin earlier than others and sometimes set others in motion I have classified primary processes, distinguished from secondary processes, which tend to be dependent on the primary ones. I have also distinguished between processes that increase cultural similarity between Japanese Americans and middle-class European Americans, or acculturative processes, and those that preserve the distinction between Japanese Americans and European Americans, or intercultural processes. The primary acculturative processes are: *economic achievement,* accompanied by middle-class life style; growing *command of American skills,* language, customs, and habits; and gradual *loss of Japanese skills,* language, customs, and habits. The secondary acculturative processes are: *geographical dispersion,* and the resulting decline of community solidarity, communication, and homogeneity; growing *individuation,* and the resulting decline of identification with (but not commitment to) family and other intimate groups; *broadening intellectual perspective* from family, neighborhood, and ethnic group to nation and world. The intercultural processes are: *changing intercultural self-perception,* arising from a shift toward participation in and management of intercultural contexts; and *cultural shifts in the perception of history.*

One might argue about whether economic achievement is truly a cultural, as distinct from a merely economic, change. I have called it a cultural change and distinguished it from other cultural changes because specific cultural problems in intergenerational relations which are closely related to it. By middle-class life style, I mean status competition based on material goods, education, occupation, and leisure pursuits and an egalitarian attitude toward child-rearing derived from middle-class education and institutions. It is harder to be specific about command of American skills and loss of Japanese skills. Reports have appeared elsewhere (Pierce and others, 1973; Clark and Pierce, 1973) on some of the methods I used to measure linguistic and cultural change. Here I need only summarize my findings by saying that there is a clear improvement in command of English and knowledge about American culture with each succeeding generation in the study; that dress, grooming, posture, gesture, and etiquette more clearly approach middle-class American norms with each generation; and that the reverse tends to be true in all respects with regard to Japanese culture, even in settings where Japanese cultural norms seem to be appropriate, such as interaction with issei or with visiting Japanese citizens. A few nisei and sansei have gained considerable knowledge of their ancestral language and culture, it is true. There are nisei and sansei who are Buddhist and Shinto priests in the Bay Area, and others who are literate in Japanese or skilled in Japanese arts, such as judo and flower-arranging. Travel to Japan appears to have become popular as well among the American-born generations. My impression, however, is that the total amount of knowledge about Japanese culture is on the wane in each succeeding generation.

Discussing acculturation as a group of cumulative processes may seem to contradict what I say in Chapter Three about the contextual and additive nature of acculturation. However, I am still not implying that people substitute American traits for Japanese traits one for one. Some people have learned a great deal about American culture while retaining a great deal of their Japanese cultural repertoire. Others, while learning little about their host country's ways, have lost much of their knowledge of native traditions and language. Here I refer to changes in group norms, not to changes in individual behavior; but it would be a mistake to consider acculturation a substitutive process when the frame of reference is the group. There are definitions of contexts shared by the whole group that require shifting back and forth between cultural styles. In interacting with an issei most nisei and sansei try to be as Japanese as possible, especially if the setting is public and the issei is not a relative. Nisei norms generally call for strictly American behavior in the presence of Caucasians, but some sansei groups have different ideas. In short, at the group level there are some predictable shifts in cultural emphasis, and we would do well to retain the concept of situationality at this level. We can depict these shifts as in Figure 1. This diagram is by no means a reliable guide to understanding Japanese American acculturation as a whole. In addition to obscuring vast individual differences, it slurs over different rates of changes in different areas of culture, and it does not even depict the all-important intercultural dimension.

Figure 1

Average Range of Cultural Competence by Generation

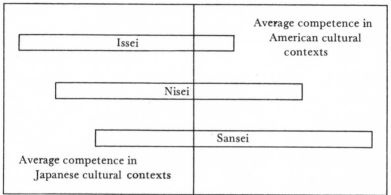

Returning to the more specific context of the family, one would expect acculturative changes of the sort I have listed to disrupt relations between parents and children and between grandparents and grandchildren. To a surprising extent this expectation is not borne out. People do not have to agree about many things or even to speak the same language to live together in harmony, although ideological agreement may certainly help. It is so much a part of middle-class American culture to think of the individual as an autonomous, integrated ego and of social relations as the communication of individual needs and impulses that we tend to believe that harmony arises out of congruent individual aims. While we recognize the necessity of suppressing feelings to preserve important relationships, we believe such suppression is somehow unfair. We feel out of character when conscious of denied feelings, and we resent it. Americans feel intensely guilty when they find their own perceptions and aims in disagreement with those of others close to them, such as family members because they see themselves as synonymous with their feelings. When a relationship is important enough—for instance, when it is supported by massive social sanctions, as in the case of motherhood—this guilt supplies the dynamic for suppressing the disharmonious feelings. At the end of such a process, we might believe we value a relationship because we are personally rewarded in it, and we are often right. However, the resolution of guilt that results in such harmony often comes about through a drastic alteration of our conscious needs and so necessarily of our perception of ourselves. Often we just live guiltily with our denied feelings rather than undergo this drastic alteration.

The result of ideal kinship relations—close, long-term co-operation in spite of fundamental differences in personal values and goals—is not very different in Japanese and in American culture. However, the dynamic that produces this result is quite different. The Japanese view conflict between role demands and inner feelings as a regrettable human characteristic that is to be corrected as much as possible by the suppression of any feelings that are disruptive. In other words, they see individuals primarily as parts of relationships or as the very roles they play, and feelings as transient phenomena which must not be taken too seriously. Many expressions of this attitude can be found in Japanese culture, but one example ought to do. The word *makoto* is used often in Japan. It is usually translated "sincerity," and it does indeed have the connotation of harmony of feeling and action. However, Americans are likely to be misled by this translation, for *makoto* is used to exhort people to behave the way society expects them to, whereas the English word *sincerity* often has the opposite emphasis. When things go badly between people, the Japanese say that they should practice *hansei*, that is, reflect on themselves. The idea is that if the disputants reflect on themselves, they will discover some feelings that are not appropriate to their roles and relegate those feelings to their proper place. (For an excellent discussion of the core differences between Japanese and American social systems, I recommend Barth's 1972 article on contract and involute systems.)

In the Japanese family, then, one need not feel guilty

about one's potentially discordant feelings and ideas. One need only keep these feelings from interfering with the business of being a member of the family. Changes in values and perspective resulting from acculturation often produce some personal distress and confusion, but they have remarkably little effect on family solidarity. This characteristic has probably helped the Japanese greatly in their adaptation to American life, although as part of the ancestral culture it too has been the victim of attrition, as we shall see when I turn to the topic of individuation. With these general remarks in mind, let us now look at some of the specific effects of cultural processes on intergenerational relations, a step toward understanding the relationship between cultural change and personal development.

Economic Achievement and Middle-class Life Style. During their struggle toward middle-class status, many nisei naturally acquired a deep concern for the symbols of achievement that went along with it, such as a good education (or the appearance of it) and good American manners. Many perceived their parents' backwardness in these respects—manifested in use of the Japanese language, performance of Japanese rituals, and holding of prescientific folk beliefs—as an obstacle to their acceptance. However, with growing confidence in their own success, the nisei may have come to accept the traditionalism of their parents more and more. Says Mrs. Minamoto (nisei, age fifty): "It's a strange thing. Most nisei grow older and value things that the issei did more and more. A strange thing. Before the war, some were ashamed to use Japanese in public. [They were] not too happy about cultural things. Now a lot of [nisei] parents say that they have to send their kids to Japan to see cultural things, that they should see them first hand in Japan." The improvement in the American image of Japan since the war has undoubtedly affected the mellowing of the nisei, as has the emerging ethnic pride of their children's generation. For whatever reason, certain folkways that were long perceived as shameful by the upwardly mobile nisei have become more acceptable to them in the old age of their parents, the issei.

The economic success of the nisei determines their ability to look after the needs of financially dependent parents and ensures their freedom from economic domination by their parents. Their economic success and independence have contributed much, I believe, to the strong sense of responsibility the average nisei feels for his parents' material security. The issei, for their part, take great pride in the material, social, and educational achievements of their children but prefer to be economically independent of them if possible. Although it is not the style of the issei to express their pride in their children directly to them, this pride is nevertheless an important source of mutual respect between the generations. Most successful nisei recognize their debt to the sacrifices of their parents, and by doing so they reciprocate parental pride. This recognition is demonstrated by the nisei's image of the typical issei: hard working and self-sacrificing.

The economic success of the nisei has also made it possible for them to demand less labor from their children than their parents demanded of them. Together with an egalitarian family ethic that the nisei have absorbed from middle-class institutions and media, this change has led both the issei and the nisei to consider the sansei somewhat spoiled. It has also prolonged the economic and emotional dependence of many sansei on their parents, a fact that does not trouble the parents much but is a major issue for many of the children, as we shall see.

If parental control over the sansei is strengthened by the economics of nisei upward mobility, it is, however, weakened by the cultural middle-class character of the sansei. More and more sansei are marrying outside the ethnic community, for instance, indicating a greater autonomy in their choice of life style that stems from their ability to melt into affluent American society. Ironically, the efforts of the nisei to live up to their parents' achievement expectations are counterbalanced by the sansei perception of this very achievement as spiritually shallow. The sansei's view is itself a product of their middle-class upbringing and education.

Command of American Skills. The growing command of American cultural skills has probably weakened family relationships more than any other factor. It has made the issei heavily dependent on their children for information about the society in which they live and has thereby weakened issei authority. For example, although the nisei believe their fathers (most of whom are dead now) were fairly competent men, they believe their mothers were less competent. The modest command of American skills of most issei women seriously limited their role in the family. Japanese mothers are supposed to provide training and advice on social skills to their children throughout their lives, while fathers enforce morality and provide economic and technical training. Once children are economically independent, fathers have discharged a large share of their role obligations.

Although some issei complain mildly about certain middle-class American traits of young people, such as their sexual liberalness, the issei are not inclined to criticize their own children. Their attitude is expressed in an old Japanese proverb: "When old, obey your children."

The effect of Americanization on relations between nisei and sansei is subtler. Both generations know their way around American society well in the sense of proper behavior, but the sansei appear to understand the meaning of social forms much better than the nisei do. This difference results in frequent misunderstandings—regarding dating and premarital sex, for example. In Japanese society, these things traditionally were controled by the family and the community. Unmarried women were never found in unsupervised surroundings, mobility was strictly limited by the absence of the automobile, and privacy scarcely existed for most boys and girls. In such surroundings, sexual self-control was hardly necessary and in fact was neither systematically taught nor much expected of the young. The situation is different in contemporary America. Mobility and autonomy are treasured social values, and boys and girls have plenty of opportunity to be together alone, especially in the middle class. Sexual self-control is considered necessary and is generally impressed upon the growing child in one way or another. He is taught the "evils" of masturbation and early sexual exploration and the dangers of venereal disease and pregnancy. In spite of their boasts to the contrary, by universal standards most middle-class American adolescents and young adults are sexually self-inhibited.

Nisei parents are generally acquainted with middle-class American norms for dating, living away from home, and so on. However, few older nisei understand the subtler matter of self-inhibition. Operating on the Japanese assumption that boys and girls after puberty are by nature licentious if left alone, parents are understandably unwilling to concede to the American norms. Their fears are substantiated and magnified from time to time by community gossip about cases of premarital pregnancy. One sansei respondent told me that girls who want to travel to Japan or to Mexico City, where there is a large Japanese community, have to announce their plans many months before departure lest the community assume that abortion is the real reason for the trip. As a result of parental anxiety and misunderstanding, ideas about sexuality are a major source of friction in nisei-sansei relations, especially where girls are concerned. Adolescent sansei often draw the conclusion from misunderstandings about sex that their parents are backward and unreasonable, and the fact that sex is a taboo topic in the average Japanese American home does not help.

Closely related to the problem of sexuality is the problem of sex-role acculturation. Sansei girls believe in sex equality more than their parents do. Girls resent the preferential treatment given their brothers and are frustrated by the fact that boys are given far greater freedom by their parents to regulate their own affairs. Since nisei mothers often support the male-dominated values of their parental culture, at least where their daughters are concerned, sansei girls sometimes consider their mothers traitors.

Loss of Japanese Skills. The major result of the loss of Japanese skills by acculturating generations has been the emotional isolation of the issei from their families. Although the principle of family cooperation and family responsibility is still strong, the loss of Japanese linguistic and other communication skills in the second and third generations has contributed to an emphasis on work and productivity at the expense of emotional communication as the symbolic expressions of family unity. Earlier in this chapter I described the perceptions that nisei and issei have of each other's generations and said that these perceptions were heavily instrumental in contrast with the more emotional perceptions held by and about the sansei.

The constraint on emotional exchange between the issei and their families might be related to two other factors: the Japanese tendency to avoid direct verbal reference to their feelings in everyday social relations and the fact that the nisei had virtually no contact with an important category of kin, their grandparents. The indirect or nonverbal nature of emotional communication in Japanese culture has been treated in detail elsewhere (for example, Caudill and Weinstein, 1969; Kiefer, 1972; Doi, 1973; Morsbach, 1972). It is a way of avoiding potentially disruptive emotional confrontation by a combination of suppressing feelings, using poetic innuendo that the listener can react to or ignore, and relying on subtle facial, postural, and gestural cues to convey feeling. Since some nisei have lost a good deal of skill at communicating with Japanese emotional language, they often fail to perceive issei emotional needs.

The effects of the absence of the nisei's grandparents are important. The ideal family in traditional Japan contained three generations. Even though only 22.7 percent of all families in Japan conformed to this ideal in 1960, 60.7 percent of a well-distributed sample believed retired parents should live with their married children (Koyama, 1962). Studies of the Japanese family indicate that the main role of the grandparent in relation to the grandchild is to develop the child's emotional expressiveness where it is appropriate. Says Vogel of modern Japanese middle-class families (1963, p. 224): "Perhaps the most common coalition pattern in homes with grandparents is for grandparents to have close positive affectional ties with grandchildren. They commonly spend a lot of time playing with children and are sympathetic with them against the strictures of the parents. But this relationship tends to be limited to the affectional sphere." Relationships between parents and children, however, tend to be intense and emotionally demonstrative until the age of about five or six. After this, they are characterized by an emotional reserve which strikes the Westerner as almost cold, but is merely careful. Older children and adults must keep their emotions under control at all times in the interest of social harmony, and discipline in this skill must begin as soon as the child is psychologically mature enough to begin learning it. Grandparents ideally provide a safety valve for emotions forbidden in the parent-child relationship, and, more important, they teach the children how to feel and to express feeling in situations where it is culturally permissible to do so. We can therefore infer that the nisei missed an important part of their socialization by not having grandparents (or friends or neighbors who had grandparents, which can be equally important). The ability to handle emotion within the framework of the Japanese American family—that is, in their relations with the issei—may never have been thoroughly taught to many nisei. In addition, many issei may not have been able to adapt their relationships with their own children to compensate for the absence of cultural input from the children's grandparents. The emotional effects of the absence of grandparents are not entirely relieved even in the case of the sansei. We have seen that the sansei do see the issei in a more emotional light than the nisei do; however, because of the great linguistic and cultural barriers separating the issei and sansei, sansei generally idealize their grandparents and seem to have little real understanding of their feelings.

It is harder to identify the effects of the loss of Japanese culture on relations between the nisei and sansei. One often gets the impression that sansei and young nisei tend to interpret the Japanese aspects of older nisei's behavior according to American standards and sometimes miss the point by doing so. For example, they regard nisei sensitivity to the feelings of others, verbal indirectness, and attempts to control others by good example rather than attack as indications of spinelessness. When the older nisei in California collected money to erect a state landmark in honor of the first Japanese settlers, a young nisei acquaintance of mine was incensed. "They should have forced the *state* to put up the money," he said. "God knows, this state owes it to us!" The Japanese perception, however, would have been that the nisei scored a great victory on two counts. First, as givers, they held higher status than the state, the receiver; second, the failure of the state to fulfill an obligation was brought to public attention, while the nisei emerged as morally impeccable citizens.

Geographical Dispersion and the Decline of Community.
One can immediately see the interdependence of geographical
dispersion and economic success, Americanization, and the loss
of Japanese skills. Upward mobility leads to outward mobility,
which leads to increased acculturation, which leads in turn to
increased upward and outward mobility. Intergenerational relations enter into the process of dispersion in a number of ways,
but the most direct and obvious way is the decline of social control attending outward mobility. With the decline of the individual's visibility in the community and the gradual attenuation of
communication networks, ethnic norms are harder for parents
to enforce. This effect of dispersion would help to explain the
recent appearance of delinquency and drug abuse among sansei
in the scattered Los Angeles Japanese American population and
the relative absence of these problems in the tight-knit San
Francisco community. Interviews with respondents who were
raised in rural communities indicate that, as one would expect,
the older generations have greater power in rural families than
they do in urban families because of the high visibility of the
individual in these small communities. For example, interracial
dating and marriage are still frowned upon, although covertly,
by most older nisei, but they can no longer keep their children
from engaging in this sort of behavior by pointing to the dire
consequences on the family's reputation. The children know
that there will be gossip about their interracial affairs, but they
also know that it is not likely to seriously threaten the family's
well-being, as it might have in the days when the family had
virtually no durable social relations outside the ethnic neighborhood. The same principle holds for political activism, dropping
out of the educational and economic achievement system, and
other forms of behavior considered rebellious by the nisei.

Nisei norms regarding the care of dependent issei parents
disparage the child who pushes the parent out of the home or
who does not contribute adequately to satisfying the parent's
economic needs. One nisei, Mr. Daibutsu, showed me a type-
written page he had gotten from his Buddhist minister on which
he had underlined the following words: "There could be no
greater illusion than the belief that one can treat one's parents
unfeelingly and with contempt and yet expect that one's own

children will someday treat one otherwise, for such people break the golden chain of affection that binds the generations and gives continuity and meaning to life." To this Mr. Daibutsu added, "A lot of people don't seem to realize this these days, but I think it's one of the wisest things I've ever read." Asked to describe the relationship between issei and nisei, two nisei respondents have different perceptions, but they seem to agree on the morality of the situation. Says Mrs. Kindaichi: "I guess they feel respectful to their parents, but not as much as the parents think they should. I think that the issei feel that the nisei don't think of them enough. Talking to friends, I feel there's a tendency for the nisei nowadays—if the parents get sick or whatever —to put them somewhere. It's very abhorrent to the issei." Says Mr. Hibana: "It's very good. They all look after their parents. They don't put them in an old folks' home. There's lots of respect. Normally, the relationship is very close." Mr. Hibana's mother, who was also interviewed, agreed with Mrs. Kindaichi, even though she herself lives with her son and his family. The director of a Japanese nursing home told me that local nisei are secretive about consulting her for fear of losing face in the community. However, some of them have installed their ailing parents in the nursing home. From these reports, and others like them, I conclude that pressure for conformity to such norms is gradually relaxing, although many people continue to believe the old ways are best.

Individuation. By individuation I mean the acquisition of the American belief in the moral rightness of individual autonomy and self-expression. The contrasting Japanese view of the proper relationship between individual and group is illustrated by Sone, who writes in her autobiographical novel, *Nisei Daughter,* about the days following Pearl Harbor: " 'I suppose from now on we'll hear about nothing but the humiliating defeats of Japan in the papers here,' said Mother, resignedly. Henry and I glared indignantly at Mother, then Henry shrugged his shoulders and decided to say nothing. Discussion of politics, especially Japan versus America, had become taboo in our family for it sent tempers skyrocketing." (1952, p. 148). Here we see a situation where personal feelings of national identity conflicted with the good of the family, and the family won out. This situation could occur in any family, but the important fact is that it is the expected course of events in the traditional Japanese family. The older nisei were raised, for the most part, in such tradition-al families, where the subordination of each member to the will and interests of the group was taken for granted. To say that the nisei were taught to avoid the expression of personal feel-ings and opinions that might disrupt the harmony of the family does not fully describe the classic relationship of individual and group. It is better to say that a basic assumption of all group interaction was that each individual had no legitimate interests that conflicted with those of the group, that group and individ-ual interests were one and the same, and that person and role were considered for practical purposes identical.

Not that this assumption accurately describes any real sit-uation. As Sone's example illustrates, social organization is al-ways full of ambiguities, and roles often conflict. A woman may be torn between her roles as wife and as mother or a child be-tween his of son and of brother. Extrafamilial roles are usually subordinate, but can also introduce conflicts. There is a basic difference between Japanese and middle-class American culture in the way such conflicts are regarded. From infancy on, Ameri-can children are groomed to live in a society where voluntary relationships, based on mutual interest and explicit sentiment, play a central role in the life of each person. The child learns that he, not his family, is largely responsible for his feelings and actions. He must decide, at first with parental guidance but later by himself, which feelings are worthy and which are not, and he must stick up for his right to express the worthy ones. Almost the whole of personality psychology in the West is based one-sidedly on this ideal (Kiefer, 1970). Moreover, the moral abso-lutism that I have described as characteristic of American cul-ture holds that the individual should be consistent in his opinions across all social contexts rather than adopt the ethic of whatever group happens to claim his loyalty at the moment. Given these principles, it makes less sense for Americans to keep their personal feelings to themselves than it does for Japanese to do so, even when self-expression threatens to disrupt relationships. It is the acquisition of this belief in the autonomy of the individual that I am calling individuation.

Two factors contribute to the process of individuation in the sansei, setting them apart from their parents. First, as I said earlier, the nisei have adopted many child-rearing practices and attitudes from contemporary middle-class America—the Dr. Spock generation. They believe their own parents were too rigid, too demanding, too dictatorial. They favor a warmer, more egalitarian relationship with their own children. However, this attitude toward children fosters individuation—a point which is rarely understood by the nisei. The practice of egalitarianism subtly communicates the idea to the child that he is important as a person, not merely as a member of the group. The lenient nisei parent is often unwittingly undermining the very sense of familial responsibility that he is eager for his children to learn. Nisei parents probably have no alternative, except perhaps to be more conscious about what they are doing. The second factor contributing to sansei individuation is the increased interaction with non-Japanese. Living in middle-class neighborhoods and attending middle-class schools, the typical sansei naturally develops a sense of the family that differs radically from the traditional Japanese norms. Nisei parental behavior often appears to be a compromise between the two cultural extremes, which forstalls open rebellion.

I used the Thematic Apperception Test to learn about interpersonal feelings and attitudes people could not or would not express more directly. The content of high school sansei Thematic Apperception Test responses indicate that they often feel disagreements with parents' values which they cannot express. Once the sansei enter college, however, they often undergo a transformation and become able to discuss family conflicts quite clearly. Miss Nakadai (sansei, age twenty-five) describes her mother:

Miss Nakadai: *She's not very frank or honest. Not direct with her kids like she could be. Like I learned sex education by accident at eighteen. I could have gone till I was twenty-six.*
Interviewer: *How do you get along with her?*

Miss N: *All right. I can't talk to her about heavy matters. As far as she's concerned, I'm a good girl in the traditional manner. I'm old enough [to have my own ideas], but she doesn't question because she doesn't want to know.*

For some sansei, the conflict over individuation takes the form of a double bind. Miss Kobayashi (sansei, age twenty-five) says her parents ask for honesty one minute and reject her attempts to be honest the next. "Sometimes I think it would be better to keep [my parents] in the dark about a lot of things," she says. "I know your parents still accept you [but] I'm not quite sure. I'm confused here. I let my mother know I have black friends. One time she discovered my grass and said, 'What else is going on?' She said, 'People will laugh at us for not knowing what's going on.' But then, they don't want to know." Later, she says, "If I talk to my parents, I'll upset them. I can't. I'll have to learn to communicate with them, in a way, on a superficial level."

The fact that many sansei see their own families as frustratingly noncommunicative on emotionally loaded issues illustrates a fundamental difference in expectations between sansei and nisei. For the sansei, the family, like other social groups, should be based on voluntary cooperation, on shared feeling, and on the commitment of individuals to each other. Theirs is an individuated point of view. It requires open communication channels and negotiated consensus. For the nisei, the solidarity of the family is an imperative, a given; to question it is foolishness, and to weaken it by airing the differences among its members is immoral.

The problem of sexuality is also relevant here. For the issei and nisei, control of the sexual behavior of children, especially girls, is *the* symbol of family cohesion, and family cohesion is the core of morality in general. Sexual rebellion is a threat to the foundations of community and honor. It is not only unfilial, it is also sacrilegious and antisocial. To the individuated sansei, however, sex is a matter of individual taste and conscience. Since feelings are what count, a girl can be a good daughter by loving her parents whether or not she sleeps alone until married. Individuation, and the sexual liberation that accompanies it, leads to endless conflict in many Japanese American families.

Broadening Intellectual Perspective. The process of broadening intellectual perspective is discussed in part in Chapter Two. There we see that the events that occupy the center of attention for many issei are filled entirely by the familiar faces of friends and kin. Although many are aware of important ethnic-group, regional, and national issues, they seldom see these issues as having a direct bearing on their own lives. Their social horizons encompass only neighborhood, church, kin, and friends. At the same time, something about the issei strikes me as timeless and universal. They remind me of Antoine de Saint-Exupéry's Little Prince, who lived on a planet so small that he could see the relatedness of everything on it and learned the essential importance of small things. The small scope of the issei's world has fostered in them a meticulous thoroughness and attention to detail. Many have learned to discriminate between the minute acts and ideas that lead to harmony and equilibrium at close quarters and those that lead to disharmony and confusion. The issei have learned to first distill the techniques of diplomacy from, and then cultivate them within the microcosm of their humble daily life. The perspective I am describing is neither morally nor functionally superior to other perspectives; some issei create struggle in their relationships by trying to manipulate others with their expertise as diplomats.

The nisei appear to have more clearly defined images of their ethnic group and their own generation than the issei do, indicating that social self-consciousness is more important to them. On the whole, they also are better informed and more thoughtful about regional, national, and international events. The nisei tend to think the issei are politically naive and culturally limited, and in fact many issei, especially women, have to depend on their nisei children for advice about issues that involve the world beyond their immediate circle of acquaintances. The tendency to seek moral or spiritual advice from the issei or to look to them as useful moral examples is rarer among nisei than the reverse—to see them as needing guidance about the social and political world they live in. One gets the feeling, however, that most nisei, like the issei, are not powerfully motivated by events outside their ethnic community. They vote regularly as individuals or as Japanese Americans, but only a few politically conscious nisei take an active part in city or statewide politics. The nisei also tend to think in terms of limited social categories such as race and generation rather than in broad moral terms, as Lyman (1973) points out.

The process of expanding horizons continues with the sansei generation. More sansei than nisei cast their social world in terms of minorities versus majority, Asian versus non-Asian, youth versus middle-aged, middle-class and poor versus rich, and so on. Many sansei have contempt for what they believe to be the complacency of the narrow, ethnic politics characteristic of their parents' generation and of their unenlightened peers. Miss Suzuki (sansei, age fifteen) is one of them.

Miss Suzuki: *I like to see a group of sansei get together like this [community meeting] because there is a broad spectrum of sansei opinion. And then there is a large group of sansei who are just apathetic, and I think they should be reached. I don't know why they don't have opinions about things, but they don't, and they're kind of being manipulated by other people.*

Interviewer: *Why is it important to reach these apathetic sansei?*

Miss S: *If you're not aware of the problems of the world or of the community, you get caught up in a self-centered bag. A lot of sansei should become aware that there is a world out there that really affects them. There are a lot of things that affect them indirectly, like the Vietnam war and the civil rights movement.*

As I mentioned in Chapter Two, the sansei who take a broad, historical view of things are generally but not always those whose parents have similar inclinations. In these families there is little conflict on the issues of morality and politics. A painful generation gap, however, is occasionally described by the sansei in terms of the relative narrowness of their parents' world views. Miss Mita (sansei, age twenty-two) is on bad terms with her parents. Asked to describe a typical nisei, she says: "Nisei equals my mother and almost everyone else's mother. Very, very emphatic about how the Japanese people have attained a position in the United States today and have had to work to succeed and be accepted. And don't trust Caucasians because they always try and make you do shitty stuff. Also racists. Like, if worse came to worst they'd let their daughter marry a Caucasian, but not a negro."

Changing Intercultural Self-perceptions. The process of changing intercultural self-perception has been treated at length under the topic of generational identity at the beginning of this chapter. This process is partly responsible for the view of many sansei that their parents have sold out to the European American culture, and have lost a valuable heritage, while their grandparents represent a more wholesome way of life, albeit often an enigmatic one to them. The reaction of the older generations to this view has been to adopt a wait and see policy. The issei are pleased by the sansei's renewed interest in their parental culture and their apparent new respect for their grandparents, but few pretend to understand or to know what the outcome will be. The nisei reaction is mixed; some admire the new sansei self-definitions and seek to emulate them; some are hurt by the sansei's rejection of their values but console themselves that this will pass in time.

Cultural Shifts in Perception of History. This chapter so far has discussed the acculturation process in terms of changes in the relationship between the ethnic individual or group and the contemporary social environment. It is also important to discuss acculturation in terms of changes in the relationship between the ethnic individual or group and the past and future, as indicated in Chapters One and Two. Habits of perception, including habits of perceiving history itself, arise out of the shared symbol system of culture. Having a generational identity means among other things having a sense of where one has been and where one is going as a member of an ethnic and historical group. These perceptions are profoundly affected by changes in such cultural factors as access to information about one's par-

ents and host society and criteria for evaluating this information. For example, the sansei's deep experience of middle-class
American culture has made them introspective and skeptical of
the American dream. At the same time, their distance from Japanese culture makes it possible for them to idealize certain aspects of it and to fail to recognize others (such as noncommuni-
cativeness) for what they are. For many nisei, being a good Japanese and being a good, quietly patriotic American citizen are in
no way incompatible (see Lebra, 1972). For others and for
many sansei, Japanese precepts of valor and loyalty demand
political rebellion and protest. Such perceptions determine the
progress and direction of cultural change, as I indicate in Chapter Two, as well as having an important impact on intergenerational relations.

Chapter V

Overcoming
Acculturative Stress

The necessities of life for most of us include both making a living in the economic sense and maintaining the will to live—that is, *amour-propre*, or self-love. Both these ingredients in turn require the ability to organize experience so that it makes sense. Making a living is based on one's ability to accurately predict the consequences of one's acts from the regularities of experience one has perceived. Self-love is based on the ability to recognize a pattern of experience called self that is on the whole more tolerable than death. At the same time, maturation is a process of responding to a diversified and constantly changing environment. Without constantly varied stimuli, our minds and bodies would remain fetal indefinitely. Our sense organs could not function at all. All growth and learning involves variation that is to some extent stressful.

Apparently, too much diversity in the human environment is pathogenic and too much sameness is stunting, suggesting that there *is* an optimum range of complexity and change for human maturation and functioning. Moreover, the complexity of man's environment is decided to a great extent by how he interprets it symbolically. That is, the relationship between man and his environment is mediated by symbols (such as the ideas *man* and *environment* themselves) that are invented and learned and that are related to the phenomenal world by convention rather than by nature or necessity. For example, while Westerners see a face on the moon, Japanese see the far more complex image of a rabbit pounding rice in a mortar.

According to a common anthropological definition, a culture is a unified symbol system that gives continuity, meaning, and order to experience or at least helps to establish and maintain a beneficial range of complexity, ambiguity, and change. This definition leads naturally to the idea that any rapid change in the makeup of a culture, including rapid acculturation, produces severe psychological stress. Much has been written about such stress by anthropologists, particularly those, like Hallowell (1942, 1950, 1951, 1952), George Spindler (1952), Louise Spindler (1962), Barnouw (1950), Berreman (1964), Mead (1956), and Chance (1965), who discuss the disintegration of nonindustrial cultures by the impact of modern European-American domination. Closer to the topic of this book, Caudill and DeVos (1956) studied the psychological stresses experienced by acculturating Japanese Americans.

I have already discussed a number of stresses experienced by my subjects as a result of their changing cultural milieu. I will discuss changes in stress over the life cycle in Chapter Eight. In this chapter, I am concerned mainly with exploring the relationship between acculturation and personal psychological stress in general. The results are necessarily partial and tentative because of the complexity of the problem. Separating stresses directly related to culture contact from those related only remotely or not at all is often impossible. Racial discrimination, for example, imposes a stress that is hard to distinguish in some cases from the confusion that accompanies rapid acculturation. Complexity also arises from the huge range of strategies people use for coping with potentially stressful situations. The researcher studying acculturation usually does not see people passively suffering stress, but people denying, avoiding, fleeing from, or coping ingeniously with many potentially stressful situations. The source of stress, or even the existence of stress, must often be inferred through an analysis of the coping strategies.

I have emphasized (in Chapter Two) the influence of contexts on acculturation. The fact that different norms operate in different social settings increases the complexity of the individual's symbolic environment and presumably requires periodic learning that is more or less stressful. The idea that the acculturating person tends to add and discard behaviors and perceptual habits as he learns to operate in different social settings is of course important in the matter of personal stress. When the perceptions and actions appropriate to a setting have become second nature, however, a person's level of stress due to complexity drops. Secondary learning, or learning how to learn (see Bateson, 1942), also lowers the stressfulness of successive new contexts.

Sources of Stress

Since my data come from a relatively short time span, I was not able to study the durations, or "careers," of stressful circumstances in detail. My short-term data, however, suggest that three main processes in the person-environment relationship frustrate adaptation and lead to recognizable periods of high stress. These processes are *cultural confusion, cultural conflict,* and *cultural alienation.* They are disturbances of the drives toward clarity, consistency, and continuity. I consider these processes part of the person-environment relationship because they appear to be products of the relationship itself, and because assigning responsibility to a given person or the other persons who are part of his environment is always questionable.

Cultural confusion occurs when a person cannot associate a definite norm with an appropriate context. This confusion arises in either of two circumstances: When more than one definite norm seems to be applicable at once (multiple norms), or when experience contradicts a person's assumptions about what is expected of him (normlessness). A person might recognize what is expected of him, but not when, or he might think he recognizes what others expect, only to be refuted. The stress that he feels in either circumstance usually can be expressed by the question, "What am I supposed to do?" I do not mean to imply that norms are generally conscious or clear-cut, but rather that they are, as Schuetz (1944) says "recipes for interpreting the social world" that are "taken for granted in the absence of evidence to the contrary." I gave an example of the first type of confusion, multiple norms, in Chapter Four. Miss Kobayashi has learned that frankness (a value associated with American culture) is asked of her in some situations, and stoic silence (a value associated with Japanese culture) in others. Her mother, however, seems to expect both at the same time—a stressful situation for the daughter.

The second type of confusion, normlessness, is frequent in both intracultural and intercultural contexts. The nisei's often mistaken belief that their sansei children would admire their stoicism and economic achievement is an example of intracultural confusion. The confusion is partly traceable to the acculturation process by which many sansei have come to value personal and expressive over social and instrumental goals. The nisei are often unaware of the normative assumptions that result from sansei values, and so they experience the conflict as normlessness. Intercultural contexts, especially those involving racially distinct people, have a built-in normlessness that automatically frustrates the learning of contextual norms, at least until the participants become familiar with each other. This built-in normlessness applies to a wide range of social events and is extremely important, but it is complex and hard to document or explain. It is based on the fact that participants in intercultural contexts regard each other as strangers. Strangers, as Simmel (1908) notes, always have a split image of each other: "The stranger is close to us insofar as we feel between him and ourselves common features of a national, social, occupational, or generally human nature. He is far from us insofar as these common features extend beyond him or us and connect us only because they connect a great many people." There is some indication that the problem of being strangers is also a feature of relations between newly acquainted members of the same ethnic group. Japanese Americans nearly always size each other up when they meet for the first time. Each tries to place the other in sociological space, as it were, to find out his origins, family background, education, occupation, friends, acquaintances, even his political views, ailments, and tastes in recreation, food, and spectator sports. There seems to be an implicit attempt in these encounters to find out just how far the stranger can be trusted as "one of us."

Participants in intercultural contexts are thus confronted in each new situation with the question: "To what extent am I perceived as a stranger?" and "To what extent, and in what respects, am I perceived as close or distant?" Because of the anxiety aroused by this ambiguity, participants are inclined to jump to conclusions about each other, with a degree of success that is at best random. I say at best, because more is involved usually than guesswork. Ambiguity leaves room for the free play of fantasy, and fantasy adheres to certain rules of its own. Much of what is labeled paranoia on both sides of interracial relations is behavior based on fantasies that have grown out of the fearful, anxious climate of normless interaction between racial groups.

The difficulty of settling the question of whether one is close or distant in intercultural relationships is shown in Miss Daibutsu's (sansei, age twenty-one) description of the hardest thing she has had to face in the last five years: "Before I got married, I went around with a black guy from back east. He happened to be black. I didn't think it would make any difference. I was naive to think that background makes no difference. I was brought up with certain ideas about how a relationship should go. His family and mine—it was hard to realize that people are different and that sometimes the differences are so big that you can't maintain certain relations with that person. Maybe these are awakenings as well as disillusionments. It's not that I'm so disillusioned, not with him. I couldn't live with the belief he had. That's pretty disturbing. There were a lot of self-doubts." Miss Daibutsu at least reached a decision about a particular relationship, however painful. More often a vague sense of confusion is too complicated to resolve, as in the following quote from Miss Kofuku (sansei, age seventeen): "Well, it was kind of difficult, changing from an all-black school to an all-white school and never feeling a part of either. I felt really strange in both schools. I don't think I ever got over this strangeness at either school, even though I had some good times at both of them. I always wondered why I was the way I was, why I wasn't black or white. It was strange that I would be right in the middle and that there would be so few people like me that I really knew; and I wished a lot of times that I would be either black or white, that I wouldn't be stuck in the middle. That's all I can remember."

Some suggestion of the variety of strategies used in the Japanese American community for coping with this sort of ambiguity in intercultural situations can be gleaned from the problems of the researcher in that community. Most people who volunteered to be interviewed seemed to accept on faith the idea that I was interested in them as individuals, and most were optimistic about my ability to understand what they told me about themselves. Some of the older nisei and issei, however, began the interviews in a formal and guarded way, which suggested that they accepted my motives provisionally but doubted my capacity to empathize with them. These people usually warmed up after several hours of interviewing, and some even expressed surprise that I seemed to understand their feelings reasonably well. A possible interpretation of their behavior is that they were in the habit of identifying intercultural contexts, however polite and genial, as having a strong component of distance and strangeness and were unprepared to have this expectation contradicted. A few of the respondents, however, ended the interviewing after one or two distant, formal sessions, and therefore were not included in the final sample. These people seemed to persist in defining the interview primarily in terms of distance and strangeness and quite naturally grew tired of the game in a short time.

The second process that is a source of personal stress, cultural conflict, results when values or beliefs held by participants in a social transaction are perceived as incompatible, so that the participants have to change values or stop interacting. By a social transaction I mean any behavior in which the values of more than one participant are relevant. Such behavior may take place in the absence of those whose values are relevant. It might even take place in an individual's imagination. The main point of transactions for this discussion is the personal significance of others. Two main types of cultural conflict grow out of the acculturation process: that resulting from perceptions of conflicting norms and values espoused by important persons and groups in the individual's life; and that resulting from perceptions of conflicting culturally biased definitions of intercultural contexts.

The first cultural conflict, norm conflict, is the type most often recognized in anthropological studies. A typical example is the conflict between American and Japanese ideals regarding dependence on parents. Issei parents and issei-dominated community institutions encourage nisei children to stay at home and accept parental support and decisions much longer than American norms indicate is good form. The children learn from their Caucasian peers, teachers, and the mass media that their acquiescence to these demands is somehow deviant, and they suffer guilt and indecision as a result of the conflict (see Caudill and DeVos, 1956). Such problems would be relatively simple if the norms of each cultural group were unanimous and specific. The truth is, however, that the bicultural individual is often exposed to a number of different socializing agents from each cultural group and that each agent often has a unique set of standards regarding any norm. Caucasian teachers, for example, tend to espouse liberal, individualistic values (albeit inconsistently) in contrast to the more conservative values of the mass media or of the working-class Caucasian neighbors of many Japanese American families.

Table 2 is a list of conflicting norms for the Japanese American teenager, such as dependence on parents, with the extreme values of each norm at opposite ends of continua. Common socialization agents are ranked along the continua according to their point of view. To give the table a rough-and-ready realism, I have chosen issues that create cultural conflict. I have tried to show roughly where I think certain important socialization agents for the Japanese American teenager would fall on the

Table 2

Relation of Socialization Agents to Conflicting Norms
for Japanese American Youth

Left norm	Agent positions (left → right)	Right norm
Dependence on Parents	F C M TPY E	Independence
Self-effacement	T F C EPY M	Assertiveness
Community	C M F Y P T E	Inner-directedness
Conformism	(T) F (E)CP (E) Y M(T)	Individuality
Sensitivity	F Y P C T E M	Toughness
Spiritualism	Y (F)PCT E (F) M	Materialism

E: American establishment—the media, traditional American values
P: Japanese American peers
Y: American middle-class youth culture
T: Teachers
F: Family
C: Community institutions—ethnic churches, clubs, and so on
M: Other minorities—blacks, Chicanos, Chinese, and so on
( ): Highly ambivalent position

cultural continua representing these issues. Japanese agents tend to line up on the left side of the figure, and non-Japanese agents tend to line up on the right. However, the overall conflict is not strictly along group lines and certainly not consistent according to the agent. The salient socialization agents and their points of view are highly specific to a particular period of life, as I discussed in Chapter Three. The degree to which an individual experiences conflict concerning any of these issues depends on who the important socializers are for him at the moment and where they stand on the issue. He may have a mother and father who are poles apart on all of them. He may have a reference group that synthesizes some extremes. As we shall see, he might take refuge in cynicism.

The second type of cultural conflict, context definition conflict, arises from culturally prescribed ways of perceiving and talking about intercultural contexts. Cultural groups in contact tend to develop a lore about each other's motives, ascribe a limited repertoire of motives to each other's actions, and block or reject each other's descriptions of their own motives. This practice is not limited to cultural groups. Mills (1940) attributes it to society in general: "A labor leader says he performs a certain act because he wants to get higher standards of living for the workers. A business man says that this is a rationalization or a lie, that it is really because he wants more money for himself from the workers. A radical says a college professor will not engage in radical movements because he is afraid for his job and, besides, is a reactionary. The college professor says it is because he just likes to find out how things work. What is reason for one man is rationalization for another. The variable is the accepted *vocabulary of motives,* the ultimates of discourse, of each man's dominant group about whose opinion he cares" (emphasis mine).

The process of context definition and management has been studied at the level of personal motivation by psychologists and psychiatrists of the transactional analysis genre (such as Berne, 1964) and the existential genre (such as May and others, 1958). It has been studied at the level of groups and institutions by the symbolic interaction sociologists (such as Goffman, 1961, 1963; Becker, 1953; Strauss, 1959). In the study of ethnic groups, context definition and management have been recognized by Berreman (1971), Eidheim (1969), and some non-anthropological writers like Baldwin (1955). So far the literature on ethnicity has been confined to the study of stigmatized groups—that is, to the process of stigmatizing and reactions to it. However, I think there are definitions of intercultural contexts that are conflict-generating but not necessarily stigmatizing. Earlier, for example, I mentioned the ideal minority stereotype that many Caucasians have of the Japanese Americans and the resulting frustration this stereotype generates for the minority group. Contextual definition conflicts are sometimes symmetrical; that is, each participant defines himself one way and his counterpart another in a mutually unacceptable exchange of stereotypes. For example, each individual defines the context as one in which he is acting idiosyncratically, out of free will, whereas his counterpart is acting predictably as a representative of an ethnic group. Insofar as the stereotype each one uses to interpret the other's behavior is cultural rather than individual—that is, shared and transmitted within the stereotyper's ethnic group—such situations are examples of cultural conflict. Using my definition of cultural conflict to study such situations would have the great advantage of giving the study a measure of badly needed freedom from value judgments. Since the study of context definition is itself a vocabulary of motives, it can easily be used to attack the dignity or even the sanity of its human objects.

Cultural confusion and conflict increases the individual's difficulty in building a sense of consistency into his life. The numberless possible strategies for dealing with inconsistency would occupy a whole series of books, and my respondents employ a wide range of them. Even though the typical Japanese American shows a high tolerance for inconsistency and a flexible identity, many pay a high price in the energy they devote to coping with confusion and conflict.

One aspect of the problem of adaptation to conflict that seems obvious to the student of culture but is often missed by the acculturating individual is that the concept of culture itself can be of great strategic value in this struggle if it is used with dispassionate objectivity. To the extent that the acculturating person can identify regularities of value and belief associated with groups in his milieu, he can also anticipate conflicts on the basis of group memberships, greatly reduce the perceived inconsistency in his environment by recognizing that others' discrete values and beliefs conform to cultural patterns, and articulate his own value choices in terms that are familiar and acceptable to the other participants in his milieu.

Because of the key importance of objective ethnological

knowledge, I am skeptical about the value of ethnic studies courses, designed for minority group students, that mix ethnology with heavy doses of ideology. The gains in self-respect that such courses offer might be more than offset in the long run by losses of useful knowledge. The decline of attention to accurate detail that ideology inevitably introduces into the study of behavior helps to perpetuate or even increase the sense of discontinuity and conflict experienced by the acculturating student. It tends to deflect the inquisitive attitude that is associated with a healthy personality in American culture.

We now come to the third source of personal stress, cultural alienation, or loss of the sense of personal continuity in time as a result of the breaking up of cultural patterns. Ordinary human self-consciousness is rooted in the abstract perception of time (Hallowell, 1949, p. 7; Cassirer, 1944, pp. 41-55). Without the ordering of experience into a sequential flow extending both backward and forward in time, the idea of self cannot be apprehended. Ecstatic experiences in the realms of religion, sexuality, and art are characterized by the dissolution of the time-bound self, but except in rare individuals such experiences are as brief and infrequent as they are intense. Acculturation can increase the difficulty of maintaining the sense that the self is all right because it can decrease the everyday continuity of thought and behavior. The resulting stress is usually felt as a vague malaise, communicable in some form of the question "Who am I?" The feeling sometimes builds to a crisis, followed by at least a temporary resolution. Such crisis and resolution can lead to a durable enhancement of the sense of self—a beneficial by-product of acculturative stress.

Cultural alienation, associated as it is with a weakened self-image, is difficult to distinguish from other sources of stress which come both from cultural change and from noncultural events. Almost any psychological stress can have the effect of weakening self-image, but for the Japanese Americans discrimination and stereotyping are particularly important. If the type of intercultural conflict I mentioned earlier, in which the acculturating individual is defined by others as merely a representative of his culture, is not recognized as such and resolved either by breaking up the interaction or by reaching an agreement, the Japanese American begins to doubt his own claims of autonomy. He begins to feel, vaguely, that his sense of himself might have been wrong. Many such encounters can lead to permanent doubt about the validity of *any* self-perception. This situation is strikingly similar to what Laing describes as the typical experience of the defined patient in a schizophrenic family (Laing, 1967; Laing and Esterson, 1964). According to Laing, the repeated failure of the patient to convince others of his individuality eventually leads to his own serious doubt that he exists at all. In Japanese Americans the combination of a culturally discontinuous environment and the denial of individuality through cultural and racial stereotypes often produces severe cultural alienation.

The stress of cultural alienation can be illustrated by examining two common strategies for dealing with it: the *guarded self* and the *reborn self*. Among nisei, a vicious circle of emotional repression is caused by a cultural emphasis on stoicism and the threat of cultural alienation. Several observers of the Japanese American personality, including Japanese Americans themselves, note that members of this group tend to feel that they are constantly under close scrutiny by others (see Caudill and DeVos, 1956; Lyman, 1973; Sone, 1953) and that they must constantly guard against the outward expression of taboo feelings or signs of weakness or inadequacy. This guardedness is partly a cultural effect of a child-rearing system that makes liberal use of shaming, that is, correcting the child's behavior with the caution "Others will laugh at you." Because of this culturally conditioned fear of embarrassment over inappropriate feelings, social relations between nisei are usually guarded and formal. The reliance on formality instead of open expression of feelings prevents the nisei from learning how to talk or think easily and clearly about their feelings. Those who lack these skills are easily confused when their assumptions about themselves are challenged. Often they do not know what their assumptions are and cannot defend them, even to themselves. The nisei are therefore encouraged by alienating situations to rely even more heavily on their already well-developed habits of stoicism and formality. They avoid situations in which their assumptions about themselves are challenged, and they rely often on cliches when they are required to talk about themselves. This habit of avoiding introspection and self-revelation is what I call the guarded self.

The skill of many nisei at guarding against introspection can be seen strikingly in their responses to projective tests. The responses are either conventional and stereotyped, lacking strong emotion or idiosyncratic detail, or they show surprisingly poor organization and form and are accompanied by unexpected expressions of confusion and anxiety on the respondent's part. When I first saw anxious responses to the Thematic Apperception Test from nisei who were outwardly calm, efficient, and intelligent, I thought the responses indicated carefully concealed but serious inner turmoil. I now think they indicate partly a simple lack of familiarity with the arts of self-reflection and self-revelation.

The conclusion that reserve is partly a response to acculturative stress is borne out by a comparison of nisei TAT responses with responses to similar cards collected in Japan from similar age groups (Kiefer, 1968). The Japanese stories show much less anxiety and perceptual blocking and are more emotionally colorful than average nisei stories. Since, presumably, shaming was experienced extensively by both groups as children, it alone could not account for the difference. Still another source of support for the connection between reserve and acculturation comes from observing Japanese Americans and Japanese citizens in the streets and shops of Japan Town. The two groups are generally distinguishable to the experienced eye by their facial expression and demeanor (as San Francisco nisei can confirm). The most important distinguishing characteristic seems to be the relative aloofness, or "cool," of the Japanese Americans.

If the guarded self is a common nisei strategy in dealing with cultural alienation, the reborn self can be loosely associated with the issei and the sansei. This is a method of coping with cultural alienation by developing, usually after adolescence, a conscious philosophy that explains one's relationship to his environment. I describe the social dynamics of the sansei version of the reborn self in Chapter Four. My knowledge of the issei version is based only on what they told me about their youth, but I think the dynamics were similar, with religion taking the part of ethnicity and with a corresponding emphasis on conformity to God's will instead of free will. In both cases, the reborn self is an increased sense of personal continuity and wholeness that accompanies a shift away from the social toward the personal. It is an increase in the sense of self-mastery, and thereby social mastery, accompanying the perception that "other people do not decide who I am." This perception involves a conscious rejection of other people or groups as sources of identity information or of self-definition in favor of the self (in the case of the sansei) or a deity (in the case of the issei). For the sansei it often but not always involves the rejection of one culture or another.

This strategy is difficult for individuals. Few people can sustain it long without the help of others; the lack of social prestige and power that contributes to the problem of alienation in the first place usually interferes with the person's ability to recruit support independently for his new identity. Nowadays one sometimes sees bicultural individuals struggling heroically to proclaim a new identity on their own in the face of what they perceive as coldness or hostility on the part of their ethnic brethren. (The ethnic media are one source of such personal statements in the form of letters from readers. Since I feel I cannot reproduce any of these statements here because of their personal nature, I refer the reader to the *Hokubei Mainichi* of January 23, 1969, and July 7, 1969, for examples.) In the issei's youth, a personal crisis probably led directly to a search for a group solution, as in joining a church. However it was manifested, the importance of the peer group in identity conversion can hardly be overemphasized.

I have covered the most common and troublesome kinds of stress that affect my respondents as a result of their bicultural background, as a guide in determining what kinds of stress a given person is experiencing at a given time and whether anything can be done to alleviate them. Having said that acculturative stress is a product of interaction between person and environment, I now summarize the contributions of each element to the equation.

Degree and kind of acculturative stress depend upon the number, cultural heterogeneity, instability, and internal inconsistency of the important social contexts in a person's life. Stress potential cannot be assessed by looking at any one—or even at any two or three—of these variables. Consider, for example, two hypothetical Japanese American children whose most important contexts are family and school. The family of one has a strong, consistent set of cultural values, but the child has had to move repeatedly between schools whose ethnic composition varies widely. The parents of the other child are confused about their own cultural identities, and they give the child inconsistent messages about values; but the child has spent several years in a school with a culturally homogeneous group of Caucasian teachers and classmates. The kinds of acculturative stress experienced by the two children are markedly different and call for different coping strategies. No simple formula can reveal the cause of either child's anxieties or produce a resolution. The first child may develop an "outsider" identity in relation to non-Japanese society and base his self-respect on his personal and cultural uniqueness. The second child may learn how to get along well in Caucasian society by minimizing the unique features of his parental culture.

A normal person in any social environment brings to it a huge range of skills and strategies for coping with stress. In general, however, the stress potential of the environment is modulated by the person's ability to recognize, simplify, select, and weigh input in order to minimize disorder. We have already seen examples of these abilities at work in the way Japanese Americans interpret history and avoid discordant relationships. With greater or less success one constantly evaluates one's acquaintances' beliefs, seeks knowledge and skills that give one social advantage in view of those beliefs, classifies one's personal associations according to type and degree of importance, schedules one's time so that important relations are strengthened at the expense of unimportant ones, and so on. I see no reason to sup-

pose that the bicultural person has a different kind of self-inte-
grating repertoire than does the monocultural person. However,
other things being equal, I think either the stress level or the
integrational skill (or both) of the bicultural individual is higher.

Acculturative Styles

I am now ready to breathe life into this discussion of individual reactions to acculturative stress by showing some typical ways people bring order to their bicultural lives. There are a
great many other styles that I do not describe here, but these
examples illustrate in action principles of acculturative stress,
such as cultural confusion and conflict, and principles of stress
reduction, such as the use of religion and philosophy as cultural
bridges. One of the paradoxes of social science is that the transformation of human passions into intellectual ciphers, like
"styles," both belittles and dignifies the human subject. Collecting and arranging like sea shells the convictions, fears, and surprising ingenuities that make up a group of lives seem to deny
their importance in the cosmic scheme of things, and, for that
very reason, the analysis of behavior refreshes our awe at the
courage of men and women who feel things strongly and act
purposefully and it deepens our compassion for those who do
not. So, while I take pause at the implied insult when I describe
the religious fervor of an aging issei as a "style," I am also encouraged by the awareness that his life itself is an eloquent challenge to that insult.

A True Christian. Religion does different things for different people, and neither the cultural background nor the age
of the issei exempts them from this rule. In this study I found
wide ranges in both the kind and degree of religious involvement—a finding consistent with studies of other elderly populations (for example, Moberg, 1965). As I showed in Chapter
One, the churches are important focuses of social activity for
most issei, whether or not the issei profess strong beliefs. Christian missions at one time also provided the issei with a few basic
survival skills and the rudiments of a Western system of values.
In addition to the literary example of Daisuke Kitagawa (Chap-

ter Two), two of my cases show a clear-cut discovery of the culturally integrating force of religious belief and practice. The two cases are quite different in a number of details. I discuss here the case of Reverend Oda as an example of an issei who fashioned of his Christianity a supracultural set of standards against which to evaluate himself and others, thereby bridging to some extent the cultural gap between races and between generations. (The other case is that of Mrs. Morita, discussed in Chapter One, who changed her church membership in order to be closer to her grandchildren.)

Reverend Oda is eighty-eight. He was born the second son of a merchant in a small Japanese city and emigrated to America in search of work in 1902, after eight years of formal schooling. Without skills, he joined a group of casual laborers and drifted from job to job for five years. His life changed when he joined a Chinese Christian mission in central California in 1907 and began to study English and religion simultaneously. I have reported in part (Chapter One) the story of his calling to the ministry. Soon after his ordainment as a Methodist minister, he went back to Japan, found a wife, and then returned to the Bay Area to preach. He and his robust seventy-three-year-old wife now have seven children, all college graduates, and nineteen grandchildren. Although retired for ten years, he keeps active in his church, he travels, and he is highly respected in the local Japanese American community. He is intensely proud of his life, past and present, and doesn't mind saying so. He claims his English is terrible and prefers to converse in Japanese.

Whether Reverend Oda's pervasive and cheerful devotion to the Christian faith would have developed under other circumstances I cannot say; nor do I know much of the history of inner struggle that brought him to his present style of life. Retracing the course of our talks, though, I find the following ideas about religion and culture to be well developed.

Christianity intensifies the sense of unity between people of like minds. It provides a broad, melodious stream to catch the many piping rivulets of individual emotion:

Interviewer: *There are Buddhists and Christians among my Japanese friends, and I don't clearly understand the differ-*

*ence in their way of thinking. Of course there are differences in
the Bible and the Sutras, but how do their hearts differ?*

Rev. O: *Well, one difference is that in Christianity we
have hymns. I think that's an especially good thing about Christianity. When people sing hymns, they feel close together, and
they feel very happy.*

Christianity is tolerant of all races and cultures. Reverend
Oda proudly mentions that his church recently elected a
Chinese American to a high office and also refers with apparent
satisfaction to the fact that his church is racially integrated. He
does not mention the fact that the Caucasian members of his
church and most issei attend separate services because of the
language problem. He emphasizes that Christian missionaries
not only helped the Japanese in America, "whether they were
believers or not," but also did a lot of good in their foreign missions in Japan.

Although there are differences between religions and cultures, human life is everywhere basically the same. Christianity
makes cultural difference unimportant: "If we talk about human society, the strong win and the weak lose. In the world of
nature, things are like that, eh?" Reverend Oda says in response
to one TAT card. To another, he says, "Human life—it is a sad
thing, but if one believes in the resurrection, it is good, it is
lucky to be a Christian."

Christianity unites people of different generations, even
though there are great cultural differences between them. "The
nisei are still okay. They pay attention to what the issei have to
say. They do this even where there is a difference in the way of
thinking between the issei and the nisei. But when you get to
the sansei, since they were raised by the nisei, they are very
close to being American, and they have gone a long way from
the Japanese ways." Later, when I ask him whether he had any
particular problems with his family, he says his family is unusually close and explains this by referring to their shared religious faith: "The community where Mary's family lives—Living-
ston—is a Christian community. The children all go to Sunday
school there. Grace's husband's family were all strong Buddhists, but now that the parents have died, Grace's family all go

to a Christian church." Reverend Oda's TAT stories are particularly revealing. In response to the two cards that show an old man, he tells of the elder giving spiritual advice while the children listen attentively. "Yes," says his wife, "just like you."

As I take my last leave from Reverend Oda, he shows me two passages from the Bible that he says interest him very much (Matthew, 16:24 and Galatians, 2:12-21). Both deal with death and eternal life, but one also deals with the conflict of two faiths and its resolution. Together, the two passages can be taken to mean that faith in Christ is more important than the answers to the questions I have been asking about family, community, and culture. Reverend Oda is gently educating me.

An Issei in Cultural Conflict. Although Mrs. Tani is a member of the same church as Reverend Oda, she has not adjusted nearly as well to a bicultural world. She was born into a wealthy family in a small Japanese town, the last of seven children. She describes her father as a stern, pragmatic autocrat who had no use for religion. At twenty, she married a first cousin and came to America, where she and her husband ran a chain of grocery stores. Her husband, who "liked sake," died in 1959 of cancer. Mrs. Tani lives alone now, by preference, although she has three children living close by and another in New York. She has seven grandchildren, two of whom she helped to raise in New York for eight years (until 1969) after their mother died.

Mrs. Tani appears physically hearty, but she is clearly an anxious person. She looks after herself and her apartment, lends a hand at her nearby children's homes when needed, and takes an active part in the affairs of her church. Every Friday morning, she babysits the small children of a recent Japanese immigrant who is studying English. In spite of all these activities, she says, "I have the feeling that a life that is too comfortable might not be good for me. Too easy. I have to do more things. Living here alone, I think it's wasteful." She worries that she might become incapacitated and have to give up her activities. She is afraid her children are too Americanized and would not have much sympathy if this happened. She left her son's home, after living there a short while, because she felt a "strain."

Mrs. Tani's major worry, however, is her grandchildren. She takes an active part in their upbringing, advising them and even making arrangements for their education. She perceives the sansei as culturally remote from their grandparents but is unable to accept this comfortably. Her point of view vacillates, showing the lack of a solution: "The issei can't touch [influence?] the grandchildren very much. Orders—they don't just speak. Giving orders or always being critical and advising is something I don't like, and I try not to do that." And: "In Japan, they did all they could for the children. Set up things for the children. That was good, but you can't do that now. Times have changed. Kids have their own ideas now. And that's good, too. The issei's bad points—some people worry about these relations too much. I think it would be good if they could be a little more openhearted."

When people with unresolved conflict in their lives are given a chance to talk at length about themselves, they often use the opportunity to criticize their own actions, as Mrs. Tani does. She chastises people who are too involved in their children's and grandchildren's lives, although she is more involved than any other issei I saw. Although frenetically active, she talks wistfully about the relief she felt when her last child was married and she could relax. From a cultural standpoint her most interesting ambivalence, however, is between fatalistic resignation and active resistance. She frequently invokes the Japanese values of patience and gratitude:

Interviewer: *What do you think is the best way for a person to get along in life?*

Mrs. T: *People should look into themselves and get rid of selfish feelings.*

Interviewer *[after having discussed dissatisfactions in Mrs. Tani's life]: Which of these changes do you think you can make?*

Mrs. T: *Rather than speak of changes I can make, I think, at times when things happen to you, to do what is correct. To live a correct life. That is my desire. It is not that I want to make changes. I want to live a correct existence.*

At the same time, she suffers suppressed anger and frustration about the neglect of the elderly by the young, about having to work so hard in her later years, and about the deprivation she suffered when young. The story of intergenerational conflict and felt deprivation is told eloquently in her response to a TAT card that depicts a man working on a farm, a young woman carrying books, and an older woman leaning against a tree—a very unusual response for an issei: "The girl's coming from or going to school. The mother looks like she's mad at the daughter. The daughter is going somewhere, face [looks] like there is a disagreement with the mother. It's hard work out there. Maybe the mother wants the daughter to help, but she's not. And she wants to do what she herself wants to do. This daughter is working alone and studying. The mother saying, 'Do what you like. It's good if you don't come back' [laughs]."

While some issei seem to have found real strength in the Japanese values of which Mrs. Tani talks and to have resolved feelings of deprivation and loss through them, these values apparently have not worked so well in Mrs. Tani's case. She speaks English well enough to have assumed considerable responsibility in the English-speaking world—first in her husband's business, then as foster mother to her two grandchildren, and now as a church member and advisor to her grandchildren. The variety and importance of her various roles, reinforced by a naturally active personality, carry a high price in acculturational stress, mainly conflict and alienation. (Another source of stress for Mrs. Tani arises when her grandchildren use their English speaking grandmother as a wedge between themselves and their own parents—a strategy closed to most sansei because of the language barrier.)

A Pragmatist. Regardless of their ability to minimize cultural complexity, most issei end up having to take a back seat to the younger generations simply because they lack the American skills necessary to manage a large family. This subordination is a source of some dissatisfaction to the issei—especially the men—who crave at least the outward forms of respect and authority in their old age. Ironically, the issei men who tried hardest to preserve their authority in this country by holding fast to traditional ideals and institutions are now likely to find themselves the most ignored.

Mr. Sano, age eighty-nine, is the one issei man I talked to who is the titular head of a three-generation household. He wields a fair amount of authority in that post and has a reputation as an effective leader in the community. In many ways he is the happiest and healthiest man I interviewed. To what extent he has deliberately arranged the circumstances that give him such authority at such a remarkable age, I do not know. However, he could not have done it unless he had decided early in his life that he would master the language, laws, and customs of his adopted homeland. Mr. Sano came to the Bay Area in 1902 and began to study English at once. As a schoolboy who did housework part time in order to put himself through school, Mr. Sano slept in the basement of a Caucasian home and earned $1.25 a week, plus board. After two years, he joined the staff of a Japanese American newspaper and continued to work on his English as a translator. He held that job for ten years, meanwhile helping to found the Japanese Association and a Japanese Christian church in the Bay Area. He became an insurance salesman in 1914.

Perhaps the best word for Mr. Sano's life is *eventful.* He remembers vividly the 1906 earthquake, when the Japanese newspaper moved into his rented room along with the Japanese Association of Oakland. In 1919-1920, when many died from the great flu epidemic, he nursed the victims in a temporary dispensary set up in his church. In 1929 he lost a large sum in the stock market crash, and in 1932 his wife of twenty-seven years died. They had had no children. He lost his insurance job during the relocation in 1942 and had to take up domestic work after the war at the age of sixty-five. He remarried the same year— this time to a widow with three sons who had been born in the United States but raised in Japan. He negotiated a difficult legal maneuver to restore the American citizenship of the eldest son, who had been drafted into the Japanese army during the war.

As he narrates this story in fluent English, Mr. Sano shows no sign of bitterness or sorrow. He sprinkles the story liberally with funny ancedotes in which he himself usually plays the trickster. My notes refer to his frequent laughter: "It is impossible to describe this laugh. It is a spontaneous, zestful, good-humored laugh, without sarcasm. It is unpredictable and it is infectious." A pragmatist, Mr. Sano seems to view life as a challenge that calls for cleverness. He mastered his own willful, pugnacious nature through Christianity, just as he mastered his old age by marrying a widow with sons. "I have never been a father," he laughs, "and now I have seven grandchildren." In the same way he has met the challenge of cultural complexity by regarding ideas and ideals as secondary to the challenge of living. There is no sense worrying about what you can't understand or control. "We don't know anything about the younger children," he says. "They say old people talk too much, so that's why they don't tell us anything. [Laughs.] Of course, we don't understand what they say very much anyway!" And: "We don't know what [the grandchildren] do because we can't go around and follow them, so [laughs]. We have just two trucks and one car and we need them for [the eldest son's gardening business]." On the subject of how to have a happy life, he says in part: "Don't complain about daily life. Do not make trouble for your neighbors and society. We can't agree with everything. Nobody can agree with everything, but others have a right to their own ways. Nobody can disturb my faith and my health."

Two Different Nisei Women. Mrs. Ohara (age fifty-five) and Mrs. Kindaichi (age forty-six) have quite a lot in common although they have never met. Both are married, with children in their late teens and early twenties. The women live settled, middle-class lives in the Bay Area. Both are high school graduates. Both met their husbands and married in relocation camps. Both are energetic, animated women, and they create similar first impressions on the interviewer. Their husbands' occupations, however, indicate some class distinction between the two. Mrs. Ohara's husband is a contract gardener, of middle income. Mrs. Kindaichi's husband is a dentist, of upper middle income.

Against this backdrop of similarity, the difference in the two women's acculturative styles is quite visible. Mrs. Ohara was raised by strict, traditional issei parents in the heart of a Japanese ghetto. She spoke almost no English until she went to school, and her school was predominantly Japanese. Mrs. Kinda-ichi grew up in a Caucasian neighborhood. There were few Orientals in her schools, and most of her friends were white. Her highly acculturated and progressive issei parents spoke English at home, and she learned her limited Japanese only after she got married and had to communicate with in-laws.

Before discussing the two women's different styles of acculturation, I must mention some developmental problems faced by almost any women their age, a subject I explore further in Chapter Eight. Our two subjects are in the process of becoming mothers of adults. This process is quite a change from being mothers of children. For the typical nisei woman the change produces a good deal of stress centering on two questions: How to give up responsibilities that have been the mainspring of one's self-perception for twenty-odd years? And where to look for new outlets for energy and new sources of identity? Arguments with children are likely to reach a peak. Forgotten dreams of self-fulfillment are likely to resurface. These problems are interwoven with those that stem strictly from cultural complexity, and neither source of stress can be understood without some knowledge of the other.

Looking at the number and variety of contexts in which these two women function reveals a major difference between them. Mrs. Kindaichi is obviously very much involved with her immediate family on a day-to-day basis, and she also has many commitments to groups outside her home, such as neighborhood, church, and school.

Interviewer: *Do you ever feel you're involved with too many things?*

Mrs. K: *Yes.*

I: *What sort of things?*

Mrs. K: *Well, between church and school, sometimes I feel I've taken on too many things. It gets hard to say no. There are so many things I want to be—so many things to get involved with. And I like to. So I find myself saying yes to a lot of things, and then it's difficult to do it all. Or to do any of it really well. In fact, my daughter says she feels I forget a lot of*

*things she tells me because I'm involved with too many things.
And I'm always having to switch gears—'Wait a minute, what are
you talking about now?' Click, click, click.*

Mrs. Ohara is also deeply involved with her family, but unlike
Mrs. Kindaichi, her social relations outside her home are confined almost entirely to her part-time job in a library.

Interviewer: *Do you sometimes feel left out of things?*
Mrs. O: *No, I don't think so. Because when I had Karen I
couldn't go anywhere. I did feel left out then. My mother told
me, "Endure it. [Mrs. Ohara says it in Japanese.] When you get
old, it will be rewarding. So take care of the children." I think it
has paid off.*

Later in the interview she is asked whether she feels too involved, and she answers, "No, not now."
     The answers to these questions begin to show us a differ-
ent sense of social relatedness and continuity of self (see earlier
discussion) in the two women. Mrs. Ohara's answer to the question about feeling left out indicates that she perceives herself
embedded in a stream of time that began many years ago and
extends far into the future. Her present and future happiness
result from her behavior some twenty years ago. This perception is different from Mrs. Kindaichi's answer to the same question: "Well, mostly when the young kids are doing something. I
like joining in, but—you know—I know I can't or I shouldn't.
Sometimes I start to, but I get a terrible look [from the kids].
That's about the only time. I'm starting to feel the age gap
much more now." Mrs. Kindaichi feels herself at the mercy of
changes over which she has no control. She sees the future
fraught with uncertainty.
     To the question, "What is the best age to be?" Mrs. Kin-
daichi answers: "I'm really looking forward to the next ten
years. My youngest child is seventeen and will be in college next
year. [My husband and I] will have more time. I'm really looking forward to that."
     To the same question Mrs. Ohara answers: "Hmm. Gosh!

[Laughs. Pauses.] What age? I don't know. [Pause.] The best age is when you don't have any worries. Gee." [She turns to her husband to ask his opinion.]

Asked to describe her character when she was young, Mrs. Kindaichi shows that she sees herself as constantly changing: "Oh, I was a tomboy. A real tomboy. Not a very good student. Wasn't at all ambitious. I guess I'm a lot more tolerant now. I think that comes with age. And I think most of these things come with age. I used to be very shy. I don't know if it was the Japanese upbringing or just a terrible inferiority complex I had there. Have. Had. Still have. I'm trying to get over it. Never saying anything. Well, lately, the last ten years or so, I have this good Caucasian friend who really gave me a kick once and got me going." Mrs. Ohara's answer shows her sense of personal continuity: "I think I'm the same. I don't think I've changed. I used to love people, say 'Hi' to everyone, and I still do."

Related to their different senses of time are differences in the ways the two women relate to their issei relatives. Mrs. Ohara's mother lives in her home and is a focus of much of her attention, showing the continuity between generations. Mrs. Kindaichi's parents live in the East, and she rarely sees them. Her mother-in-law lives nearby but becomes a focus of concern only when she needs Mrs. Kindaichi's help. Mrs. Ohara sees a person's ability to relate to others as the foundation of a tolerable old age, as the following excerpt shows:

Interviewer: *Pretend you are sixty or seventy years old. How would you like to be?*

Mrs. Ohara: *Sixty or seventy? Oh, cheerful, cheerful and healthy. The main thing is to get along with other people.*

Mrs. Kindaichi wants to be self-sufficient. In answer to the same question she says: "I'd like to be as active as I am right now. Able. Phew! It's not that long."

Value conflicts between parents and children are frequent in families in which the children are reaching the age of independence. The contrast in the way the two women handle these conflicts is striking, and it points to fundamental differences in self-perception. Mrs. Kindaichi is openly critical of her children, both to the interviewer and to the children themselves. Asked to describe a typical family disagreement, she says: "We yell a lot. [Laughs.] Long into the night. We were just talking about that. It only involves two or three people, and the others make a critique afterwards. You try to make them admit they're wrong after a while, instead of trying to explain your position. It may take a long time, but you usually work it out. If one person withdraws or something, another will talk to them." What happens in Mrs. Ohara's family when there is a disagreement? In her words: "We just let it ride. Then somehow it seems to smooth out. It is always—[laughs]—I think that's how it goes. No use antagonizing." Mrs. Ohara's daughter, Karen (age twenty-two), confirms her mother's statement: "When I'm in a bad mood I'm rude to [my mother]. I take advantage of her. Not like other people. When I get in a bad mood, I try to be rude. Like, last time I was in a bad mood, I got to her by saying things about my brother. How she should encourage him to move out. She listened and then changed the subject. It got to her. She doesn't know how to show her reactions sometimes. She'll give out a nervous laugh. Doesn't know what to do, so she goes on to the next subject." Americans are inclined to think of such suppression of feelings as that of Mrs. Ohara as no strategy at all for coping with conflict, but the apparent guilt in Karen's remarks about needling her mother supports my use of the term *strategy* in referring to such suppression and shows that the strategy works.

The two women have different strategies for handling interpersonal conflict and, along with these, corresponding strategies for handling inner turmoil. Mrs. Kindaichi is on friendly terms with her own aggressive feelings; Mrs. Ohara is not. To the question, "What do you do when you get tense or irritable?" Mrs. Kindaichi answers: "Yell a lot. [Laughs.] I hate to admit it, but I guess that's what I do." Mrs. Ohara says: "I, uh, knit or sew, listen to the radio. [Laughs.]"

The overall pattern of Mrs. Kindaichi's self-perception, then, is one of autonomy, lack of connectedness with others, and self-acceptance. Mrs. Ohara, in contrast, sees her life as a continuous gift from others, which she continuously struggles to repay. It is not surprising that Mrs. Kindaichi's TAT responses often picture people as isolated and at cross-purposes, while Mrs. Ohara's stories are full of nurturing relationships. A final example of these different themes is the two women's descriptions of the turning points in their lives. Mrs. Kindaichi says: "The war first. Pearl Harbor. I certainly found out who my friends were. Then camp. Then getting married. Gosh, that was in a period of two years. Then moving to this house. When the last kid was in school all day. What a free feeling that was! Of course, I filled that up quickly. I guess those are the major ones. Different phases of my life." Mrs. Ohara says: "Oh, I think when I had Karen, and when she'd cry I didn't know what to do. What all mothers go through. What my mother did for me. I realized how much my mother meant to me. Mother's love. I don't know how to put it. That's when I grew up. [Laughs.] Took things for granted [before then]."

A Young Machiavelli. Gallows humor is entertaining when there are no real gallows around, which is one reason why people who are clever, young, and well endowed with life's comforts are often tempted to cynicism. Part of the reason for Jack Morita's acculturative style is that others are charmed by it. Jack, now twenty-two, is the oldest child and only son of a nisei chemist and his issei wife. The family has lived in the heart of Japan Town since Jack's father returned from Japan in 1946 with the girl he had met and married in Tokyo during his tour as an Army interpreter. The family lives in modest middle-class style. Jack's grandmother has a flat nearby where she visits with her family and issei friends on her days off. Usually she lives with a Caucasian family for whom she has kept house for forty years.

Jack seems unusually responsible for his years. A graduate of a local business college, he is already working carefully on ambitious long-range financial plans. He has begun to develop his reputation in local society as well, and he contributes generously to civic organizations. He reads the financial newspapers religiously and knows the latest status symbols and who possesses them. All this he does in a consciously self-serving way, or so he says. "I'm sort of different than most kids of my generation. I'm a dirty old capitalist, that's why. You need money to do what you want to do. Get a B.A. in social welfare and you'll starve the rest of your life." So he sees himself as an oddball and a loner where his peers are concerned, not only because of his ambitions, but because of his culture. "I'm in a different position than most sansei. My father is nisei and my mother is Japanese. [Japanese holidays] are celebrated here. Japanese is spoken here, and there are more Japanese things in the house."

In his perceptions of relationships outside the family in general, Jack portays himself as a critical observer, a nonparticipant—one who understands but does not seek to be understood. He studies people and situations, to see where a profit can be turned.

Interviewer: *Ever argue with your parents about sex?*

Jack: *No. What's there to argue about? You don't talk about it with them. They won't know what you're talking about. That question doesn't pertain to me anyway, because my social life is nil. I have better things to do with my time. You talk about the stock market, girls don't know what you're talking about.*

He describes a typical nisei: "Oh, he still sort of has a part of that concept, 'You have to do best.' That nonsense. A lot of the issei's views rubbed off onto the nisei." And a typical sansei: "He's mixed up. I'm not mixed up, but most of my friends don't know what they want to do."

At the moment, Jack looks at his own family as a setting where he can turn a profit. He is on good terms with his parents because it is foolish to antagonize one's benefactors. "It's a working relationship," he says. "There are no major problems. Everyone knows his place and what he's supposed to do. When anything comes up, big discussions are mutual. For the kids, it becomes a selling technique. If we push, they'll go our way." This manipulative attitude is an outstanding feature of Jack's whole TAT profile, indicating that at the moment his character is deeply and broadly imbued with manipulativeness. His response to the card depicting the farm scene will do for an illustration: "Why can't they get any pictures relevant to the times? We have a family here who runs a farm in the Midwest. It's a poor family, because they have no car. It's a dead picture. This young, vivacious, good-looking girl is in her prime. She's thinking how to get into the big city, find a rich old guy. It turns out she goes back to the farm, but she's dreaming how to get out. What if she gets in *Playboy* foldouts, or something?"

There are obvious advantages to such a cynical attitude for a bicultural person, besides the benefits he might reap from its entertainment value. Cynicism probably makes it easier for him to protect his sense of identity and integrity against too much ambiguity. Financial gain represents a kind of acultural value, a transcendant goal like Reverend Oda's faith, that enables him to rise above cultural conflict. However, the question of why Jack Morita has chosen a Machiavellian manipulativeness instead of some other strategy is a difficult one. His situation suggests some possible answers.

First, one of the main cultural conflicts in his life centers on economic success itself. Many sansei reject what they perceive to be the venal attention to such values on the part of American culture in general and the nisei in particular. Still, as the only son and oldest child in his family, Jack carries a heavy responsibility for keeping his family's name and fortune in good order. He has an uncle living in Hawaii who is a physician and apparently financially successful. One gets the impression from Jack's grandmother that this uncle is her favorite. Jack's parents, more traditional than the average for their generation, probably place more stress than their contemporaries do on both economic success and family honor. In short, Jack is caught between peers who outwardly reject economic self-interest as a major value, at least until they are old enough to have economic responsibilities, and parents and grandparents who expect him to apply himself vigorously in this very area. Second, Jack is clearly more conversant with many economically important aspects of American culture than his parents are. He advises them on such things as stocks and status symbols. He has been thrust precociously into the role of a cultural broker between his family and the economic world, and he has discovered that he can use this role to his own advantage. One is tempted to say that he has developed a taste for the role of the cynical insider because through it he exercises some control over his parents.

These observations in themselves might explain much of Jack's behavior; however, looking at his father's behavior, we find another explanation—this one peripheral to Jack's cultural situation. Although Jack's father shows none of his son's outward cynicism, his TAT shows a marked tendency to view human relationships as manipulative, suggesting that he unconsciously behaves as though people are always on the make. As to why this tendency developed in the father, I can only speculate on the basis of his life history. Jack's father was raised mainly by his paternal grandmother (some issei brought their parents with them to America), since both his parents worked full time as domestic servants when he was small. Moreover, the parents appear to have used a large fraction of the income they gained at such sacrifice to send their eldest son, Jack's uncle, to medical school, leaving Jack's father to shift for himself. This neglect might easily have undermined Jack's father's trust in others. At the same time it created a situation in which he could manipulate the relationship between the five persons involved—his grandmother, his mother and father, his older brother, and himself—using the guilt these five must have felt about the fact that they had neglected him.

Cynicism is thus one response to cultural conflict that is attractive to the young. If a person is consistently rewarded for behaving in a cynical or manipulative way, this behavior might become a dominant adaptive strategy for him for a time—at least until others stop chuckling.

An Inward Pilgrim. Mr. Chikai, mentioned in Chapters One and Two, is thirty-two. His whole life, as he now presents it, can be viewed as a private search for internal harmony and order. He has parried all attempts of others (including me) to define him, eschewing family, religion, community, ethnic group, and career alike in favor of a fully developed individuality. Having left, at nineteen, the town in Hawaii where he grew up, Chikai has had too many addresses to bother listing them all, but he mentions

New York, Chicago, and Arizona, as well as many places in San Francisco. As his occupation he lists "research botanist," and adds, "I've been a factory worker, newspaper boy, musician, carpenter, sales clerk, media specialist, dishwasher, photographer, and gardener, among other things." His apartment is full of paintings and posters he has done. He rarely sees any of his relatives, although he likes most of them well enough. He has never been married, although he has loved and lived with a number of women of various ethnic backgrounds. He has attended five different universities for periods of between one and six years but fails to mention whether he has a degree from any of them. He has thoughtful opinions on almost every subject we discussed and original ideas about many, making it impossible to identify him with any political or philosophical doctrine. He is intellectually interested in Asian American studies programs and in ethnic community self-help organizations. Occasionally he lends a hand with them, but he is not a leader or a hard-core activist.

One gets the curious impression that Mr. Chikai is a man of high principles, but it is hard to put those principles into words. He is obviously devoted to aesthetic values. He does not criticize people much, nor does he idealize them. He values spontaneity and honesty, as the following excerpt indicates:

> Interviewer: *What do you do when you get mad?*
> Mr. Chikai: *Well, I try to work it out.*
> I: *Do you ever yell?*
> C: *Yeah. Sure. That's therapeutic and immediate. It's up front.*
> I: *Do you yell at most people?*
> C: *Generally.*
> I: *Anyone you wouldn't yell at?*
> C: *No . . . I would generally yell at whom I feel warrants it at that particular time. But I couldn't say beforehand that I would do it or I wouldn't.*

He clearly mistrusts prefabricated ideals and solutions to life's problems. He feels that self-confidence and inner strength are the greatest virtues a person can have, but he has no communicable sense of how to get them, although he feels he has them himself. "I don't know if parents can teach [their children] anything," he says. "I think it's generally the other way around, or should be. Parents should be there when the kids need them. That's all parents can do, really." Any experience is educational, he says, if you have the right attitude. A person and his life are always changing, and it doesn't help to have formulas:

> Interviewer: *Do you have time for everything you want to do these days?*
> Mr. Chikai: *Well, you know, I don't worry about things like that. You just do what you want to do. You know, you can't learn everything there is to learn in this world. You make some concerted effort in that direction, you try to be aware of everything, but you can't. It's physically impossible. Why worry about it? Why make a problem out of something that isn't a problem? When a problem comes up, you deal with it.*

By persistently questioning the definitions and values of others, and persistently monitoring his own sense of solidity and worth, Mr. Chikai has worked out a life style that is unusually self-sufficient. The remarkably vivid, rich, and dreamlike quality of his TAT stories shows that he has easy access to levels of consciousness that are repressed in most people. Asked what the major turning points in his life have been, he says in part: "I think the most critical one in recent times—it really crystalized a lot for me —was a simultaneous thing of two events. I went away one summer and was a counselor at a summer camp. And the day that I got back from camp I came home to find out that the chick that I had been living with had split. It had been a nice, warm summer of working with all those young people and seeing some of my problems reflected in them. And then coming home to an empty house with only a pregnant cat who subsequently gave birth to eight kittens. And I think from there on things really crystalized themselves into some very definite patterns." This story suggests what is apparent from Mr. Chikai's life style: that he has discovered an inner strength that frees him from dependence on others.

Mr. Chikai sees the unfolding of his life as a drama in which he is partly actor and partly spectator. The process itself is supra-individual and supracultural.

Chapter VI

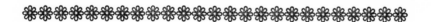

Culture and
Personal Development

Ethnology, the comparative study of small cultural groups, leads us on a search for the pervasive underlying patterns, themes, or unquestioned assumptions that lend regularity to human experience within whole societies and mark off boundaries between them. This search leads to the view I discussed in the last chapter, that rapid change and great variety of thought and action are exceptional and often unhealthy. Anthropologists have long looked at urbanization and industrialization as processes of pattern breakdown and conflict creation

163

and have written much about American culture from this point of view (for example, Hsu, 1961; Kluckhohn, 1949; Henry, 1963; Sapir, 1922; Spiro, 1951). According to this intellectual habit, the life cycle of the individual is a biological process that is (or ought to be) given social meaning by a unified set of cultural rules. Through cultural institutions and rites, the individual ought to be helped to anticipate each coming stage in his development and to prepare for it. An overarching mythology or world view ought to explain the changes that are necessary and suppress those that are not. Personal needs and social demands ought to be in harmony so that there is a close fit between culture and personality.

This useful way of looking at human behavior requires careful attention to the stages of life when biological changes are rapid and severe, the periods of maturation and senescence. Outside these periods, the individual personality is considered stable. Changes in basic style of thinking and feeling are expected to be only additions to and elaborations on earlier patterns, even where circumstances have altered outward behavior quite a lot. It is puzzling that we tend to think of enculturation, or the learning of one's native culture, as additive and acculturation as substitutive, even though the opposite view makes just as much sense.

Another way of understanding the conventional anthropological view of the life cycle is to keep in mind that the separation of biological and cultural development it assumes is purely intellectual, since the two processes are never separate in fact. In complex societies this distinction is obvious, since the unfolding of the genetic code in human maturation is inevitable, whereas progress along a culturally approved life course is not. We can predict with fair accuracy what an American child will look like when grown—especially if we have seen its parents—but we can say precious little about its adult behavior. The case is different among the Zuñi or the Tiwi. In such societies, much of adult behavior is prescribed early in life according to the position of the new member in a fairly stable social organization. It is possible to develop in the child, as soon as he is biologically ready to learn them, traits and skills that will serve him well when grown. From this example it is easy to assume that biology, custom, and personality move forward in lock step under normal circumstances.

Such terms as *basic personality structure* (Kardiner and others, 1945), *modal personality,* and *national character* have been used by anthropologists to describe broad patterns of psychological functioning that are laid down in early life and persist with only minor changes until extreme old age or death. Kluckhohn (1949, pp. 178-180) provides an excellent example of such a description. He divides the personality into core and peripheral areas, the core being the stable structures developing out of childhood experience, and the peripheral being the plastic realms of attitude and belief that are open to socialization influences throughout life. What sort of behavior, exactly, belongs to each sphere? Unfortunately, Kluckhohn is content to leave that question unanswered. Other illustrations of this habit of linking early socialization and adult personality in anthropology are the questionable ideas that life cycle ceremonies involving preadult participants mark transition to new statuses for the young but not for their elders, and that funerals are meant to restore social equilibrium rather than mark irreversible changes in the lives of the survivors. So pervasive is this emphasis on childhood socialization that Clark writes, "What we need in anthropology, and what I hope to see developing, is an ethnography of adult life" (1973, p. 86; see also Plath, 1973).

In this and following chapters, I take a small step along the path toward an ethnography of adult life. Specifically, I look at the whole life cycle as a series of challenges to the personality and assume that normal people can and often do make major changes in their habits of thinking, feeling, and behaving in response to such challenges.

From such a viewpoint, culture appears more complex and variable, but is no less useful as a concept. Within a single society, one expects to find variations in value and belief with age, or rather, with developmental position, corresponding to major changes in authority and responsibility during the life cycle. The individual's appreciation of his cultural world is profoundly colored by the lenses of age status through which he surveys all. The pioneering work of Caudill and Scarr on value orientations and age in Japan (1962) shows a useful application of this idea. Looking across societies comparatively, one sees that the nature and timing of age subcultures is part of the pattern that makes each whole culture unique. The events that mark the passing from one age status to another (such as marriage, coming of age, and so on) and the roles and attitudes appropriate to each status vary from culture to culture. These variations illuminate the economic, political, and spiritual patterns of cultures (Clark, 1967; Clark and Anderson, 1967, pp. 3-30).

The developmental approach raises new questions about the relationship between biology, culture, and personality. Each of these words is a taxonomic tool that must be suited to the work at hand. The usefulness of any definition is determined by its precision or clarity (we should know what it includes and excludes) and by its versatility or durability (we should not have to change it each time we want to say something new). Like any tool, a definition can be highly specialized and precise or very versatile and handy, but rarely both. The fact that these properties tend to be mutually exclusive, especially when they pertain to the descriptions of complex ideas, is shown by the tendency of stable folk definitions of words like *personality* to be vague, and of precise scientific definitions to proliferate and mutate like fruit flies as people think of new things to say. In 1937 Allport reviewed fifty definitions of the term *personality* widely used in psychology. The number undoubtedly has been squared since then.

What I say about culture and personality is not very complicated so blunt, versatile definitions are best. By the term *personality* I mean those fairly persistent habits of feeling, thinking, and perceiving that, taken together, make up a discernable pattern or style of behavior by which a person gets what he needs from his environment. My focus is functional, but we might also be interested in how the elements of personal style fit together, which is a structural problem. The unit of observation is the individual, making us aware of differences and similarities between persons, although we can refer to personality trends as group characteristics. By the term *culture* I refer to the sum of individual habits that characterize a defined group. This concept comes into play when we make comparisons between groups.

I view both culture and personality as quite plastic in practice, always subject to profound changes. While there must be biological limitations to change, we as yet have so little knowledge about such limitations that it is dangerous to speculate about them. A corollary of this way of thinking, I think of stress as a feature of the person-environment relationship that is neither abnormal nor undesirable in itself. As I suggested in Chapter Five, one might even think of it as a basic human need.

What evidence have we, then, that predictable and important changes in personality functioning occur throughout the life cycle? Psychologists are no more unanimous in their answers to this question than we would expect, and I certainly cannot review all the arguments here. Some people apparently change a lot during their adult lives, and others change little (Clark and Anderson, 1967, pp. 415-416; Lowenthal and others, 1967, p. 172; Alker, 1972). The direction taken by the personality in adult life is affected by social class and culture (Clark and Anderson, 1967; Rosow, 1967; Kiefer, 1971), by sex (Neugarten and Gutmann, 1964), and by urbanization (Clark, 1967; Youmans, 1969), as well as by genetic and biographical pecularities.

Attempts to cull major developmental trends from all this diversity have produced some interesting ideas, however. Cumming and Henry (1961) found that European American midwesterners of modest to middle income tend to disengage from their social environment as they age, with beneficial effects. Gutmann (1969) found that males in several societies seem to move from a realistic and active style of confronting and mastering their environment to more passive styles and then to styles characterized by illogical fantasy. Neugarten (1964, pp. 198-199) and Lowenthal (1967, p. 269) noticed an increased consistency and decreased complexity in personality with age. Frenkel-Brunswik (1964), in an unusual study of the biographies of four hundred Europeans, noted a shift of emphasis in the personality from biologically based concerns toward the demands of ideals, conscience, authority, and practical affairs. This shift occurred for most people in their late forties and was often quite dramatic.

Shifting our attention from findings to theories, we find considerable interest in the concept of identity and in the microcosmic changes in behavior as a person moves from one social setting to another. It has long been suspected by the intellectual descendants of Mead in sociology (for example, Goffman, 1959; Blumer, 1969) that self-perceptions, and hence values and styles of behavior, are highly plastic; luckily, some recent research in psychology, such as that of Gergen (1972), supports this idea. We should therefore expect fairly continuous lifelong personality change in people living in complex, rapidly changing societies as they move through a series of changing milieus. Interactionist theory, which stresses the influence of the immediate social environment on thought, is thus an attractive framework for studying the life cycle and is useful for explanation. Although the focuses of interactionist and psychoanalytic theories of development are different, the two are not incompatible. Once the essential plasticity of adult personality is granted, psychoanalysis too offers useful explanations.

Any discussion of theory brings us up against the problem of the ways in which development and history are responsible for personality change. Viewed phenomenologically, from the standpoint of a single life span, there is a certain annoying pedantry about this issue. A person's circumstances change, and he must make many adjustments with little or no attention to whether the change has resulted from his own maturation or the epochal changes around him. But for fashioning a social science it would be useful to separate changes that occur over and over in the development of succeeding generations from those that make up the larger drift of history. The speed of historical change in industrial societies is overwhelmingly frustrating, since the student must do a whole series of extended longitudinal studies on succeeding generations to really sort out developmental regularities. Perhaps this rapid change is why there is no genuine theory of personality development over the life cycle—only an embarrassment of hypotheses.

I am aware of such theoretical and methodological problems, but in this book I am concerned mainly with understanding overall change in a small group of relatively healthy people and only secondarily with a general theory of developmental change over the life cycle. I am dealing with a short, turbulent, and unique slice of history, not with history in general. I offer an example to anthropologists of how the attitude of developmental studies can expand on the study of change, and I offer an example to developmentalists of how their ideas look when applied to another culture.

I have described development as a process of individual response to environment. This functional description is vulnerable to all the limitations of a functionalist system of reasoning. An adaptive response for the individual might be maladaptive in the long run for the group of which he is a member. Further, the environment makes many conflicting demands on the individual, so that advances in one area often cancel out those in other areas and overall adaptation must be seen as a compromise or juggling act in which conflicting needs are kept in the air. Such conflict is the essence of tragic drama and is treated in social science under such rubrics as *scheduling* (Murray and Kluckhohn, 1962) and *side-betting* (Becker, 1960). A number of examples are described in this book, such as the use of the *guarded self* among the nisei—a response to ambiguity that avoids painful identity confusion but at the same time tends to alienate the nisei from their self-conscious sansei children.

Another serious limitation of functionalism is revealed by the model of the person-environment relationship as an ecological system, change in any part of which is linked with changes in many others. Whatever temporal perspective we take in looking at human behavior—evolutionary, historical, or developmental—we see examples of adaptive changes that turn out to have been mistakes once their effect on large systems has come to light. The gradual growth of the cerebral cortex and associated structures in man's ancestors over perhaps a million years' time finally produced a creature, probably only forty thousand years ago (Washburn and Harding, 1970), whose habit of interfering with his natural environment may well have marked him for eventual extinction. For example, the eradication of diseases and improvements in agriculture have resulted in staggering new problems of overpopulation that may contribute to man's extinction. Likewise, in an individual's lifetime, thorough personal adaptation, in the form of competitiveness, to a competitive world, might seriously hurt one's chances for a serene old age (Clark and Anderson, 1967). In short, adaptation can be really assessed only after the fact—that is, only when all the major effects of a developmental change have been accounted for.

My pessimistic view is not presented out of idle ill humor. It is meant to counterbalance an assumption implicit in much developmental literature that health, sanity, adjustment, and maturity are general conditions that can be measured or prescribed *en masse* for a given stage of the life cycle in a given society. The study of personal development over the life cycle might help to reveal some common developmental problems and some of the specific, obvious effects of some common developmental strategies on carefully defined person-environment systems. Beyond that, such study can make no claims as a guide for insight, planning, or therapy. Such measures of adaptation as morale, energy, or even physical well-being are treacherous if separated from the whole person-environment system in which they appear, and prognostications based on them are always doubtful. Still, some developmentalists would say, some general characteristics, like intelligence or flexibility, might have a predictable affect on a person's chances of continuing to adapt well throughout life under a wide variety of circumstances. Only a rigid nihilist or a confirmed transcendentalist would deny such a possibility. However, social science has yet to develop measurements of these general adaptive characteristics that are accurate enough to be of much use in individual cases. Until such measurements are available, we must be very careful when making predictions that might affect people's lives. Predictions about whether individuals will succeed or fail at any developmental task tend to be self-fulfilling when they are used as guides for action.

Chapter VII

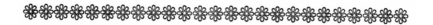

The Life Cycle in Traditional Japan and in America

Now that I have spoken up for the flexibility of both personality and culture and presented the human life cycle as a process of continuous change, I must limit this view. On one hand even the simplest society offers its members a few major options, such as the choice of an occupation, a special role in community religious life, or a mate. Within the culturally approved course thus chosen, there is always room for the expres-

171

sion of a certain amount of personal idiosyncrasy or style. On the other, even the dizzying complexity and uncertainty of such choices in societies like our own is limited by rules of propriety that are at least dimly perceived by each of us according to our membership in a class, gender, occupation, or age group. Part of the cultural environment through which the person passes in the course of aging consists of expectations based on age and social position. By observing his elders, a person builds up some sense of what the next stage of his own life will be like. His culture, we can say, presents him with a map of the developmental territory ahead. The clarity and simplicity of this map is a function of society's orderliness and simplicity and of the pace of its progress, as well as of the individual's personal experiences and thought processes.

If we are to understand the process of personal development in the residents of Japan Town, then, we must know something of the symbolic environment—the cultural environment of shared symbols and expectations—that in part directs and constrains that development. We must try to understand their perceptions of what is a desirable and what is a possible future at each stage of their development and look for the cultural patterns that might help to explain these perceptions. In the discussion that follows I concentrate on the major differences between the life cycle expectations that the issei brought with them from turn-of-the-century Japan and those that each generation now faces as a result of the cultural and historical changes I have discussed in earlier chapters.

A few cautionary words are in order before I discuss the cultural influences on our subjects' personal expectations. First, I am dealing with two complex and rapidly changing societies and so must confine myself to the most general terms in discussing them. My discussion is confined to the underlying patterns that seem to be common to a wide variety of life styles and careers thought normal in each society. These patterns suggest themselves because their explanatory value appears broad and powerful; rarely have they sprung full-blown from the lips of my respondents. They are the shared assumptions about what life styles are possible and desirable at each stage of the life cycle. These assumptions can rarely be articulated by those who hold them, and yet they are extensive in their effect on perception and behavior. It is almost ridiculous to ask how much these general cultural patterns affect behavior, because they are themselves constructs derived from behavior.

Second, as we shall see, these general cultural patterns include a variety of options for action. In the course of development a person is likely to choose one option over another according to his position in the society and according to the developmental demands of his age. As his position shifts with age so will his choice of the options offered by his cultural map. Whether he exercises a particular option is less important, for our purposes, than the fact that his perceptions of the culture guide his choices of the options that he can exercise. For example, from a broad cultural viewpoint, the relationship between father and son is often ambiguous on such issues as how much authority and how much mutual affection should pertain and when and in what areas authority ought to be transferred to the son. My data on Japanese Americans indicate that young men tend to emphasize the affectionate character of their relationship with their fathers to counterbalance the authoritative; that middle-aged men tend to emphasize the authoritative with their sons; and that old men tend to emphasize, as they did with their own fathers when young, the affectionate, egalitarian character of the relationship with their sons and grandsons. The map laying out the proper behavior between fathers and sons is thus redrawn by the individual as he crosses it, although its general outlines are preserved. If the other people in the map reader's social environment disagree with his drawing of it, he can console himself that his behavior falls within the range of culturally defined normality. The mellowing of a grandfather often results, as Gutmann (1969) suggests, from a shift in emphasis away from a culturally approved authoritarianism toward a culturally approved affectionateness, encouraged by his waning ability to override the opinions of the younger generations.

A third caution is that the traditional Japanese life cycle influenced differently the different individuals and generations in America. The physical removal of the issei from Japan altered their expectations of the developmental process, but the change was by no means uniform or predictable. Most issei originally intended to return to Japan and resume the true Japanese life style at some indefinite future time. Furthermore, they tended to keep in touch with their elders at home by letter and by occasional visits, so that the chain of enculturation was not always broken or even seriously weakened. At some point in their American adventure, however, most issei seem to have realized that they were going to grow old in America, surrounded by an Americanized second generation. The defeat of their homeland in 1945 also raised the alarming question of whether the life cycle they had observed in childhood would continue to be a possibility for anyone, anywhere, ever. Such revelations seem to have had different effects on different issei. Some did their best to create around them an old-fashioned Japan, as they remembered it, in order to deviate as little as possible from their original hopes. Others reversed course dramatically, scrapping their original hopes in favor of what seemed a more realistic and in some cases a greatly superior plan. However, Japanese norms have continued to exert a strong unconscious influence over even these issei. Many issei, especially women, left Japan in order to *escape* from the traditional life cycle they expected, or at least from certain aspects of it.

The effects of Japanese life cycle norms on the nisei and sansei are difficult to discuss for several reasons. The nisei are now at an age of life during which the differences between Japanese and American norms are not as great as at other ages, so it is difficult to say which pattern they are following. In addition, the nisei are the only generation in our study who are heavily involved in the lives of both their parents and their children and therefore in both Japanese and American perceptions about age and aging. Of all the difficulties that biculturalism has caused the nisei, the problem of charting their future is perhaps the greatest at the moment. On one hand, they clearly see the attractiveness of the issei style of aging. On the other, they have profound doubts whether their own children will support them emotionally or materially as they have supported the issei. Most nisei have in fact absorbed unconsciously a generous dose of

Japanese expectations about the life cycle from their parents and their peers, as we saw in the case of Mrs. Ohara in Chapter Five and as we will see again in the next chapter. The influence of the Japanese pattern of development on the sansei has yet to be learned, for the most part. I have already discussed some of the conflict between them and their parents over age norms governing young adulthood, but the sansei have scarcely begun to think about middle and late life.

Traditional Life Cycle

Let us now look at the traditional Japanese view of the normal or expectable life cycle. Some features of this traditional view can still be found in modern Japan, but many of them have disappeared from all but the most remote and conservative places. Perhaps the most striking feature of this view, from a European-American outlook, is the group-centeredness of personal development. Each change in a person's life was scheduled according to fairly clear-cut expectations, and was the focus of concern of the groups the person belonged to. Idiosyncratic changes were avoided, if possible, or somehow normalized to fit into the wider patterns of group life. Some of the many customs illustrating this principle are described in the following paragraphs.

Age Reckoning. Age was reckoned not from date of birth but from the first New Year's Day after birth. In other words, all children born in a given year were considered one year old on the first day of the next year, regardless of birthdate. As a result everyone of a given age passed simultaneously to the next age, and important age transitions become a matter for communal celebration.

Astrology. Many Japanese still believe to some extent in the Asian astrology, which assigns character traits on the basis of year of birth. There are twelve zodiacal signs, which follow one another in fixed sequence, one per year, yielding a cycle of twelve years. People of like signs are thought to be alike and to have affinities or antipathies for people of certain other signs. Since women born in the Year of the Horse are thought to

make poor wives, the birth rate drops markedly each time the
cycle reaches that year. This belief system further emphasizes
the solidarity of age mates.

Inductive Magic. There used to be a custom of blocking
children's ears for a few days whenever a child of the same age
died in the vicinity for fear that they might die also if they
heard others talking of the death. This custom showed that the
sense of kinship between age mates was not merely for the sake
of convenience but had cosmological or magical overtones.

Unlucky Years. The *yakudoshi* belief complex, which I
will discuss in more detail later, was a belief that certain years
of everybody's life (different for the sexes) were predestined to
be unlucky. It suggested that everybody reaches certain crises at
precisely the same age.

Age Grading. The custom of forming distinct age grades
was widespread in Japan at one time (Norbeck, 1953). Although there were many local variations, Norbeck describes a
typical system as follows: Until the age of about six, children
were considered infants and had no social personality. From
about seven until about thirteen, they were considered children
and had few organized roles in the adult community. From
fourteen or fifteen until marriage—a stage whose beginning was
often marked by puberty ceremonies—a person was considered
a youth. Youth organizations often performed important ritual
and economic activities in temple and village life. A strong bond
between age mates was expected to develop at this time. The
period from one's own marriage until the marriage of one's son
was formally middle age. Most adult roles were performed during this stage, as well as some ritual specialties such as the performance of funeral rites. After the marriage of a son, a person
was considered semi-retired and again had few duties outside his
own home. However, after formal retirement, an individual (especially a man) joined the ranks of the *elders* and again assumed
formal community duties, usually religious. Each of these stages
was denoted with special terminology, and in many places the
rules setting out the duties and rights of the members of each
age grade were detailed and explicit. Formal rituals marking
transitions from one grade to another varied widely. Beardsley

and others (1959, p. 289) list nine types of transition rituals that had been witnessed by living respondents in an agricultural village.

Seniority System. According to the seniority system, children were never failed in school, and men who held jobs in large organizations always advanced slowly but steadily, in step with their age mates, with little attention to individual differences in ability.

In the traditional Japanese life cycle, then, people developed and aged in cohorts. There was little reward for reaching a developmental stage ahead of one's age mates. In fact, too much preconsciousness, as well as unusually slow development, was regarded as cause for shame by ordinary people.

By American standards, Japanese children were indulged during about the first five years of life. The ideal child at this stage was contented, quiet, and physically robust. Physical contact with older relatives, especially the mother, was continual and affectionate. Children usually slept with their mothers until weaning, which was gradual, usually coinciding with the arrival of a new sibling. It was not considered unnatural for a child to nurse until the age of ten or twelve, although such behavior was discouraged in the interest of appearances. Even during early childhood, children were impressed with the seriousness of their social responsibilities outside the family. They were carefully taught the polite ways of speaking and bowing, and they learned to fear the ridicule of others. They learned that they were looked upon as representatives of their family in all dealings with the outside world and that they therefore carried a heavy responsibility. Around the age of five, the knowledge of this responsibility brought them to a new phase of development. Now that they were spending a good deal of time in the company of nonrelatives, especially if they went to school, they had to learn self-control. Strong displays of emotion met with ridicule, as did lapses in politeness or in consideration for others. Children became truly social beings. They took on statuses in the community at large. For example, in the urban community where I studied in 1965-1966, the question, "How old is your child?" was answered with the child's age in years or months for preschoolers, but with the child's grade in school if he or she was over five.

In many places, the age of thirteen conferred adolescent status. After this age, the sexes were segregated for bathing and sleeping. In ancient times, this was the age at which boys of the warrior class underwent a coming-of-age ceremony, during which they had their heads shaved and received their swords. In modern times, this is the age at which boys had their heads shaved and received their military-looking middle school uniforms with their first long pants. From this age until marriage is generally conceded to have been a difficult period for boys in traditional Japan. They were given increasing responsibility for work and for "manly" behavior, but they were totally under the domination of their older male relatives. Ethnographic observation (Embree, 1939; Smith, 1956; Beardsley and others, 1959) of the apparent stress and discontent of young men in rural Japan is borne out by studies using projective techniques. In a large normalization study using the TAT, Marui (1958) found evidence of considerable repressed hostility towards fathers in adolescent boys.

In spite of the other difficulties of adolescence, however, sexual mores seem to have been fairly relaxed in traditional Japan, with the exception of upper-class girls. In some rural villages, adolescent boys and girls slept apart from the adults in separate youth houses, with the inevitable results. The institution of night-crawling was also widely practiced. A boy would creep into a girl's room at night with a towel wrapped around his face as a disguise. If she rejected him, both could afterwards pretend ignorance of the incident and so avoid embarrassment. The disguise was also a handy pretext for letting the culprit escape unpunished if the girl's parents should catch wind of him. Such indiscretions were permissible at a time when marriages often did not appear on official records until the birth of a healthy child and were easily broken up until that time. The cult of virginity seems to have been a preoccupation mainly of the elite, although promiscuity was frowned upon by all classes. Further, prostitution was a respectable and time-honored institution in traditional Japan. An occasional visit to a brothel, if a boy could afford the price, carried no special stigma.

Marriage was an important transition for men and women alike, because it conferred social maturity. However, its meaning was different depending on the sex and family position of the newlywed. Brides of heirs (usually first sons) were in the unenviable position of being under the severe eye of their mother-in-law and being a virtual servant in their husband's home until they had produced a child. Marriage had little effect on the style of life of the heir himself, because he remained in his natal home and had few obligations to his new wife aside from his responsibility for her general health and safety. Second sons and their wives were different. Because of the practice of primogeniture, second sons were generally expected to establish their own households. This practice did not mean the severing of ties and obligations to the parental household, but it did mean they had at least a small measure of privacy.

Wives were supposed to defer to their husbands in all major decisions, although this was not always the case. Within her own home, the Japanese wife found ways of exerting some authority. Outside the home, however, men were not expected to defer to their wives in any respect. Wives seldom accompanied their husbands except on ceremonial or obligatory occasions, and when they did so, they walked several paces behind, with bowed heads. The cohesion of the male peer group and its significance to its members continued even after the marriage of its members.

Significant to the discussion of the sexes is that for men, the first *yakudoshi,* or unlucky year, is the twenty-fifth, and for women it is the nineteenth. These designations might well have corresponded at one time to the typical age at marriage of the two sexes and thereby testified to the stresses experienced by the bride and groom. Marriage was traditionally arranged by the families of the principals and was not a matter of personal choice. If either principal objected violently, the families would usually have to drop the match. But even so, personal suffering seems to have been almost customary for newlyweds.

The birth of the first child was perhaps the most important event of all in the life cycle of a woman. Her status within the lineage of her husband, as well as in society, changed markedly. Mothers bore most of the responsibility for the socialization of children, and they reaped most of the recognition for raising productive, virtuous people. The proper life for a woman was considered to be one of self-sacrifice in the fulfillment of this duty. It was she, more than her husband, who toiled and fretted over every difficulty the children encountered and who triumphed with their every advance. The birth of a child, then, was one of the most ceremonial events in the parents' life. Before the birth, there were visits to shrines to offer prayers for a safe delivery. Afterwards, there were rituals for disposing of the afterbirth and preserving the umbilicus (which in some places was returned to its owner upon his death by being placed in his coffin). There were congratulatory visits and gifts from all neighbors and acquaintances of the family. On the seventh day after the birth a naming ceremony was held. At the age of thirty-three days, the newborn was dressed in red ceremonial dress and taken to the local Shinto shrine, where it was formally introduced to the gods who were given money and incense, after which mother and grandmother partook of a ceremonial meal.

The second *yakudoshi* is age thirty-three for women and forty-two for men. These are the so-called great *yakudoshi*, the most dangerous years in one's life. The origins of this belief are now lost, but there must have been a time when these years marked the climax of a stressful or ambiguous period in a person's life. Of many possible speculations, two appear to me worth mentioning. First, women's *great yakudoshi* might have marked the average age at the time of the birth of the last child. In 1960 this average was 28.7 years, but the fertility span has been decreasing for some time (Morioka, 1966). In a fertility-conscious peasant society, the unlikelihood of another child would mean at least an unofficial change of status for a woman. Her feelings of self-worth, long focused on her value as a fertile womb, would have to find other sources of support. Second, a man's oldest child would have been likely to reach puberty about the time of his great *yakudoshi* (and his wife's third *yakudoshi* at age thirty-seven). In 1960, the average age of a man at the birth of his first child was about twenty-nine years (Morioka, 1966). This age is just right for my hypothesis but is probably a couple of years later than the average in premodern times. However, the greater infant mortality rate might have compensated for this discrepancy by lengthening the average time it took in ancient times to have a child live till puberty. Judging by the conflicts over sexuality and aggression that appear to have long afflicted male adolescents in traditional Japanese society, it is possible that a man's normal identification with his children throughout their lives could reopen the father's adolescent conflicts in his middle age. Fathers and sons probably often reinforced each other's discomfort, especially in households where the father's parents were still healthy enough to wield plenty of authority.

The marriage of a child was another important life cycle event, because it established lifelong relationships with in-laws, and, in the case of sons, was an important step in ensuring the future of the lineage. Wives were carefully chosen for their health as well as their breeding, and husbands for the status and economic security offered by their families. The marriage of an eldest son was particularly important, because it added a new member to the household and advanced the cycle of family development. The change in status from mere mother to mother-in-law as well was particularly important. The suffering of new brides under the near-absolute authority of their unfeeling and often jealous mothers-in-law is a story as familiar to Japanese as is the tragic love triangle to Westerners. Many young Japanese mothers have looked forward with a frank gleam in their eye to the day when the cycle would advance them to the age at which they could have their revenge. This very force has probably helped to assure the dominance of the male in the Japanese family by dividing the women against each other. Mother-in-law and bride are constantly competing for the loyalty of the men in the house as their allies in this eternal struggle.

Some relief from the struggle between wives and mothers-in-law could be expected to accompany the appearance of grandchildren. Another well-known bit of lore is that grandparents and grandchildren were in many ways closer than parents and children. I have already discussed the role of the grandparent as the emotional socializer of the grandchildren. In addition, grandparents traditionally took an active part in the practical care of grandchildren and probably exerted a conservative influence on child-rearing attitudes. As the head of the household, a grandfather exerted considerable influence on decisions bearing on his grandchildren's upbringing.

Formal retirement from household headship was mainly a male transition. In ancient times, it was in many places fixed by custom at the age of sixty and accompanied by ceremony, but in the present century this custom has declined. In farming and entrepreneurial families, where retirement from work is not mandatory at a given age, the turning over of the family headship to the heir tends to be a gradual and unceremonious affair these days. In spite of the traditional notion that reaching the age of formal retirement is a result of both luck and wisdom and is desirable, the stress of this achievement also seems to have been recognized. The third *yakudoshi* for men was the sixty-first year, the year following retirement.

To the cyclical view that old age in modern Japan is a blissful second childhood—a view widespread in anthropological literature—Plath (1972) makes an excellent rebuttal. Presumably, the well-being of old people compared to the rest of society was greater a century or so ago, when urbanization and industrialization had yet to seriously challenge the traditional family system, with its backbone of Confucian ethics. Respect for one's aged parents was and still is an important value in Japanese society, and when economic and other values were in harmony with it, it was probably a fact more often than it is today.

In a careful study of the typical life cycle of the Japanese agricultural family, Morioka (1966) shows an economic process that supports the Confucian value of respect for the elderly. The three-generation preindustrial agricultural family's economic fortune followed a cyclical pattern, as the ratio of able hands to hungry mouths fluctuated over the life cycle. When the household consisted mainly of strong young adults and adolescents and their still vigorous parents, per capita income was likely to be highest. When there were small children and weak elders in the house, the fruits of labor were spread thin. Moreover, the elders tended to be in their declining years precisely when the grandchildren were too young to pull their own economic weight. However, there were many tasks on a farm that required patience, practice, and the knowledge of long experience rather than physical vigor. The normal elderly were likely to have a good knowledge of weather and soil conditions and to have acquired skills such as tool mending, sewing, and the diagnosis and treatment of human and animal diseases. They could do light housework, tend fires and floodgates, cook, and—perhaps most important of all—look after children while the parents were in the fields. In short, their old age coincided with a time when the family badly needed whatever economic help they could contribute. Thus the gratitude and respect of younger generations were a natural result of contribution made necessary by these economic conditions.

This picture is far off the second childhood model of aging in Japan portrayed by Benedict (1946). It is my impression that, while the elderly are less morally constrained than the middle-aged, most would still find the idea of indulging themselves like children morally flabby and downright insulting to their character. The main complaint of the elderly I interviewed in an urban apartment village near Osaka was that there were too few opportunities for them to be useful there, in contrast to life on a farm or in a shop. During a brief visit to friends in the countryside, I was able to see the contrast myself; there the grandparents were busy and productive. In 1970 the Japanese Ministry of Welfare issued the results of a study which purported to show that hard work in their later years and a cheerful disposition are the distinguishing characteristics of those who live to a ripe old age (*Hokubei Mainichi,* October 17, 1970).

Perhaps the most striking period of the traditional Japanese life cycle, to a Westerner, is that following death. In Japan, a person did not cease to function as a member of a family when he died (Plath, 1964, p. 307):

As a corporation, the Japanese household includes both living and dead members, and both are essential to its existence. All members are responsible for the welfare and continuity of the corporation, and all should be mutually concerned for their

*co-members. The dead provide a spiritual charter guaranteeing
the right of their household line to a separate existence. The
living provide the material stuff, both productive and reproduc-
tive, that keeps the line in motion. The living carry out household business. The dead remain passive except episodically; they
serve mainly as moral arbiters and sources of emotional security.*

The presence of the dead was symbolized by the Buddhist memorial tablets, each inscribed with an ancestor's special
memorial name, that were kept in the house. Offerings and
prayers were regularly made to the ancestors through these tablets, and many people were in the habit of holding silent conver-
sations with them on matters of personal and family importance. Graves were also visited for the purpose of communicating with or simply feeling emotionally close to the dead. These
life cycle practices are still preserved today in the Buddhist
practice of memorial services for the dead, called *hōji*, ("invok-
ing the [Buddhist] law") or *senzo kuyo* ("offering sustenance
to the ancestors"). These services consist of the reading of prayers and sutras at the household Buddhist altar by priests called
in for the purpose, accompanied by the offering of incense to
the departed by relatives and neighbors, and followed by a communal feast and sake drinking. These ceremonies are ideally
held frequently during the first year after a death and then on
the anniversary of the death in certain years up to the centen-
nial. The ceremonies varied in length and elaborateness, lasting a
day or so and employing anywhere from one to ten priests.

Prior to my research, I thought it might be very important to the elderly in San Francisco's Japan Town to feel confi-
dent that their children would carry out these traditional Japanese duties after their death; but such concern did not seem to
be the case. The issei would simply shrug when asked whether
their children would perform them, saying, "Who knows?" This
attitude puzzled me until I talked with a Buddhist minister
about the meaning of the ceremonies. He explained that the real
benefit of the ceremonies is to the *living*; through the memorial
services they learn the connectedness of all lives and they learn
the humility and patience that, in the Buddhist view, give joy to

life. These ideas are part of a vast and subtle difference between the Japanese and American cultures—a difference in the whole perception of self and time. The traditional Japanese view sees the individual life as a single segment of a continuous cord. Life and its circumstances are gifts from countless prior generations, whose repayment flows on to the generations of the indefinite future. Benedict grasped this principle, but took the one-sided view that it produced a wearying sense of ceaseless obligation in the individual. It often produces an uplifting sense of gratitude for life and an equanimity in the face of death as well. It is of a piece with the overall pattern of personal development I have been discussing. Japanese life is group life; the changes experienced by a person throughout his life are also experienced by the groups of which he is a member. Those groups share intimately the credit for his achievements and the responsibility for his difficulties, and he shares the credit and responsibility for theirs. These influences extend outward, both in space and in time, from his biological presence.

How has modernization and Americanization affected the fabric of the traditional Japanese value system? I described in Chapters Two and Four some of the perceptions my respondents had of their own and each other's generations and the main historical and cultural processes bearing on these perceptions. As far as their personal expectations of the life cycle are concerned, I have also discussed the difficulty of making general statements about the effects of history and social change. However, I think one can identify a complex, cumulative process which accounts for some widespread and irreversible changes in individual life expectations. This process, which has been identified in other works on the subject of urbanization such as those of Redfield and Singer (1962) and Simmel (1902-03), might be called the shift from a sociocentric to an egocentric locus of development. I designate it with the term *individuation,* which I explain in detail in Chapter Four.

In this space I can give only a rough outline of the effects of individuation on personal development. Urbanization and industrialization increase economic specialization, decrease the size of the typical residence unit, increase the separation of the various spheres of human activity (work, worship, education, leisure, and so on), greatly increase the rate of obsolescence of knowledge, increase geographic mobility, and prolong life. Taken together, these processes have two important effects on life expectations. First, definitions of roles become much vaguer and more unstable, so that expectations are much less clear. Second, the effects of and responsibility for developmental changes fall less and less on intimate groups such as family and community and more and more on individuals.

One can easily see how the ambiguity of roles comes about. The separation of work from home and leisure, at least in the case of males, reduces contact between generations, as does the shrinkage of the dwelling unit from the extended to the nuclear family. The removal of the aged from mixed residential neighborhoods to nursing homes and "golden ghettos" furthers the process. The pace of social change assures that much of the know-how of previous generations can be discounted anyway, so that parents and grandparents can be less relied on as models. The increased complexity and specialization of skills, together with the decline of handicrafts, results in the removal from the home of technical education, which in turn further contributes to the generation gap. Meanwhile, both the increased heterogeneity of life styles found in a typical urban neighborhood and the mobility of its residents decrease the availability of developmental models within the community and lead to a further relaxation of norms and greater ambiguity of possibilities.

The discovery of this complex process has led many to conclude that urbanization is accompanied by the breakdown of family solidarity; however, the idea that the urban family is prone to drifting apart is usually overstated—a fact especially appreciable when one looks at family participation in the life-long development of its members. The dismantling of the extended family household into smaller residential units is indeed a pattern that follows urbanization and a rising standard of living (Shanas and others, 1968). However, residential dispersion is different from the breakdown of family ties. The rapid communication and transportation techniques that also accompany industrialization increase the ability of dispersed residential units to keep in close touch, and most families in urban industrial societies do keep in touch this way. Such separate households have advantages for grandparents in an urban society, for the grandparents themselves as well as for their offspring. Where it is economically feasible to do so comfortably, old people tend to prefer living separate but close.

There is little doubt, however, that on the whole the idea of individual life as a process of independent growth and self-fulfillment gains ground with urbanization and industrialization. Along with the shift from ascribed to achieved status described by Linton (1936) comes a similar shift toward privatization, or the experience of the self as spatially and temporally disconnected from the social world. The important events of one's life come to be seen as only those that impinge directly on one's biological presence. Personal time begins somewhere around the event of one's conception and ends with one's death. Gains and losses tend to be assessed on a personal rather than on a group basis. There is a dwindling appreciation of the attitude expressed by the Japanese proverb, "If you even brush another's sleeve, your fates are linked." In Chapter Eight I discuss the main developmental problems now faced by each generation. The cultural patterns outlined in this chapter will provide yet another backdrop against which we can see the intertwined effects on the individual of history, culture change, and psychosocial maturation.

Chapter VIII

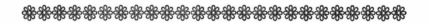

Problems of Development: Issei, Nisei, Sansei

My task in this chapter is to describe the main developmental problems of the Japanese Americans. I underplay personal idiosyncrasies and deal with each sex in each generation as a homogeneous group. My intent is to enrich our understanding of Japanese American life by comparing their developmental process with developmental processes in other times, places, and cultures. In addition to the published studies of adult personality development that I mention in the preceding chapters, I draw on many of the findings of the life cycle studies of my colleagues at the Human Development Program (for example, Spence and Lonner, 1971), and I use for comparison my experience with Japanese middle-class families in Osaka in 1965-66, having asked similar questions of them.

The Issei

The issei departed radically from the expectable Japanese life cycle in a number of ways. First, simply leaving their native culture was an adventure far from the experience of their compatriots. For the majority that expected to return to the normal cycle in Japan at a later time, leaving was viewed as time out from life as usual. Perceiving that life at home went on normally without them, the issei felt that coming to America meant a temporary delay for some of their plans and that therefore the days they spent here were precious and not to be wasted. The conservation of time and other commodities was a familiar feature of their native culture, but in America it had a new urgency. One of the epithets most frequently heard on the lips of the issei was *wastetime,* used to describe anything trivial or inefficient. Their life was to be devoted to the acquisition and saving of things that would be of use when they rejoined the mainstream of life in Japan. Money escaped the *wastetime* category, but it was not necessarily the only or even the main exception. Education in both Japanese and American skills and culture was of major importance, as was the cultivation of spiritual values. We have seen, for example, how churches and study groups were given a strong early priority in the issei culture.

The dissatisfactions and anxieties of living outside the mainstream of Japanese life must have been considerable. Many issei sojourners soon began to weary of the sense of urgency they felt about returning and discovered aspects of their lives away from home that were satisfying in themselves, as the new requirements of living gradually took on the familiarity of custom. If they did not get used to life in the United States, they at least got used to not getting used to it. Taking time out from some developmental processes was mitigated by taking time in again with others that had been postponed. Marriage was for most issei men such a resumption, but it had to be adapted to their special situation. For one thing, by the time they made the decision, most men had already postponed their marriage well past the normal age and in their mid-thirties took wives ten or more years younger than themselves. In order to save the expense of going home to select a bride, many issei married girls who were familiar to them only through letters and photographs, and both partners of such matches were often disappointed at first.

Men who followed this practice soon found themselves middle-aged with young wives and children. The practice undoubtedly contributed to the heavy sense of responsibility and the firm authority of the issei men as a group before the war and therefore to the severity of the demotion in family and community status they experienced during the relocation. The fact that many issei men had to take on menial jobs in their advanced age also resulted from this demotion and from the fact that their young sons, whose careers were delayed by the relocation, were unprepared to assume the burden of dependent parents directly after the war. On the positive side, the age gap between the issei men and their families helped to assure that those who were fortunate enough to marry had vigorous wives and children in their economic prime, during their advanced old age. There are few widowers and few men with chronically ill wives among the issei today. Moreover, this pattern is, as one would expect, highly desirable from the man's point of view. Both the issei men interviewed who had been widowed earlier in life had remarried and were satisfied that they had done so. A healthy wife can be expected to provide comfort and companionship to an old man, even if she may often undermine his dignity by babying him. Wives of our elderly subjects tended to take an active part in the interviews, offering help and advice, sometimes when it was not solicited. When shown the TAT cards, one issei man brusquely handed them to his wife and said, "You! Tell him some stories about these!" Before my protests had any effect, the wife had obliged with several well-constructed stories. The great pity that Japanese Americans almost unanimously express for old issei bachelors also attests to the advantages they see in having young wives in old age. Such men are considered lonely, frustrated, and without hope.

The effects of the age gap on the issei women is another matter. Mostly very young and inexperienced when they reached America, the issei women were greeted by much older prospective husbands who had already acquired some understanding of United States culture. The Japanese norm of deference to one's husband was reinforced not only by the seniority and experience of the issei male community, but by their tight-knit cooperativeness and cultural sophistication. This disadvantage could make life very difficult for a reluctant bride. Going home to mama—a forceful threat in the hands of rural Japanese brides in those days—was nearly out of the question, since it amounted almost to divorce under the circumstances. Wives tended to remain quite ignorant of the world beyond their families and neighborhoods. This ignorance has increased the dependency of the aged issei woman on her ethnic community and on her children and seriously undermined her usefulness as the socializer of grown children and grandchildren. On the positive side, putting an ocean between herself and her traditionally autocratic mother-in-law gave the issei woman greater autonomy in her own arena, the home. Another advantage was that the alliance between mother and child, traditionally formidable anyway, could use father's age to his disadvantage if he went afoul of the alliance between his wife and children.

The age differential meant a greater likelihood of prolonged widowhood for issei women. I sampled for vertical, not horizontal family structure; as it happened, all but one of my issei women were widows, and the nonwidowed woman's husband was incapacitated with a stroke. I could not systematically study the effect of widowhood with this biased sample. Perhaps I could not have anyway, given the reluctance of issei widows to discuss their deceased husbands in any terms other than ideal stereotypes. The death of a husband is sure to be met with ambivalence when the years preceding it have been devoted to nursing him in his advanced senescence, but Japanese widows are not constrained to a long period of mourning and are generally forgiven if they enjoy their new freedom a little. Further, widowed issei women have little trouble finding the companionship of their peers. The homogeneous age structure of the community and the frequency of widowhood result in a variety of associations made up mostly of women in the same developmental stage. Relatively early and prolonged widowhood is a normal pattern of aging for the subculture of issei women, and the new widow as well as her relatives can find many acceptable models for their adjustment to new roles.

Although one might expect the loss of the Japanese language by the third generation to have a great effect on the ability of the issei to adjust to old age, such a conclusion is not borne out by observation. The inability of the generations to converse limits the amount of substantive knowledge that they can exchange, but it has surprisingly little effect on the exchange of moral outlook. As I explain in Chapter Four, Japanese culture makes greater use of innuendo, gestures, and facial expressions for communication than does American culture. Anyway, close relationships in any culture often seem to get on well when words are left out of them. The issei are aware that examples speak louder than commands, and they consciously strive to influence their children and grandchildren silently. The most serious limitation on their influence, then, may not be the lack of English but the lack of experience with the problems of mainstream American life.

I now turn to the important developmental problems the issei face today. Although my intention was to be as inductive as possible in searching for such problems, obviously not everything could be studied. Implicit in both the interviews and the analysis then, was a set of developmental issues of typical importance to the aged, derived from the pancultural study of personality. The great issues of personal development most important for the issei can be reduced to five categories of personality needs: *companionship, authority, autonomy, productivity,* and *acceptance of death.* Many other labels, such as morale, self-esteem, social involvement, could be used to classify the same data. There is much overlapping of behavior and needs in any such scheme. For instance, the desire to keep working might be aimed at the satisfaction of all these needs, and conversely, the need for autonomy might be reflected in ideas about religion, family, leisure use, health, and so on. I have chosen this particular analytic outline because I think it corresponds fairly closely to those points on which my data are richest and because it is relatively, not completely, free of culture-bound associations. Students of psychoanalytic ego psychology will recognize familiar ideas here. My inclusion of productivity derives partly from the works of Jung and Erikson.

Companionship. By now it should be clear that the local Japanese American community offers many opportunities for companionship to the healthy issei. First, the great majority of issei living in Japan Town have a spouse or other kin either in the same house or close by. Of twenty-one issei who answered a questionnaire distributed at a senior center, mostly widows, only two said that they were living alone. Three nonwidows were living with a spouse, and the other sixteen respondents were living with other relatives. Families as a rule include the elderly in many of their leisure activities whether or not they live in the same household, and most make some effort to see that the elders can be with their friends regularly. Observation of church groups, hobby classes, and senior center meetings shows a striking contrast with parallel urban Caucasian groups. Among the issei, the level of noise and motion is high, many activities are shared, and personal space is minimal—there is much close face-to-face interaction and touching. The issei interviewed might have been more socially active than the average, since many were originally contacted for my research through social groups; however, only three of my issei subjects did not have regular social activities outside their homes and families more than once a week. Two of these issei were physically weak.

The relationship between health and companionship is significant. Most issei who are healthy enough to live at home but too weak to get out often can and do receive visitors and talk with their friends daily by telephone, even though they are

much more restricted in their social activities than healthier issei. However, two conditions impose severe social isolation on
an unknown number of issei, ambulatory mental illness and
long-term hospitalization. Any prolonged emotional distress
that does not have an immediate and identifiable cause is likely
to be labeled mental illness in the Japanese American culture, a
label that always carries intense stigma. Emotionally disturbed
issei tend to shut themselves off from family, church, and
friends and suffer in isolation. In addition to observations of
this phenomenon, data on mental hospitalization show that
while Japanese have a low rate of admission, they tend to remain in the hospital comparatively longer than other groups.
This finding suggests that those who do reach hospitals may be
severely deteriorated by the time they seek help (Kitano, 1968).
Japanese-speaking ministers and mental health professionals
have had very little success so far in finding and helping emotionally disturbed issei. One important source of help seems to
be the messianic ethnic churches. Because of the sensitivity of
this problem and limitations on my time, I was unable to study
the role of these churches adequately.

The possibility of severe physical disability is regarded by
healthy issei with horror, mostly because of its social consequences. They know that some nisei place their disabled parents
in nursing homes and leave them there to languish in relative
isolation. The problem of physical disability is similar to that of
the isolation of the mentally disturbed. Nisei typically react
with intense shame and guilt when the presence of a dependent
old person in the home leads to severe emotional strain within
the family. Rather than let such strain be known, many nisei
prefer to cover it up for as long as possible. Eventually the family's tolerance of the burden gives out and they decide to move
the issei elsewhere. By this time, family relationships may have
deteriorated to the point where any contact with the issei can
scarcely be tolerated by the others, a condition aggravated by
the guilt surrounding institutionalization itself.

The issei believe that such neglect is the result of a decline in filial piety, but I offer a more precise explanation. First,
as I explained in Chapter Four, most nisei think of their parents

mostly in terms of their health and productivity, a way of thinking that may be out of keeping with the emotional needs of issei who have few contacts outside the family. This disparity might be partly a result of the fact that the nisei missed the socializing influence of their own grandparents when they were young. Second, although women of all ages, especially nisei, are generally more involved in day-to-day interaction with the elderly than men are, the burden of responsibility for major decisions regarding dependent issei falls on the shoulders of the nisei men. This sex role difference is reflected in attitudes. When I asked subjects how young people feel about the elderly, I got the following results: Nisei and sansei women are almost four times as likely as men to give an opinion on this question, and in all three generations, all those who said the young feel supportive toward the elderly are women, and all those who said otherwise are men. The TAT results are also interesting. In response to the card which shows an elderly woman and a young man, often called the mother-son card, themes of conflict and filial guilt are frequent (twenty-five out of forty) throughout the study sample. Such themes are virtually absent (two out of forty-three) in response to another card, which shows both sexes in two adult generations. A possible interpretation of this finding is that the role of Judas often falls on nisei men in relation to their mothers.

So far I have been discussing the social structural features of the problem of companionship for the issei. The healthy and active issei live in a social world that offers many opportunities for rewarding human contact. It is a small world, and culturally a fairly homogeneous one, when compared with urban industrial society on the whole. Concern for the well-being of the elderly is a strong value holding the generations together, even though the nisei may not clearly understand some of their parents' emotional needs.

Cultural patterns bearing on the conduct of interpersonal relations in general also affect the way the issei manage the companionship problem. In many ways Japanese culture disciplines, trains, and prepares the young for the tasks of later life. A wide combination of values and beliefs aims at the mainte-

pression of dominance in the traditional culture, and it places the recipient in a subordinate position, at least until he is in a position to return each favor with one of equal value. One who is repeatedly or continuously in debt to another becomes a social subordinate in his own eyes, whether or not his benefactor treats him as such. Under the traditional value system, however, dependent elders are not regarded as subordinates, because whatever they receive from society, especially from their descendents, is considered repayment for their life's labor. But in order for this system to work it must be recognized by the parties involved; this condition is not clearly met in present-day Japanese American culture. The issei face a double problem, then, in their premature loss of authority and their demeaning dependency.

Needless to say, the problems of authority and autonomy vary in extent from individual to individual and family to family. In six of the families interviewed and in several others I saw casually, issei refused various kinds of important help proffered by their children. In several cases the issei refused to live with their children's families. In other cases they refused assistance with necessary chores or offers of financial help. These issei were usually not able to explain clearly this behavior, saying only that human relations are smoother if they are reciprocal. Their feeling was not that they had no right to depend on their children, but that the children did not understand their obligation. Under the circumstances, they preferred a difficult and restricted autonomy to an unwanted dependency. This struggle for autonomy is also found in intergenerational perceptions about personality. For instance, one of the interview questions was, "What makes it possible for an old person to live happily?" Seven out of the eight issei who had an opinion answered *personal qualities* of the old person. In contrast, eight out of fifteen nisei answered either *support from others* or *health*—over both of which the elderly have no direct control. Apparently, the issei perceive themselves as more autonomous than their children perceive them.

This pattern of responses is not so different from one frequently found among aging European Americans. What makes it interesting is that the help-rejecting issei are part of a culture in which lifelong interdependency among members of intimate groups is the normal pattern and the one that these issei's children outwardly support. Moreover, the issei seem perfectly willing to accept limited help when it is willingly offered by friends, community organizations, or anthropologists who are not compelled by custom to help them. The great sensitivity of the issei to the feelings of others is augmented here by anxiety touched off by their early loss of authority. Some issei are extremely sensitive to being perceived as helpless by others.

Doi (1973) thinks that the need for indulgent support from others is a cornerstone of Japanese personality and that the satisfaction of this need is normally taken for granted in the parent-child relationship. There is much to support Doi's view of the Japanese, and the exception in the case of the issei is an important acculturative change from that traditional characteristic. It may be that needs for support have been transfered to a large extent from the family to the issei peer group. As I mention later, a great deal of support is shared among members of issei groups in the forms of sympathy, food, and even physical care of dependent members.

In the preceding chapter I briefly mentioned another way of handling such perceptions on the part of issei males. In the responses to a TAT card showing the faces of a young man and an elderly man, often called the father-son card, a strong contrast emerges between the generations. The nisei men see the father figure in a solid position of authority over the son. The sansei men see the son rebelling against or escaping from the authority of the father. The issei men see the relationship as one of mutual affection and concern. The issei attitude supports the proposition that issei men tend to compensate for their loss of authority by shifting their emphasis to the emotions. This proposition is contrary to Caudill's finding (1952) that the issei use intellectualization as a defense. The discrepancy might be explained by the fact that both the issei and the nisei have gotten a lot older since Caudill's study. My finding is also supplementary to Gutmann's conclusions (1969) from the study of aging men in three cultures. Gutmann found that among the Highland

Maya, the Navajo, and the Kansas Citians, men's attitude toward the mastery of their environment tends to change from an active one to a passive one as they age.

Productivity. The problem of autonomy is closely related to the problem of productivity for the issei. All but two of the seven formally interviewed issei men had income-producing work at the time, and both of the retired men were otherwise active in their community. Three of the working men—ages eighty-one, eighty-two, and eighty-five—still held jobs consisting mainly of manual labor, and each expressed his pride and gratitude in being able to work hard at his age. Three of the ten issei women interviewed—ages sixty-five, sixty-nine, and seventy-four—had regular, income-producing work, all of it involving physical labor. While the women put more emphasis on support from their families than on the ability to work as a source of morale, they too seem to be grateful for the opportunity to contribute to their own economic maintenance. The worth of the individual to his group in Japanese culture is measured to a fair extent by what he contributes concretely toward the group's goals (see Plath, 1964b), and as I have repeatedly said, self-worth and group worth tend toward an explicit unity. The nisei and sansei image of the hard-working issei derives from the issei's general task-orientedness, which often emphasizes group goals. When anything needs doing, an issei is likely to set about it quietly but intensely, without being asked and without agonizing about whose responsibility the job is. Work builds social harmony, and harmony builds happiness. A major part of the issei perception of productivity, then, has nothing to do with any permanent or material effect on the world; productivity is often the simple building of human bonds. For this reason, the issei seem to derive an unusual sense of satisfaction from the performance of simple routine work of the sort that gadget-happy America has come to refer to as drudgery. A spotless house, a well-ironed dress, a bountiful garden are not only aesthetically pleasing and morally instructive, they are statements of the owner's concern for the sensibilities of others and of his or her willingness to work tirelessly for a basically social cause.

An important part of almost any social gathering including the issei, or at least the issei women, is the sharing of food. Issei women seem to be at their happiest when watching something they have prepared being eaten with gusto. The culinary consumer might be her husband, an issei friend at a pot luck, a grandchild at a picnic, or an anthropologist taking a coffee break in her parlor. When I invited one of my issei respondents to dinner at my house, she showed up with a pailful of her own cooking big enough to feed six hungry people. The issei do not expect to be reimbursed for this type of giving. It is another form of productivity that they find satisfying in its own right. Recreation, too, often has a similar productive component for the issei. Many issei devote much time to the study of art, flower-arranging, poetry recitation, music, needlework, and the tea ceremony and other domestic arts, which have a kind of social productivity as their goal. Some issei have taken up the serious study of English in their old age with the same motivation.

Part of the issei's concern with the culturally traditional has to do with the form of productivity that Erikson (1963, pp. 266-269) calls generativity, or passing on the important meanings and values of one's own life to the next generation. We have seen that the traditional Japanese concept of time portrays individual life as a segment of a continuous filament. If there is little passing on of values, the filament of time is weak. Being able to die peacefully requires a sense of having been a strong segment, of having given back at least what one received from life. Says the elder Mr. Uchida: "As I told you, the war made a fundamental change [in our lives]. And after that, our younger generation [went] to work anywhere, [in] any direction. And we see we can establish our finer foundations in this country. Since the war, we have a strong foundation to live in America, for our younger generation. The nisei and sansei have the same hope and desire—to be good American citizens—as their Japanese ancestors had. That way, we see that they are enjoying life and working very diligently to establish the family and teach their children as the issei did." The issei have fought hard to preserve some of their values, not just for the sake of maintaining their authority or for the aesthetic satisfaction that they derive from tradition, but because preserving and carrying them forward was an important part of the issei's life work. It was their product and their legacy, as well as their responsibility as parents.

With a few exceptions the issei have long since relinquished their role as the primary socializers of their children. Although they see themselves as a moral restraining force and example, they rarely try to manage their children's careers or social lives and do not seem very disturbed about major filial decisions they disagree with. Where the issei still take an active part in the management of family business—as in the cases of Mr. Sakai, Mr. Sano, and Mrs. Kawada—they are usually genuinely needed in their leadership role. The issei differ from many aging European Americans in this respect. Recent work on the adult development of American women (Spence and Lonner, 1971) indicates that many of them suffer considerable anxiety regarding the careers of their grown children, over whom they no longer have any control. These women are haunted by the fear that they have somehow failed to complete the tasks of motherhood and are unwilling to relinquish the role. This anxiety results partly from the relative lack of criteria for judging parental success in the American culture. There is no clear-cut notion of what a successful mother does or what she achieves by being one; nor does she get much feedback from peers about whether and when she has succeeded. Japanese criteria are simpler, and information about one's performance of the parental role is more available from peers in the community. Most issei appear to have done quite well in the terms of their own culture. Family reputation in the tight-knit community is a good indicator of parental performance, and I did not find any families whose reputations were bad enough to raise the issue of issei failure in the parental role.

While some kinds of productivity derive from autonomy and authority, others involve relinquishing them—relaxing and giving in to primitive impulses. Cultivation of the traditional arts can be a return to the bosom of the mother culture, as cultivation of the soil is to Mother Earth. Jung (1931) speaks of the creative process as a natural force against which man struggles only at his peril. Religious and philosophical ideas, also products of this type, are highly cultivated among issei men, in keeping with the masculine role in Japanese culture. They quickly warm to questions about the meaning of life and death, the development of character, and the secret of happiness. They freely offer speculations that show an appreciation for life, a contemplative, aesthetic understanding. For example, Mr. Fujii was asked what makes him angry.

> Mr. Fujii: *Well, in people's relations with each other, they are sometimes unreasonable. That's because human beings are emotional animals.*
> Interviewer: *Do you feel sorry afterwards?*
> Mr. F: *At such times, I feel as though I'm talking to myself—as though I'm talking to a mirror.*

Other examples include Mr. Ono's response to the mother-son card of the TAT: "I think a mother has a very great influence on her children, whether they are young or old. I watch my wife around the kids, and I watch my daughter-in-law. There is a very pure and beautiful love between a mother and a child." And Mr. Uchida's account of a recent trip to Argentina: "I like to understand things about the places I travel. Such as in South America, the way the native people live, and what their history is, especially what kind of government do they have, and thirdly the economic condition. For instance, we saw a nice capitol in Argentina, but the guide told us the capitol building was for rent because some general did away with the Congress. Because of that sort of thing, some are very rich and some are very poor."

If it is possible to draw together the various forms of issei productivity—work, art, heritage, and philosophic insight—and name the goal toward which they all strive, that goal is neither abundance nor novelty, but rather harmony. As the traditional arts, such as flower-arranging and the tea ceremony, seek to nourish inner poise through the balancing of natural forms, materials, and movements, so work harmonizes human relations. As leaving a legacy balances the pendulum of life and

death, so philosophic creativity settles a personally satisfying order on the ceaseless flux of experience. This sense of productivity is based on the principles of social organization and ethics
that I have described as typical of Japanese culture. It is a conservative rather than a generative productivity. Like a bonsai
artist who by patient attention both limits the growth of his
trees and bends them toward ever-greater perfection, the proper
work of the issei is to order the resources at their disposal into
an ever more harmonious microcosm. In reality the work often
goes awry and the sense of harmony eludes the aging issei. However, as Clark and Anderson concluded in their study of aging
(1967), the chances of high morale are best for the aging person
who has productive goals, but whose goals do not require maintaining a youthful capacity for bringing the world to heel.

Acceptance of Death

Mr. Daigen: *I feel life fading away. Fading—and I can't
stop it.*
Interviewer: *Do you worry about growing older?*
Mr. Daigen: *No. If you get over eighty—I'm ready to kick
the bucket. [Chuckles.] I'm over eighty-one. I'm ready. Dying
is not at all a worry.*

It would a sign of weakness for an issei to show much
fear of dying, so we cannot place great credit in interview responses as the above alone. This one is typical of issei expressions on the subject. However, the words just quoted take on
validity in view of what followed. A few months after the interview, Mr. Daigen died quietly. Independent support for the idea
that the issei have little fear of death comes from ministers of
various Christian and Buddhist churches in the community.
These ministers also agree that acceptance of death is not typical of Japanese Americans in general, only of the issei generation. The nisei are said to have much more difficulty discussing
death or handling the deaths of others than have the issei. How
is the issei equanimity to be explained? When I discussed the
question of an afterlife with a group of four issei women, they
showed little anxiety but were also skeptical of afterlife theo-

ries. Other individuals, like Reverend Oda, show a firm conviction in the idea of eternal life and seem to draw great strength
from this conviction. Filial care of the spirit after death, as I
said earlier in this chapter, does not seem to be an important
concern for any issei.

Three related attitudes about death are strongly developed in Japanese culture and seem to help those issei who have
lived in accordance with Japanese tradition to face death. First,
Japanese culture shows a deep reverence for nature. From the
use of natural materials in architecture to the worship of natural
phenomena in the popular Shinto faith, Japanese people
demonstrate in their everyday lives satisfaction with things in
their original, unprocessed state. This culture pattern is more
than a romantic philosophy, as visitors to rural Japan often remark. Living close to nature in the way valued by the traditional culture involves shivering in winter, sweating in summer,
and ignoring the bites of insects and the stinks that attend life
in the ripe. The Japanese are often critical of the intellect's arti-
ficiality. They use approvingly such terms as *no-mind* and speak
of a person who insists on logic as argumentative. Their reverence for nature is expressed in such concepts as the "is-ness" of
things (*yūgen*) and the pity of things (*mono no aware*). Buddhism teaches that all life is suffused with a unifying force, the
Buddha nature. According to this view, death is natural and the
fear of death therefore amounts to the fear of nature—a sad
error of perception. This is probably one reason why suicide
was traditionally considered an acceptable solution to a wide
variety of personal difficulties and why the fear of either the
bodies or the souls of the dead is not strongly developed in
Japanese culture, although it is not altogether absent either. In
short, it is considered incorrect and gauche to struggle against
nature's inevitabilities. One who lives long is lucky, and one
who dies young is unlucky, but the prolongation of life at great
expense shows a lack of dignity. When the physical powers have
waned and the business of life has been set in order, death is
appropriate. It is almost as though one who knows his proper
place dies at a reasonable age. Plath (1972) cites a popular Japanese folk tale in which a particularly robust old woman be-

comes so ashamed of her abnormal vitality that she resorts to knocking out her teeth with a stone.

Second, the clear sense of their responsibilities and obligations to the world, together with their conservative attitude toward productivity, seem to help the healthy issei achieve a sense of the completeness and wholeness of their lives. On the subject of death they are likely to say, "I have finished up my work in this world. I am ready any time."

The third and most important attitude that helps the Japanese accept death is their perception of time. Meyerhoff (1955) reminds us that it is the consciousness of aging and death that, more than anything else, gives human psychological time its irreversible quality and that this quality is fundamental to our whole perception of the world, including the self. The meaning of death is in turn conditioned to a great extent by whether we perceive time as continuous and suprapersonal or as discontinuous and personal. Just as the Western tendency to perceive time as personal leads toward our Grim Reaper symbolism and our peroccupation with the destructiveness of time in philosophy and literature (Meyerhoff) so the suprapersonal tendency in Japanese thought leads toward a relatively sentimental portrayal of time and its effects. A common metaphor for death in Japanese literature is the falling of cherry blossoms. The metaphor comes from nature and carries a suggestion of renewal.

These attitudes toward death, however, make sense only when they are supported by other cultural norms. A person who sees himself as a deviant or a failure will probably find the approach of death threatening or mocking and out of keeping with the naturalistic ethos, and his deviant perception may well deepen his isolation and self-disgust. An old person without the support and gratitude of family or followers may have great difficulty seeing time in suprapersonal terms and consequently feel overwhelmed by the significance of the end of their personal time. For these reasons, social isolation in old age is particularly tragic for the issei.

A Note on Disengagement. Much attention in American social gerontology has been devoted to the disengagement theory of aging developed by Cumming and Henry (1961). In essence the theory was put forward to explain research findings that did not fit with the common American notion that old people continue to want the same level of social involvement that characterizes their middle age. Cumming and Henry find that among older people living in Kansas City the withdrawal of psychological energy and affect from social relations often accompanies the gradual decline in social activity and loss of social roles found among the elderly. They hypothesize that a mutual disengagement of individual and society in old age is normal and even desirable. Later work like that of Havighurst, Neugarten, and Tobin (1968) questions whether disengagement is the best way for people to grow old or simply an aberration of our era and culture to which many people are subjected whether they like it or not. The large literature on the subject of disengagement indicates that it interests many scholars. For this reason I want to comment on its relevance to the issei.

First, neither the level of social activity nor that of psychological involvement found among the physically healthy issei shows a process of disengagement. Most issei spend a great deal of time interacting with a variety of other people and are extremely interested in maintaining this activity. The fact that they see the same dozen or so people day after day or that the range of cultural background represented by their consociates may be quite narrow is probably a lifelong characteristic of their social life. Second, the psychological process of disengagement requires a perception of one's self as fundamentally distinct from one's social roles—a perception that is alien to the issei. Behind the Westerner's perception of himself as purposefully engaged in and thus potentially disengaged from his intimate social relations lies a long history of philosophic individualism and a personal biography that includes early independence training and the self-conscious acquisition and dismantling of many relationships. What is continuous about the Westerner's self-feelings is the stream of sensations, moods, and ideas that he feels originate inside his own skin. The issei, however, cannot disengage from his social roles because he is those roles. He feels that his stream of sensations, moods, and ideas is a product of the harmonious or disharmonious quality of his relations with the social and natural world. As I have written elsewhere (Kiefer, 1971), the issei resemble a very large sector of humanity in this respect.

The Nisei

If the developmental task of the issei can be said to be preserving harmonious order based on traditional values, the task of the nisei is constructing a new developmental map out of fragments of two cultures. This task is monumental—in fact, the personal rigors of accomplishing it go far in explaining the single most salient characteristic of nisei personality: their grim determination to achieve a comfortable level of wealth and prestige. The immensity of the nisei's problem and its central importance to the topic of adult personality development becomes clear if we again juxtapose basic characteristics of the Japanese and the American value systems. The American ethic of competitive self-reliance and respect for the individual often runs directly counter to the Japanese ethic of social harmony and stability through the merging of individual and group. Moreover, simply having to adjust to two different cultures puts a serious strain on the ethic of harmony itself. The situation amounts to a psychological knot: The more perplexing grows the problem of reconciling harmony and individuality, the more elusive grows the desired harmony.

Developmental change compounds the problem in various ways. As I said in Chapter Three, the socializing influences and their specific cultural contents shift as the person adopts new roles and loses old ones. Many compromises between the two cultures become uncomfortable and must be revised. As the first Japanese American generation to have the problem of adapting to two cultures, the nisei find precious few models that might serve as examples for each stage of their lives, and they are constantly facing uncharted developmental territory. Moreover, the weight of personal developmental decisions is usually cumulative. The young have the freedom to make mistakes and defer decisions because they have time ahead of them

ısibilities for others. As the time be-
ı grows shorter and the effects of earli-
ıns add up, this freedom melts away.
ıl compromises becomes more acute as
ıkes a mistake in middle age, life might
ɔrrect it. Previous decisions have closed
ılity (see Becker, 1960). For example,
isei who has a grown child with plural-
ıght be attracted by his child's views,
ɔ adopt them easily. Having sired a
rtgage and a new car loan, he must
keep up his income. Having elected to be, let us say, a lawyer,
he is unqualified to be a community organizer, minister, or social worker. Having built up a clientele, he cannot choose his
friends, hobbies, or political views on a whim. Either he is stuck
with his present ethnic identity, he faces changes of dizzying
proportions, or he must live with inner conflict.

With this in mind, let us turn to some acculturative problems—the *Protestant ethic syndrome, mother-guilt, masculinity
and feminity,* and *body concern*—that appear to bother a large
number of nisei, partly by reason of the developmental tasks
which their generation now faces. The problems may have been
solved at earlier stages of development only to become problems again by the social and physical demands of middle age.

The Protestant Ethic Syndrome. When the nisei were
young, it appeared to most of them, though not always consciously, that certain values were widely accepted in both cultures and could therefore be pursued safely and with relatively
little conflict. These values, known as the Protestant ethic
syndrome, were material success, education, cleanliness, honesty, hard work, sobriety, and politeness. The current developmental tasks of the nisei must be understood in the light of this
set of goals, chosen early in their lives and gradually dignified
by the passage of time. We must also consider the irony that the
same years whose passage bound the nisei to their precarious
course also witnessed the erosion of the same values among the
educated classes in America to make way for a more aesthetic,
socially conscious, and self-expressive ethos.

Although the conflict generated by the Protestant ethic syndrome between the nisei and the sansei does not often lead to direct confrontations between nisei parents and their children, its subtle presence is a personal concern in both generations. Sansei accusations that the nisei are competitive, flashy, and devoted to a spiritually shallow materialism are sure to echo in their parents' minds the injunctions from the issei to strive for harmony through cooperation, to be modest and frugal, and to place human values above material ones. The fact that the nisei now have adult children whose ethics resemble those of the issei in some ways more than those of the nisei has reopened an acculturative wound that had been partly forgotten. The problem of nisei-sansei conflict over materialistic versus spiritual values is compounded by two other developmental events: the economic independence of their children, and the approach of retirement. When the children were at home, the nisei took the very sound position that their own values rested on the necessity of providing well for the family; now, many are having to revise either the values or the justification. The onset of retirement means that work for profit can no longer serve as the keystone uniting a dual cultural identity. The younger Mr. Uchida struggled hard to succeed as an architect and now has a large, expensively furnished home in a neighborhood that is best described as sedate. But there is a newly acquired Japanese flair to his life style, and he seems almost embarrassed by his prosperity: "As far as material things are concerned, we have a '56 station wagon and a '57 Volkswagen, and that's about the sum of it. As far as values are concerned, I suppose we want enough to—I guess that's the important thing—make enough to— Oh, what? We don't aspire to having a boat or a second home or go on trips abroad." Mr. Kawada, the restaurateur (who owns a second home), feels that his life has become easier since he gave up trying to become wealthy:

Interviewer: *What do you feel is the best way to get along in life?*

Mr. Kawada: *First of all, try not to set too high of a goal. Try to do a good job at what you do do. A lot of people set unobtainable goals for themselves, and it makes them unhappy.*

It may not be too hard to disparage material success once one has achieved it, but to shrug off the habit of self-denial and the rigidly task-oriented approach to life is another matter. Observers of the California nisei have almost unanimously recognized their emotional flatness and lack of insight, which I discussed in Chapter Five under the concept of the guarded self. This technique for avoiding conscious identity conflict fits in well with the Protestant ethic syndrome because it makes the nisei frugal, reliable, highly rational, and hard-working as business colleagues and employees.

We have already discussed the sansei challenge to their parents' adaptive habit of self-denial. Self-denial is likely to create other problems as a life style when the nisei retire. Many nisei women whose children have left home find themselves with oceans of free time and realize that they have never learned how to enjoy leisure. Goals of self-expression through creative careers—goals which had gathered dust along with other daydreams in the attic of the spirit for decades—begin to press again for recognition and resolution. But for most nisei, the habit of self-denial appears for the moment to carry enough inertia that these goals remain a wistful fantasy. Mrs. Kofuku, for instance, is a pleasant and highly intelligent forty-three-year-old nisei mother. Her oldest child is just leaving home, her youngest is ten. Although she has been satisfied with her life so far, she has begun to feel that something is missing. She says that her "personality hasn't changed much" since she was in relocation camp. She has a college degree, but when asked whether she would like to revise her life, she says, "I don't think I'm well enough educated." And when asked to name some accomplishment that made her proud, she has to go all the way back to her high school graduation: "I was at the top of my class, and received many scholarships. [My father] was so happy and so proud." Throughout her interviews, a subtle sense of stagnation haunts her perception of herself. She is concerned about "having an interest" when she gets old.

Mrs. Kindaichi, however, is struggling toward a sense of growth. She says she is more outspoken than before, because of a Caucasian friend who "gave me a good kick and got me going" (see Chapter Five). She sees the fledging of her children as an opportunity to develop still further: "There's lots of times when the kids are young you keep quiet for the sake of the family, just give up a point. Later on, when you get the chance, you express yourself. I don't think that's good, but that's the way it went. [My husband and I] are in a new phase, where the kids are grown." The great difficulty of finding new goals and new techniques for self-expression for themselves may help to explain the permissive attitude the nisei have toward their children. Given the dedication to parental roles typical of the nisei as a group, one suspects that many nisei are searching for liberation vicariously, through the sansei. This suspicion raises an important question for the future: Will the nisei be able to relinquish their parental roles when it becomes necessary for their mental and spiritual health? As we shall see, this question is one of the more important developmental problems of the sansei.

I close the discussion of the Protestant ethic syndrome with quotes from an interview with a Buddhist minister, a man whose profession represents the spiritual values of traditional Japanese culture (Omatsu, 1973):

The only group that [Reverend X] is worried about is the middle-aged nisei, who he thinks will experience an acute spiritual crisis as they grow older and face the inevitability of death.

"People who don't struggle to seek don't have a chance to find out meaning in life," Reverend [X] believes. He says that he has had a hard time talking with the nisei generation about matters such as death because they have not struggled with spiritual questions enough. Explaining this point in detail, he notes: "As history shows, the issei had to work to support their families, nothing but work. The nisei were educated by the issei to build up their lives the same as the [white] people. So you see the majority of nisei people out to buy cars and homes. They don't think about spiritual matters."

The minister is probably right about the spiritual crisis facing the nisei. My analysis suggests that nisei materialism started out as a tentative solution to a very difficult spiritual problem, that is, the problem of how to integrate Japanese and American values. This solution has precipitated a new problem in the course of history and personal development.

Mother-guilt. Guilt is something that everybody would like to be rid of, since it is an unpleasant sensation at best. But it would be hard to conceive of a human society in which guilt does not play an important part. We are often motivated to help each other out of the fear of guilt, and our actions are just as socially beneficial as if they had been motivated by pure altruism. In discussing the problem of companionship for the issei, I noted that nisei often feel guilty about conflict with their mothers. Given the typical childhood experience of the nisei, guilt toward the mother has probably been a strong feature of their personalities throughout life. The Japanese technique of socializing children includes an extremely close bond between mother and child and an attitude of passive suffering on the mother's part when the child misbehaves (Kiefer, 1970). The bond is based on close physical contact and a relative absence of independence training, so that the child's self-concept and sense of well-being are closely tied to his perceptions of his mother. This technique for socialization works extremely well. The child learns at an early age that misbehavior hurts his mother, and his close identification with her makes the hurt intolerable to himself. This dynamic is reinforced by the mother's total dedication to the well-being of her family at the sacrifice of her own comfort.

The dramatic quality of maternal self-sacrifice might best be illustrated by the role of the mother in preparing and serving food. Kitagawa is aware of the tremendous significance of family meals in the Japanese American culture: "The family table, under normal circumstances, is an institution around which the life of the family as a unit is centered. It is where children 'eat and drink' their parents' love and care for them, as materially symbolized in the meals earned by the father and prepared by the mother. Even in a completely secularized family, the family table is a sacrament of parental love for children and of the intrinsic unity and solidarity of the family" (1967, p. 86). The dramatic quality of family meals is underscored by the fact that many nisei remember them more vividly than any other aspect of their childhood. They remember their father's stern enforcement of order and quiet and his admonitions against wastefulness. They remember early feelings of ethnic self-consciousness over the kind of food they ate. But mostly they remember that their mother served their father first, then the children, and that she often spent the entire mealtime on her feet, serving and cooking. Many mothers would not eat until everyone else had his fill. If there was nothing left, they would go hungry or prepare themselves a bit of some inferior food. The fact that such scenes were absent in the relocation camps probably functioned to increase rather than decrease nisei guilt, since many must have perceived their flight from the family table as taking advantage of a situation that caused their parents to suffer. Even now, many nisei associate fundamental feelings of gratification —receiving warmth or love, being filled with pleasant sensation as with good food—with the image of their mother cheerfully slaving over a hot stove.

Hurting one's mother, then, is a formidable consideration in relationships between issei and nisei. The quality and intensity of guilt feelings associated with hurting change along with the structure of the relationships. For example, nisei women perceive issei-nisei relations in a more positive light than men do, and the guilt that stalks the mother-son relationship is relatively absent when both sexes of both generations are interacting. Nisei women generally spend more time interacting with their mothers and mothers-in-law than nisei men do, but the men carry a greater share of the responsibility for decisions affecting the aged. Given the need of dependent issei women for material and emotional support and the greater role of nisei women in providing that support, we would expect to find that feelings of guilt toward the mother are less noticeable in nisei women than in men, and in fact the TAT responses support this expectation. More nisei men's stories than women's stories in-

clude themes of guilt when the characters perceived are elderly women.

What are the effects of mother-guilt on the behavior of
nisei? Guilt almost certainly contributes to the sense of duty
that many nisei feel toward their aged parents. It may also help
to explain some of the anxiety that many nisei feel about their
own adequacy. Guilt probably has a lot to do with the very
strong desire to compete and to achieve economic wealth that
most nisei seem to have. Issei mothers often mention their children's achievements as an important source of satisfaction in
their own lives. What could be more natural for a nisei than to
feel that his success expunges his sense of guilt toward his mother? Hard work and thrift not only satisfy American and Japanese norms (America is a guilt-ridden culture, too), they can
also be perceived as self-punishment. Women have an advantage
over men in this respect. The nisei mother can work off her
guilt by the same self-sacrifice for her own children that her
mother showed for her. The situation is more difficult for men.
In Japan a guilt-instilling childhood is followed by an adulthood
during which a man is expected to be obedient and extremely
respectful to his mother. American norms label such adult behavior immature and require an autonomy that may cause conflict in the nisei, as Caudill (1952) notes. Big trouble comes to
both sexes, therefore, with the arrival of financial security, their
own retirement, the independence of their children, or the
death of their parents—and thus the end of the need to achieve.
If mother-guilt has not been resolved by this time, the nisei
must find new outlets for their altruism and salve for their con-
sciences or suffer more self-doubts.

Masculinity and Femininity. The developmental tasks of
autonomy and productivity are thoroughly conditioned by sex
roles, which are in turn limited by cultural tradition. The ideals
of masculinity and femininity that the issei held up to their children were traditionally Japanese for the most part. The masculine ideal required the maintenance of dignity through perfect
control of the emotions. Physical toughness, courage, rationality, circumspection and reserve in dealings with others, and a
definite disdain for the "weakness" of women and children

were part of the pattern. A good man was educated and world-
ly-wise. The model of femininity incorporated all the characteristics of motherhood discussed here. Although special categories
of women in Japan, such as merchants and geisha, were traditionally exempt from conforming to the mainstream feminine
model, for most women it called for shyness and reserve outside
the home and patient dedication to the family inside it, marriage being taken for granted. Emotional volatility and natural
lustfulness, while not necessarily part of the ideal, were associated with the Japanese feminine identity.

The traditional sexual ideals might pass today as common
old-fashioned American sex roles if it weren't for certain Japanese assumptions about relationships between the sexes. Since
the clearly defined, autonomous ego is nurtured neither in the
growing child nor in the adult, Japanese men and women typically require intensive support from each other in a way that
Americans generally look upon as immature. The Japanese male
is likely to suffer serious feelings of inadequacy if his wife fails
to reassure him constantly of his status in the family by taking
an indulgent and subservient attitude toward him, as the cultural norm demands. Women also depend heavily on the approval of their husbands, although their identification with their
children makes the problem of support less critical for them.
American norms for the relations between men and women conflict with Japanese ideals in a number of subtle ways. First, by
granting more autonomy and equality to women, the American
norms undermine an important source of male self-esteem and
at the same time create some sexual identity confusion among
nisei women. Second, by favoring an image of masculinity
which is more overtly aggressive, autonomous, and outgoing
than the Japanese ideal, American culture challenges nisei male
identity still further. Nisei men have a hard time competing
with Caucasians for jobs that require aggressiveness and are by
the same token at a disadvantage when competing for the affec-
tions of women.

A nisei couple, presented with multiple challenges to
their sexual identities, may have several difficulties. The wife
might work extra hard at supporting her husband's ego in the

Japanese style, meanwhile chafing under the comparison of her role with that of a more Americanized woman. Or, the wife might herself adopt the American view that she is at least her husband's equal if not his superior in some respects, leading to a vicious circle in which his frustrated need for ego supports gradually weakens him while she takes his increasing passivity and withdrawal as justification for greater and greater indifference or contempt. An underlying difficulty is that some nisei women were required by their parents to marry nisei men, even though they felt poorly adjusted to such a marriage. A middle-aged nisei man who faces waning physical prowess and, possibly, receding career goals can seldom handle these difficulties easily. He may try to defend his sexual identity by acting tyrannically toward his wife and children or by spending every spare minute in male-dominated activities outside the home—such as sports, cards, or wenching—where his masculinity is not seriously challenged. The sexual maturing of their children can also inflame such sexual identity problems. Parents see their children facing many of the challenges that they themselves face and feel with a new poignancy the need for personal solutions. Some intergenerational conflict over sexuality may result from nisei anxiety over sexual identity. Such conflicts are invariably passed on to the children of the principals in one way or another. This is not to say, however, that all nisei suffer from sexual identity problems, or that male peer group activities function mainly to bolster the sagging masculinity of the participants.

Body Concern. In American society, as in any other, attitudes toward physical illness and weakness are closely linked with attitudes toward dependency in general. American women tend to be hypochondriacal, probably because they feel guilty about asking for attention and tenderness in more direct ways. American men, however, have such a horror of dependency in any form that if they can admit their physical weaknesses at all, they can do so only when the need is urgent. Outwardly the nisei resemble other Americans in this respect. Women are more outspoken than men about their physical ailments, and men tend to deny physical problems at first (Syme, 1973). However, there is something unique about the way the nisei perceive their bodies. They are unusually given to joking about the signs of aging, both in themselves and in their friends. Their year-round passion for team sports and the importance of such events as the annual Nisei Olympics show a preoccupation with fitness. In the interviews, nisei men seemed more inclined than their Caucasian counterparts to dwell on physical problems once they have come to light. I compared the TAT responses of my nine nisei men with those of fifteen Caucasian men of about the same age as the nisei. I found as I had expected that the nisei mentioned health and physical characteristics in their stories much more often than the Caucasians did and that the nisei's physical preoccupations were more often with illness or fatigue. The underlying concern with health among the nisei is noted by Caudill (1952). Caudill says that the combination of a strict cultural taboo against interpersonal violence and aggressiveness coupled with the absence of traditional Japanese outlets for sensual enjoyment led to hypocondriasis among the nisei. That is, most nisei have acquired the habit of taking out their normal anger and frustration on themselves in the form of psychosomatic discomforts rather than confronting the external source of their difficulty. Although this behavior seems to be equally evident in Japan, there the individual is likely to be on better terms with his body because there are many ways that he can express his needs for physical care and comfort. Sickness and drunkenness are legitimate reasons for seeking physical nurture, and the healthy person has access to an elaborate cultural repertoire of bathing, massage, and so on. A similar interpretation is suggested by Doi (1973). Doi views a certain need for nurture, or "passive object love," as the basis for much of Japanese culture. Without the many culturally approved channels for getting the nurture he is conditioned to want, the typical Japanese as Doi presents him would be in an almost continuous state of frustration, which would be likely to show up as psychosomatic ills.

The average nisei is probably much better adapted psychologically to life in the United States than the average Japanese would be. In fact, I have no data indicating that nisei are actually sicker than non-Japanese. It is possible that the latent hypocondriasis of the nisei is simply a greater awareness and acceptance of their own bodies than Caucasians have. So-called psychosomatic disorders (an idea which presupposes the typically Western dichotomy between mind and body) are frequent enough in the American population. Perhaps the difference between the ways nisei and Caucasians talk about health can be explained by the idea that illness is a subject too threatening to a typical Caucasian to even appear in his waking fantasies.

Depending on the interpretation of nisei concern with health and vigor there are two possible prognoses for the generation as it ages. If the nisei are interpreted as hypocondriacs suffering from cultural conflict between their need for nurture and their desire for autonomy, they risk psychosomatic illness or chronic depression from feelings of physical deterioration. If body awareness—something Caucasians lack—is interpreted as an extra in the nisei's cultural tool kit, aging might turn out to be easier for them than for non-Japanese Americans. Perhaps each interpretation has limited applicability.

In the Japanese American culture, one often hears references to the issei as pioneers, which indeed they were. They confronted a wilderness of prejudice and economic hardship and carved from it clearings that would support themselves and their families. The nisei, however, have forged onward from those clearings to explore a whole new cultural horizon. It is a horizon which constantly changes as the nisei age, requiring new trails and new bridges. The nisei are pioneers too, now facing a culturally uncharted wilderness of old age. Being nisei is probably both a help and a hindrance in the task ahead. Had they lost their cultural identity as a group, they would have to rely exclusively on non-Japanese models of the developmental territory or seek purely personal ones. Their range of choices would have been restricted, though sometimes to their benefit. However, the solidarity of the nisei as an ethnic community and their close communication and mutual support probably save them from much of the alienation felt by most people facing their later years in a highly mobile and rapidly changing society.

The Sansei

In his popular book *Future Shock,* Alvin Toffler claims that Americans in the mid-twentieth century are suffering grievously from a hypertrophy of choices—there is so much available abundance in our environment that our brains short-circuit when a choice must be made. In my view this is a useful idea, but it applies more to youth than to the middle-aged, more to the well-educated urbanite than the rural bumpkin, and of course more to the affluent than to the poor. Being predominantly young, well-educated, urban, and affluent, the sansei might be understood as victims of abundance. They are thoroughly attuned to the American culture of the 1970s—perhaps more so than European Americans a generation older—and they are in a position to take what the culture offers. Given the emphasis on academic and professional achievement in the Japanese American culture, this advantage already poses a weighty developmental problem for the sansei. As young people, their developmental task is to find an adult identity. They must discover and develop their talents, they must sever their dependence on their parents, they must form intimate social ties outside their families, and they must find socially acceptable outlets for their vast energy. In many cases they must resolve acculturative dilemmas handed down by their parents and come to grips with their feelings of estrangement as people with Asian faces in an overwhelmingly non-Asian society. The complexity of these tasks in an era of overabundance is hard to imagine.

The combined effects of history, acculturation, and personal development are for purposes of description a particular set of characteristics with a particular distribution in the sansei personality. These characteristics are: *autonomy conflict,* the *war of the sexes,* and *lost aggression.* These labels are a convenient means of referring to the effects of the processes of acculturation and development and are not strictly isolable traits. This discussion is an attempt to describe complex patterns, not construct theory.

Autonomy Conflict. We are by now familiar with the different perceptions of what makes up a person and a person's relationship to society in both Japanese and American culture. Such characteristic perceptions are crucial to the developmental tasks of youth. As people grow, they acquire habits, responsibilities, skills, memories, and material baggage that help to solidify and anchor the boundaries of the self. The boundaries are never really fixed, but a person hopes that the amount of work that goes into revising them will gradually diminish. Adolescence and young adulthood are times of comparative flexibility of these boundaries. The kind and degree of anxiety a young person experiences while growing up depends partly on the perceived inconsistencies and discontinuities—the gaps and rough spots—in his progress toward an adult identity. For the sansei, cultural conflict over autonomy is a great jagged hole in the path. A typical sansei needs guidance in settling on a self-concept, and yet his many socializers give him conflicting messages about his responsibilities to himself and to others. How long should he remain economically dependent on his parents? Under what circumstances must he speak his mind or keep quiet? Which of his desires and interests should be cultivated and which should be suppressed? The answers to such questions are hard enough in any complex society (this is one reason why adolescents in such societies are so susceptible to fanatic dogmas), but where two fundamentally conflicting self-concepts are at hand, the problem can become desperate.

Because the key cultural difference between these self-concepts has to do with one's relationships with other people, especially one's intimates, the observer finds in the sansei pervasive concern over the issue of autonomy versus dependence. The issue appears in many aspects of their behavior, expressed in many ways: personal freedom versus conformity and security, development versus stagnation, aggression versus docility, artistic or intellectual achievement versus economic or domestic achievement, career versus marriage, sexuality versus inhibition. Sometimes the conflict over autonomy is clearly felt, as in the case of Miss Bijin (age twenty). Asked to name the hardest thing she has had to face in the last five years, she says: "One thing that comes to mind is that I'm [still too] close to my family. I think part of it is because I'm a girl. Girls are generally closer.

Guys usually get out sooner. My brother has had more breaks, so I'm closer. [My parents] are hanging on. This drawing away process is necessary, but it will be hard. I really appreciate what they've done, but I know I'll never be an individual if I don't do things on my own."

More often, conflict over autonomy comes out as a more diffuse anxiety over one's ability to behave purposefully and independently. The sixteen-year-old Mr. Kawada, son of the restaurateur, says repeatedly that it is hard for him to make decisions:

Interviewer: *Is there anything that you're afraid of now?*
Mr. K: *Ahh, well. Let's see. Well, ahh, being afraid of— everybody's afraid of getting killed or dying. Right now? I guess passing in school and failing a test comes to mind. [Pause.] You can be afraid of not making the right decision at the right time.*

Mr. Kawada also says that the hardest thing to face in the last few years was deciding how to spend a large sum of money he'd saved. He also seems to feel guilty about his dependence on his parents: "Maybe I've been spoiled too much. I've gotten too much of what I wanted. I've gotten away with a lot that maybe I shouldn't have." The overall tone of his interview indicates that he is struggling against passivity. The interview as a whole is very difficult for him, because it forces him to objectify himself —to make decisions about what he really thinks.

Internal conflicts that nisei parents have about their own identities often complicate the difficulty of sansei autonomy. Many sansei complain that they get mixed messages from their parents about self-reliance. For example, they are told to obey teachers and other authorities, but they also learn from their parents' attitudes that the same authorities can't be trusted unless they are Japanese Americans. They are urged to distinguish themselves academically, but they are encouraged to forgo the authority that accompanies such distinction.

The problem of autonomy conflict appears to be more open among sansei women than men. Thus, for example, there is more disturbed behavior evident on the part of women. They act out their conflict by dating and sometimes marrying men their parents strongly disapprove of, by arguing violently with their parents (especially their mothers), and by taking drugs. In Los Angeles County, where the drug problem among young Japanese Americans is the most serious, a community volunteer organization reported in 1971 that twice as many girls as boys had to be treated for drug overdoses the previous year. Moreover, the women are more articulate about the autonomy problem than the men are and spend more time talking about it. Many sansei women's interviews showed a real need for sympathy and understanding concerning identity conflict. The respondents often actively sought the interviewer's support and approval, in contrast to the men, who generally showed a take-it-or-leave-it attitude.

The reasons for this important sex difference are complex. Clearly young women are much more restricted than young men in the Japanese American culture in terms of what they are allowed to do while under their parents' guidance, what life goals are considered legitimate for them, and how they are allowed to express themselves. The difference, in other words, between mid-twentieth-century American urban middle-class norms and Japanese American norms for the autonomy of women is greater than the difference between the norms for men. As a result, the inner conflict for Japanese American women is greater. This problem is magnified in a peculiar way by the overabundance of choice. The rate of change of women's roles has been greater than that of men's roles in the last few years; consequently a young woman faces more ambiguity about what she can, can't, must, and mustn't do. She must now consider many alternatives that were until recently out of the question. The range of new alternatives is even greater for Japanese American women because both their looks and their manners resemble sufficiently European American ideals of femininity and enable them to compete economically and sexually with non-Japanese women. The range of choices open to sansei men is more restricted because they face a higher degree of subtle discrimination in both areas. Their range of choice of education and career and of marriage partner, for example, is more clearly defined

than that of their sisters. However, sansei women do not therefore suffer more than men over autonomy conflict. Because
men are expected to be more decisive and self-controlled than
women, the nagging feeling of doubt about one's ability to as-
sert, to decide, and to stand alone that plagues many sansei men
must be threatening to their masculine identities.

The War of the Sexes. The problem of finding an adult
identity is further complicated for many sansei by cultural differences in sex role definitions such as those mentioned above.
For sansei women, the difficulty is to find a comfortable way of
relating to men. Many nisei mothers have had great difficulty in
this area also because of conflicting cultural sex norms and because they were coerced into marrying nisei. Unconsciously, for
the most part, such women resent the circumstances of their
marriages and convey the idea to their daughters that men in
general and Japanese American men in particular are less than
ideal partners. This theme shows up in sansei women's TAT
stories, where men are frequently portrayed as unreliable and
weak or self-centered and manipulative. Many young sansei
women do not want the sort of feminine role their mothers had,
and they see an opportunity to escape from it by either marrying outside their ethnic group or not marrying at all. Most often
neither of these solutions is acceptable to the nisei. Grandpar-
enthood is a career goal for the typical nisei mother, and she
subtly pressures her daughters to get married. Whereas the rate
of interracial marriage has risen sharply in recent years, most
nisei would still prefer to see their children marry a Japanese
American.

Of course, not all sansei women are bent on avoiding marriage to a sansei man. Many think of such a match not only as
the proper thing to do, but also as the most desirable. They may
recognize that intraethnic marriages are unusually stable and
that the children of such marriages have a good chance of turning out to be high achievers and having fewer identity problems
than children of mixed marriages. Some sansei men also prefer
to date and marry interracially. But even the sansei man who
intends to marry a sansei may have his work cut out for him. He
is likely to perceive that he is at a disadvantage in competing

with non-Japanese men. Roughly twice as many Japanese American men as women marry within their ethnic group, because
women are better able to compete for outside mates. How a
sansei man responds to the situation depends on how he feels
about himself and his ethnic group. If his feelings of self-worth
are already wobbling under the pressure of autonomy conflict,
he is likely to see it as further evidence that he is not as masculine as other men. This lack of self-confidence will show in his
behavior, which in turn will be considered unmasculine by some
of his peers, and so on in a vicious circle. The Japanese American culture encourages men to compensate for such self-doubts
through academic, athletic, and economic achievement.

Lost Aggression. Giving orders, making decisions, and
having possessions are all forms of power that people typically
crave at one time or another. In American society, power is supposed to be doled out on the basis of competitive achievement;
everyone is supposed to have an equal shot at it. If such reward
is not forthcoming as a result of culturally prescribed effort and
self-sacrifice, a person may believe that his effort and ability are
not being recognized, and this belief in turn leads to feelings of
aggression. Adolescents and young adults in our society must
pay particular attention to the way they handle such aggression,
because they are developing an adult sense of themselves. They
are participating in adult roles where performance is measured
in terms of power, and yet their elders are typically loath to
recognize their claims.

In Japanese American culture, the problem of aggression
is complicated by the emphasis on harmony. The outward display of aggression is considered immoral, childish, or both under most circumstances. The traditional Japanese ideal is simply
not to have aggressive feelings; failing that, one is at least supposed to keep them to himself. Even though this ideal carries
less weight than it used to, many sansei men still have difficulty
recognizing and dealing with their aggressive feelings. Part of the
problem is that Japanese and American standards of aggression
have not been thoroughly integrated in the nisei personality.
Nisei parents expect their children to compete and achieve, and
yet they also expect them to be self-effacing, patient, and obe-

dient. They expect their children to be honest, but not when it comes to expressing their feelings. The relative strength of an individuated identity (Chapters Four and Six) among the sansei leads them to recognize this contradiction.

Among sansei men there are several styles of handling aggression. Some, the more energetic and emotionally positive, find indirect ways of expressing aggression that are acceptable to them, especially through wit and humor. Mr. Chikai and Jack Morita (Chapter Five) are examples of this type. Others find less constructive, indirect means of expression. Some social activists are motivated in part by the need to express pent-up hostility through displacement, or scapegoating. However, a great deal of aggression is simply repressed, being too threatening to handle overtly. The TAT stories of the sansei men who have not discovered direct means of expression show an unconscious preoccupation with self-assertion coupled with feelings of guilt. In the following example nineteen-year-old Mr. Kimura first addresses the picture of the elderly man and the young man, the father-son card, by making the figures equals, engaged in engineering, his own specialty. This fairly competitive story, however, is too uncomfortable for the teller, and he shifts to one in which the son is the unhappy subordinate in a line of work similar to that of the teller's actual father. Finally, the son attacks the father passively—by failing.

Subject: *Gee, these people aren't smiling either. [Chuckles] Okay, these two guys are business associates. And, uh, they have a fairly large company, they manufacture all sorts of things —it's a diversified company. They make, uh, oh parts for all kinds of aeronautical stuff. These two guys are two big bosses. And, uh, things have fallen down recently in the electronics business and they're kind of thinking about what they're going to do. One guy doesn't look too happy. And, uh—can I change that, the whole story?*

Interviewer: *Yes.*

Subject: *Yeah, now I see it. An older man and a younger man, so I'll call it father and son. And, um, yeah, they're in business together. And the father started the company and the son is working under him, and eventually he'll be the head of the company. And, uh, they still manufacture things and, uh, and not electronics parts or aeronautical parts because I can't see a father and son working like that together. So I'll say they work together making, uh, household goods. And the father says that when he retires he'll have to keep the reputation of the company up. But, uh, the son looks like, you know, he kind of doesn't seem too interested at the moment in what his father's saying, so I think eventually the company will sell out to another one. Even though they're one of the largest ones, their production rate will fall down and the son will be working for someone else, or else he'll just quit and become a bum. [Laughs.] That's all for that one.*

Mr. Misono, an eighteen-year-old sansei, registered with his draft board as a conscientious objector. This act took a lot of courage and hard work, and he seemed to be entirely sincere in his objection to violence of any kind. Mr. Misono had great difficulty relating to his father, a successful businessman who took frequent trips to Japan leaving his wife and children behind. He was preoccupied with the problem of aggression, and he divided the world into two spheres, victims and aggressors. The victim sphere was represented by nature, femininity, and spiritual and religious values. The aggressor sphere was represented by technology, masculinity, and economic and political values. He talked of the capitalists raping Mother Nature, and used other sexual metaphors for political processes. He was in the habit of getting up in the middle of the night to ride his bicycle through the streets of San Francisco's downtown financial district—an activity that elated him. He had few close friends, but his closest ally and confidant was a Catholic priest; this relationship was an unconscious compromise between the masculine-aggressor and the feminine-victim spheres. The most interesting thing about this sansei man was that he appeared, in spite of a very keen intelligence, to be completely unaware of the aggressor-victim symbolism that strongly influenced his political convictions.

For sansei women, the problem of aggression is more

Chapter IX

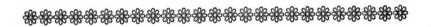

Conclusions and Implications

Let us not forget when we make claims about the advancement of knowledge that we are defining knowledge as the appropriateness of a certain way of talking about things and not as a step along some path toward perfect wisdom. Since several millennia of philosophic effort have failed to bring us closer to such an ideal, any work like this book must be judged according to its usefulness or beauty. I have two views of the usefulness of social science. For one, I see it as a formal art, like music or

230

poetry—a form of communication cherished by a small group of people who find personal satisfaction in the contemplation of its highly specialized rules and who are blessed with the freedom to indulge their taste. For another, I see it as a technique for putting the symbolically codified concerns of daily life into new combinations that can stimulate new activities on the part of almost anybody—again, like what we usually call the arts. Since man's actions and perceptions are at the mercy of his way of talking about things, a review of his grammar and vocabulary can often make him feel better. In this spirit I will now discuss this book as a contribution to the advancement of knowledge, although I do not insist that others draw the same conclusions. I begin by examining the ethnography of adult development and aging as a form of consciousness, and then summarize my findings concerning Japan Town.

Ethnography is the study of the patterned meanings attached to behavior in groups. It associates shared meanings with their contexts, and therefore concentrates on human interaction processes. When ethnography is applied to the study of adult personality development and aging, it requires a view of the person as a role player in varying situations, using multiple strategies to attain his goals. It often leads to the view that the maintenance of certain kinds of interaction is itself a high priority goal, and that the meanings shared in specific interactions can supersede or even replace meanings prevalent in participants' other interactions. Because of this, the ethnographic approach to personality study encourages the view that personal goals, attitudes, and perceptions—including perceptions of the self— can vary markedly over short periods. In a complex urban environment, where people move daily between groups with quite different shared meanings, the ethnographer perceives personality as quite naturally and easily flexible. Personality may be called the style in which the individual adjusts his needs and habits to fit the many immediate social and physical facts of his environment. Personal development is then nothing other than the cumulative, irreversible changes that history and personal development bring to contextual adaptation. Important people enter the individual's life, grow, and leave; his capabilities and quirks develop, flourish, and atrophy; history shifts the scenery around him. Some of these changes are radical and require the development of new skills or the overhaul of parts of the environment; but even so, radical personality change is rare. One gains respect for the characteristic adaptability of the individual.

As a style of thinking about personality development, ethnography draws attention to the fact that people seem generally unaware of their chameleon-like flexibility. They have identities, and they see themselves as solid and continuous. When a sudden change in the environment or the continuous presence of contradictory demands threaten this sense of wholeness, the individual suffers intense anxiety. Sane people appear to prefer even a degraded whole identity to a confused or inconsistent one, as Spradley (1970) has shown in the case of Skid Row tramps. To the urban ethnographer, a large part of the problem of adaptation is maintaining the illusion of inner consistency amid the facts of change. This view is different from the implicitly psychoanalytic one that pervades much of developmental literature, in which the problem is seen as the overcoming of rigidities of style laid down early in life. These two points of view, moreover, lead to different therapeutic emphases. The ethnographic model of the plastic personality emphasizes helping the individual maintain his sense of consistency while employing adaptive skills of which he already has a large repertoire. The psychoanalytic model emphasizes loosening the self-concept so that new adaptive skills can be taught. The best therapeutic strategy probably results from a mixture of these two points of view.

I have suggested in this book some of the ways people maintain the illusion of inner continuity and consistency. For one thing, people construct and reconstruct their biographies and their histories, explaining to themselves and others in the process how they came to be who they are. This process appears to be largely unconscious and haphazard in most people most of the time. It is stimulated by the discontinuities in one's environment, and, depending on the individual's education and belief system, it takes the forms of folklore, religious cosmology, historicism, or private introspection. For another thing, people develop strategies for protecting their self-feelings from too much dissonant input. They surround themselves with others who support their self-disclosures and vocabularies of motive through ethnic, occupational, familial, regional, political, religious, linguistic, and social class separatism; and they learn and adopt the vocabularies of motive of the diverse groups and settings in which participation is important to them. Furthermore, most people make at least a little effort to anticipate and prepare for the future stages of their lives. In relatively stable societies, there tends to be a well-developed lore at hand for this task, but in more unsettled ones the task can become hopelessly difficult.

Another important result of the ethnographic perspective is the view that different sociocultural milieux present very different problems and resources to the person struggling to maintain a workable identity and that consequently very different strategies may be called for in different societies at different stages. Identity maintenance is crucially affected by the number, variety, size, power, accessibility, moral rigidity, homogeneity, and permanence of reference groups in a person's milieu—as well as the changes in all these factors over the life cycle—and by the moral content of the meaning systems and roles that are important to him. I have tried to show how, for instance, introspectiveness and individuation might adapt people to some stages of life in some societies but become detriments to functioning at other times and places. Again, learning how to assimilate and use many value systems interchangeably might itself be a stressful and even dangerous process, but it might lead to vigorous self-esteem and high morale in the long run, under the right conditions.

The ethnographic perspective therefore discourages the search for statistical associations between adaptation to life changes on one hand and personality traits on the other. Whether or not introspectiveness is an asset in handling widowhood, for instance, depends on what operative or potential relationships survive in the widow's milieu, what customary meanings are attached to her situation and behavior in each of those relationships, and what her practical and psychological needs are. What is even more unnerving to the ethnographer about the survey approach to personality change is that it usually takes one very restricted kind of interaction (the interview) as a yardstick for all interactions, and regards contextual variation as unimportant! The same remarks apply to the study of the relationship between stress and illness—a popular but odd preoccupation of developmental psychologists apparently based on the dubious idea that illness originates inside the physical organism, while stress originates outside. The degree of stressfulness of an event appears to the ethnographer to depend partly on the degree to which the subject attributes such qualities as uniqueness, importance, avoidability, and unpleasantness to that event. It even depends on whether he perceives it as an event at all. This perception in turn depends heavily on the shared meaning systems in which the subject participates. A concrete example is the way nisei subjects show keen discomfort when taking the TAT. In most of their ordinary interactions, introspectiveness is not valued, but intelligent performance is. Their self-conscious habit of assuming that their competence is under constant scrutiny gives them considerable trouble when they confront an unfamiliar task. At the same time, I have no doubt that the average nisei could learn in a matter of hours how to avoid excessive TAT anxiety if he perceived the usefulness of such a skill.

Attention to individual development throughout the life cycle enriches the study of cultural change in some interesting ways as well. For one thing, attention to the need for personal continuity reveals some attractive explanations for the fact that ethnic self-identification persists while outward cultural differences between contiguous groups fade. The simple ambiguity of interethnic relationships, like that of relationships between strangers, helps to explain continued ethnic self-segregation and the persistence of ethnic stereotyping. Increased personal rewards in intercultural contexts hastens the disappearance of outward cultural differences between groups, but it may also actually strengthen ethnic self-awareness by greatly increasing the importance of small differences in shared meaning systems, such as vocabularies of motive. A developmental view of cultural change also shows clearly some limitations of the unilinear and unidirectional concept of acculturation. The unilinear idea may still have some applicability when the units of analysis are whole ethnic groups or communities, but the attempt to rank individuals, small groups, or even generations within an ethnic group on a unidimensional continuum of acculturation appears futile. Psychologically, acculturation can be viewed as an adaptive strategy, and as such it is an innovative behavior that is added, tentatively at first, to existing skills and habits. Gradually new cultural material is thus woven into contextually defined role behavior. If developmental or historical processes alter the adaptive value of the new behavior, it may be dropped from the individual's repertoire. The concept of identity helps to explain the integrating role of conscious religious, political, and philosophical belief systems, as well as less conscious defensive habits, by minimizing the sense of personal disintegration and confusion that can result from living in a changing bicultural environment. Although all the subjects in this study were reasonably healthy, I have little doubt that too much diversity and discontinuity is sometimes partly responsible for problematic personality traits as well. Jack Morita's cynicism, discussed in Chapter Five, was no real cause for alarm, but it could eventually become a character defect if allowed to run wild. I believe more specific ethnographic studies of deviant identity processes in bicultural individuals are needed. Erikson's study of Gandhi (1970) is a good beginning in this direction, and I think firsthand observation of less famous individuals may reveal some widespread identity patterns—in both the mentally healthy and mentally ill—in acculturating groups. In Chapter Five I have given some examples of such patterns.

Now let us turn to the substantive findings of this study. One of the major hypotheses at the beginning was that acculturative changes in values with each succeeding generation in an immigrant group would greatly complicate relationships within families, and especially that they would create difficulties for the elderly. The study suggests that there are marked differences in life styles, values, and goals between generations in an acculturating community, that by no means all of these are a result of acculturation, and that conflicting values tend to be applied situationally in such a way that they do not often seriously disrupt intergenerational relations. The maintenance of family bonds itself remains a strong value and generally supersedes other values when the context is a family. Value differences between the generations are often perceived clearly by the actors in intergenerational relationships, with the effect of simply complicating the problems of identity maintenance. The situation brings to mind a scene from a French movie, *The Baker's Wife,* in which a priest says to a lecherous parishioner, "Don't forget, I'm your confessor!" The other answers, "Father, unless we both forget that, communication between us will be impossible." Although the elderly have to some extent lost the respect and empathy of their children because of changing values and customs (and the lack of grandparents in the issei-nisei home), few have lost material support for these reasons.

Acculturation accounts for only part of the generation gap in the Japanese American community, a large portion of it deriving from historical and developmental differences between generations that result in different interests and resources. One way to look at intergenerational conflict of this kind is to use a quasi-political model. At certain stages in their development, the generations are in competition for power within the institutions of the community. This competition was true of the issei and nisei before the war, and the problem was to some extent solved by the relocation. It is true now of the nisei and sansei, but meanwhile neither of the younger generations has any persistent power conflict with the issei, and each tends to support the issei in its own way. The nisei, for their part, seem to be gradually relinquishing their power in many community institutions to the sansei, and much of the friction between these two generations can be expected to burn itself out in the next couple of decades. The granting of greater autonomy to youth groups, mentioned in Chapter One, is an example. The presence of the resident alien Japanese in Japan Town adds an interesting complication to this picture. Their economic weight is considerable, and although they are outside the generational power struggle, they are often able to siphon off power that would otherwise belong to the nisei businessmen. One is tempted to see a certain ironic similarity between this situation and the nisei usurpation of issei power three decades ago, although the wartime situation was in no other way comparable.

Another starting hypothesis of this study was that individualism and the work ethic together make it very hard for many Americans to accept old age, and that cultures that emphasize other values should produce a different aging experience. This hypothesis is not difficult to form, looking at American culture. One sees that our moral aloofness from human weaknesses and needs was once a means of getting closer to God and later became a bitterly lonely proclamation of our personal might in a godless world. One sees how our glorification of human progress makes nature an enemy, wielding the terrible weapon of decline and death, against which youth is our only shield. It is not at all surprising, then, that the issei generally confirmed the hypothesis. But let us look at the lessons of the issei adaptation in more detail. The most important lesson from the issei is a very old one, but one that bears repeating anyhow. Life is lived in society, and for ordinary people society exacts a heavy price in self-denial in return for the conditions of a humane and peaceful old age. It is analogous to the mastery of a satisfying craft: the habit of self-discipline generally seems to improve both the craftsman and his art. Like craftsmanship, successful aging depends on the careful mastery of communicative skills. This learning process is itself arduous, but once completed, it is an avenue of self-expansion.

A second lesson is that culture is not a stamping die, turning out a narrow range of personalities that fit nicely into the jigsaw structures of society. Culture allows many strategies of aging and many possible meanings for the private conditions and events from which we construct our biographies. In any culture there are those whose appreciation of their lives leads to an anxious and forlorn old age and those whom we might call successful agers. It helps greatly, I think, to understand this fact thoroughly. The struggle to wrest meaning from life is never final until our last breath, and this very endlessness may be (as Kafka would have it) the meaning we seek.

A third lesson is that history is a gigantic obstacle to an applied developmental psychology based on long term predictions about values and social conditions conducive to health in late life. If the issei's children had grown up Japanese, as their parents often wished, perhaps they would still be scraping out a sour living in ethnic ghettos. If the war had not happened the way it did, when it did, most issei would probably be growing old in Japan, where a dramatic upsurge in the life span has created a new "problem population" of old people who are idle, lonely, and poor. If Japan had not reemerged as a world superpower in the last decade, showing pride in their national culture would not be nearly so easy for the issei. If immigration had not been cut off when it was, the issei might have melted into the ethnic landscape and lost their identity as a generation. The adaptive skills we now see in issei personality might be badly suited to a different historical niche.

A fourth lesson is that being part of a minority itself might have some large benefits for the aged. The issei are few in number. In any West Coast city (except Los Angeles) most issei are likely to know each other at least by reputation if not by sight. They are a little community unto themselves, tightly bound by the sharing of a unique identity. To be a member of this group may not guarantee the friendship of other members, but to some extent it guarantees their understanding. It means the sharing of a set of beliefs and practices that have now largely vanished from the earth. It means the sharing of a series of unique, unforgettable memories. Between issei, a word or a gesture can convey meanings that volumes could not convey to anyone else—even to most nisei. Perhaps there have been times in human history, before medicine ensured that many would live to old age, when grey heads were rare enough that their meeting signified mutual recognition and support. Almost certainly, the technology that creates a vast class of elderly and keeps reminding them of their anonymity does not make aging any easier.

Bibliography

Alker, H. A. "Is Personality Situationally Specific or Intrapsy-
    chically Consistent?" *Journal of Personality,* 1972, *40*
    (1), 1-16.
Allport, G. W. *Personality: A Psychological Interpretation.* New
    York: Holt, Rinehart, and Winston, 1937.
Arendt, H. "Truth and Politics." *New Yorker,* Feb. 25, 1967.
Barnouw, V. "Acculturation and Personality Among the Wis-
    consin Chippewa." *Memoirs of the American Anthropo-
    logical Association,* 1950, No. 72.
Barth, F. (Ed.) *Ethnic Groups and Boundaries.* Boston: Little,
    Brown, 1969.

Barth, F. "Analytical Dimensions in the Comparison of Social Organizations." *American Anthropologist,* 1972, *74* (1-2), 207-220.

Bateson, G. Comment on "The Comparative Study of Culture and the Purposive Cultivation of Democratic Values" by M. Mead. In L. Bryson (Ed.), *Science, Philosophy, and Religion: Second Symposium.* New York: Conference on Science, Philosophy, and Religion, 1942.

Bateson, G. *Steps to an Ecology of Mind.* New York: Ballantine, 1972.

Beals, R. "Acculturation." In S. Tax (Ed.), *Anthropology Today.* Chicago: University of Chicago Press, 1962.

Beardsley, R. K., Hall, J. W., and Ward, R. E. *Village Japan.* Chicago: University of Chicago Press, 1959.

Becker, H. S. "Becoming a Marihuana User." *American Journal of Sociology,* 1953, *59,* 235-242.

Becker, H. S. "Notes on the Concept of Commitment." *American Journal of Sociology,* 1960, *66* (1), 32-40.

Befu, H. "Corporate Emphasis and Patterns of Descent in the Japanese Family." In R. J. Smith and R. K. Beardsley (Eds.), *Japanese Culture: Its Development and Characteristics.* New York: Viking, 1962. Also published in *Anthropology,* 1962, No. 34, 34-42.

Benedict, R. *Patterns of Culture.* New York: Random House, 1934.

Benedict, R. *The Chrysanthemum and the Sword.* Boston: Houghton Mifflin, 1946.

Berger, P. *Invitation to Sociology.* Garden City, N.Y.: Doubleday, 1963.

Berkowitz, L. "The Case for Bottling Up Rage." *Psychology Today,* 1973, 7 (2), 24-31.

Berne, E. *Games People Play.* New York: Grove, 1964.

Berreman, G. "Aleut Reference Group Alienation, Mobility, and Acculturation." *American Anthropologist,* 1964, *64* (2), 231-250.

Berreman, G. "Self Concept and Escape from Stigmatized Ethnicity." Paper presented at the annual meeting of the American Anthropological Association, Nov. 19, 1971.

Bettelheim, B. "Individual and Mass Behavior in Extreme Situations." *Journal of Abnormal and Social Psychology*, 1943, *38*, 417-452.

Blumer, H. *Symbolic Interactionism: Perspective and Method.* Englewood Cliffs, N.J.: Prentice-Hall, 1969.

Bosworth, A. R. *America's Concentration Camps.* New York: Norton, 1967.

Broom, L., and Kituse, J. I. *The Managed Casualty—The Japanese American Family in World War II.* Berkeley: University of California Press, 1956.

Broom, L., and Rimer, R. *Removal and Return: The Socioeconomic Effects of the War on Japanese Americans.* Berkeley: University of California Press, 1949.

Brown, F. J., and Roucek, J. S. (Eds.) *One America.* Englewood Cliffs, N.J.: Prentice-Hall, 1945.

Campbell, J. *The Masks of God: Creative Mythology.* New York: Viking, 1968.

Cassirer, E. *An Essay on Man.* New Haven and London: Yale University Press, 1944.

Caudill, W. "Japanese American Personality and Acculturation." *Genetic Psychology Monographs*, 1952, No. 45, 3-102.

Caudill, W., and DeVos, G. "Achievement, Culture, and Personality—The Case of the Japanese Americans." *American Anthropologist*, 1956, *58*, 1102-1127.

Caudill, W., and Scarr, H. A. "Japanese Value Orientations and Culture Change." *Ethnology*, 1962, *1* (1), 53-91.

Caudill, W., and Weinstein, H. "Maternal Care and Infant Behavior in Japan and America." *Psychiatry*, 1969, *32* (1), 12-43.

Chance, N. A. "Acculturation, Self-Identification, and Personality Adjustment." *American Anthropologist*, 1965, *67* (2), 372-393.

Chrisman, N. "Ethnic Identity Among Working-Class Whites." Paper presented at the annual meeting of the American Anthropological Association, Nov. 19, 1971.

Clark, M. M. "The Anthropology of Aging, a New Area for Studies of Culture and Personality." *The Gerontologist*, 1967, *7* (1), 55-64.

Clark, M. M. "Contributions of Cultural Anthropology to the

Study of the Aged." In L. Nader and T. W. Maretzki (Eds.), *Cultural Illness and Health*. Washington, D.C.: American Anthropological Association, 1973.

Clark, M. M., and Anderson, B. G. *Culture and Aging: An Anthropological Study of Older Americans*. Springfield, Ill.: Thomas, 1967.

Clark, M. M., and Pierce, R. C. "Acculturation Types." Paper presented at the annual meeting of the Society for Applied Anthropology, Apr. 12, 1973.

Cohen, E. *Human Behavior in the Concentration Camp*. New York: Norton, 1953.

Cumming, E., and Henry, W. E. *Growing Old: The Process of Disengagement*. New York: Basic, 1961.

Doi, T. *The Anatomy of Dependence*. Tokyo: Kodansha, 1973.

Dore, R. P. *City Life in Japan*. Berkeley: University of California Press, 1958.

Eidheim, H. "When Ethnic Identity Is a Social Stigma." In F. Barth (Ed.), *Ethnic Groups and Boundaries*. Boston: Little, Brown, 1969.

Eisely, L. *The Unexpected Universe*. New York: Harcourt Brace Jovanovich, 1964.

Embree, J. F. *Suye Mura: A Japanese Village*. Chicago: University of Chicago Press, 1939.

Embree, J. F. "Acculturation Among the Japanese of Kona, Hawaii." *Memoirs of the American Anthropological Association*, 1941, No. 59.

Erikson, E. H. *Childhood and Society* (Rev. Ed.). New York: Norton, 1963.

Erikson, E. H. *Gandhi's Truth*. New York: Norton, 1969.

Frenkel-Brunswik, E. "Adjustment and Reorientation in the Course of the Life Span." In B. L. Neugarten (Ed.), *Middle Age and Aging*. Chicago: University of Chicago Press, 1964.

Freud, S. *Totem and Taboo*. New York: Moffat, Yard, 1918.

Freud, S. *Group Psychology and the Analysis of the Ego*. London: Hogarth, 1948. Originally published 1921.

Gans, H. J. *The Urban Villagers*. New York: Free Press, 1962.

Gergen, K. J. "The Healthy, Happy Human Being Wears Many Masks." *Psychology Today*, 1972, 5 (12), 31ff.

Girdner, A., and Loftis, A. *The Great Betrayal.* New York: Macmillan, 1969.

Gluckman, M. "Tribalism in Modern British Central Africa." *Cahiers d'Etudes Africaines,* 1960, No. 1, 55ff.

Goffman, E. *The Presentation of Self in Everyday Life.* Garden City, N.Y.: Doubleday, 1959.

Goffman, E. *Asylums.* Garden City, N.Y.: Doubleday, 1961.

Goffman, E. *Stigma.* Englewood Cliffs, N.J.: Prentice-Hall, 1963.

Green, V. "Situational Change and Selection Versus Assimilation in Understanding Multi-Ethnic Societies." Paper presented at the annual meeting of the American Anthropological Association, Nov. 19, 1971.

Grodzins, M. *Americans Betrayed, Politics and the Japanese Evacuation.* Chicago: University of Chicago Press, 1949.

Gutmann, D. L. "The Country of Old Men: Cross-Cultural Studies in the Psychology of Later Life." *Occasional Papers in Gerontology,* No. 5, April 1969.

Hallowell, A. I. "Acculturation Processes and Personality Changes as Indicated by the Rorschach Technique." *Rorschach Research Exchange,* 1942, *6,* 42-50.

Hallowell, A. I. "Personality Structure and the Evolution of Man." In *Culture and Experience.* Philadelphia: University of Pennsylvania Press, 1955. Originally published 1949.

Hallowell, A. I. "Values, Acculturation, and Mental Health." *American Journal of Orthopsychiatry,* 1950, *20,* 732-743.

Hallowell, A. I. "Acculturation and the Personality of the Ojibwa." *Journal of Projective Techniques,* 1951, *15* (1), 27-44.

Hallowell, A. I. "Ojibwa Personality and Acculturation." In S. Tax (Ed.), *Acculturation in the Americas.* Chicago: University of Chicago Press, 1952.

Hannerz, U. *Soul Side: Inquiries into Ghetto Culture and Community.* New York: Columbia University Press, 1969.

Hansen, M. L. "The Third Generation in America." *Commentary,* 1952, *14,* 492-500.

Henry, J. *Culture Against Man.* New York: Random House, 1963.

Horinouchi, I. "Educational Values and Preadaptation in the Acculturation of Japanese Americans." Sacramento, Calif.: Sacramento Anthropological Society, Sacramento State College, 1967.

Hosokawa, W. *Nisei: The Quiet Americans.* Englewood Cliffs, N.J.: Prentice-Hall, 1969.

Hsu, F. L. K. "American Core Value and National Character." In F. L. K. Hsu (Ed.), *Psychological Anthropology.* Homewood, Ill.: Dorsey, 1961.

Ichihashi, Y. *The Japanese in the United States.* Stanford, Calif.: Stanford University Press, 1932.

Jung, C. G. *Seeleprobleme der Gegenwart.* Zurich: Rascher, 1931.

Kardiner, A., Linton, R., Du Bois, C., West, J. *The Psychological Frontiers of Society.* New York: Columbia University Press, 1945.

Kiefer, C. W. *Personality and Social Change in a Japanese Danchi.* Unpublished doctoral dissertation, University of California, Berkeley, 1968.

Kiefer, C. W. "The Psychological Interdependence of Family, School, and Bureaucracy in Japan." *American Anthropologist,* 1970, *72* (1), 66-75.

Kiefer, C. W. "Notes on Anthropology and the Minority Elderly." *The Gerontologist,* 1971, *11* (1, Pt. 2), 94-98.

Kiefer, C. W. "Loneliness in Japan." San Francisco: University of California, Human Development Program, 1972. Mimeographed.

Kitagawa, D. *Issei and Nisei: The Internment Years.* New York: Seabury, 1967.

Kitano, H. H. L. *Japanese Americans: The Evolution of a Subculture.* Englewood Cliffs, N.J.: Prentice-Hall, 1968.

Kluckhohn, C. K. M. *Mirror for Man.* New York: McGraw-Hill, 1949.

Koyama, T. "Changing Family Structure in Japan." In R. J. Smith and R. Beardsley (Eds.), *Japanese Culture: Its Development and Characteristics.* Chicago: Aldine, 1962.

Laing, R. D. *The Politics of Experience.* New York: Ballantine, 1967.

Laing, R. D., and Esterson, A. *Sanity, Madness, and the Family.* London: Tavistock, 1964.

Lebra, T. "Acculturation Dilemma: The Function of Japanese Moral Values for Americanization." *Council on Anthropology and Education Newsletter,* 1972, *3* (1), 6-13.

Leighton, A. H. *The Governing of Men.* Princeton, N.J.: Princeton University Press, 1945.

Levy, M. J., Jr. *The Structure of Society.* Princeton, N.J.: Princeton University Press, 1952.

Linton, R. *The Study of Man.* New York: Appleton-Century-Crofts, 1936.

Lowenthal, M. F., Berkman, P. L., and Associates. *Aging and Mental Disorder in San Francisco: A Social Psychiatric Study.* San Francisco: Jossey-Bass, 1967.

Lyman, S. M. "Generation and Character: The Case of the Japanese Americans." Reno: University of Nevada, n.d.

Lyman, S. M. "Japanese American Generation Gap." *Society,* 1973, *10* (2), 55-63.

McFee, M. "The 150% Man, a Product of Blackfoot Acculturation." *American Anthropologist,* 1968, *70* (6), 1096-1103.

McLuhan, M. *Understanding Media: The Extensions of Man.* New York: McGraw-Hill, 1965.

McWilliams, C. *Prejudice—Japanese Americans: Symbol of Racial Intolerance.* Boston: Little, Brown, 1964.

Marui, F. "Studies on the T.A.T.—Studies of Standard Responses to the Japanese Edition and Their Clinical Application." ("T.A.T. ni kan-suru Kenkyū—Nihonban no Hyōjun Hannō no Kenkyū to sono Rinshōteki Ōyō"). *Psychiatria et Neurologica Japonica,* 1958, *61* (13), 1767-1834.

Matsumoto, G., Meredith, G., Masuda, M. "Ethnic Identification: Honolulu and Seattle Japanese-Americans." *Journal of Cross-Cultural Psychology,* 1970, *1* (1), 63-76.

May, R., Angel, E., and Ellenberger, H. F. *Existence: A New Dimension in Psychiatry and Psychology.* New York: Basic, 1958.

Mayer, P. "Migrancy and the Study of Africans in Towns." *American Anthropologist,* 1962, *64* (3, Pt. 1), 576-592.

Maykovich, M. K. *Japanese American Identity Dilemma.* Tokyo: Waseda University Press, 1972.

Mead, M. *New Lives for Old.* New York: Morrow, 1956.

Meyerhoff, H. *Time in Literature.* Berkeley and Los Angeles: University of California Press, 1955.

Mills, C. W. "Situated Actions and Vocabularies of Motive." In J. G. Manis and B. N. Meltzer (Eds.), *Symbolic Interaction: A Reader in Social Psychology.* Boston: Allyn and Bacon, 1972. Originally published 1940.

Mills, C. W. *The Sociological Imagination.* New York: Grove, 1959.

Miyamoto, S. F. "Social Solidarity Among the Japanese in Seattle." *University of Washington Publications in the Social Sciences,* 1939, *11* (2), 57-130.

Moberg, D. O. "Religiosity in Old Age." *The Gerontologist,* 1965, *5* (2), 78-87.

Modell, J. "Class or Ethnic Solidarity: The Japanese American Company Union." Paper presented at the annual meeting of the Pacific Coast branch of the American Historical Association, Aug. 28, 1968.

Modell, J. "Socio-Cultural Adaptation of Issei Immigrants to the Mainland United States." Paper delivered at the annual meeting of the American Anthropological Association, Nov. 20, 1970.

Morioka, K. "Life Cycle Patterns in Japan, China, and the United States." Paper presented at the World Congress of Sociology, 1966.

Morsbach, H. "Aspects of Non-Verbal Communication in Japan." Glasgow: Department of Psychology, University of Glasgow, 1972.

Moynihan, D. P. *The Negro Family: The Case for National Action.* Washington, D.C.: Department of Labor, 1965.

Murray, H. A., and Kluckhohn, C. K. M. "Outline of a Conception of Personality." In C. K. M. Kluckhohn and H. A. Murray (Eds.), *Personality in Nature, Society and Culture.* New York: Knopf, 1962.

Neugarten, B. L. "Summary and Implications." In B. L. Neugarten (Ed.), *Personality in Middle and Late Life.* Chicago: Aldine-Atherton, 1964.

Nietzsche, F. *Thus Spoke Zarathustra.* W. Kaufman, trans. New York: Viking, 1954.

Norbeck, E. "Age-Grading in Japan." *American Anthropologist,* 1953, *55,* 373-384.

Omatsu, G. "Buddhist Church." *Hokubei Mainichi,* Jan. 10, 1973, p. 1.

Parsons, T. *The Social System.* New York: Free Press, 1951.

Pierce, R. C., Clark, M., Kiefer, C. W. "A 'Bootstrap' Scaling Technique." *Human Organization,* 1973, *31* (4), 403-410.

Plath, D. W. "Where the Family of God Is the Family: The Role of the Dead in Japanese Households." *American Anthropologist,* 1964a, *66* (2), 300-317.

Plath, D. W. *The After Hours.* Berkeley: University of California Press, 1964b.

Plath, D. W. "Japan: The After Years." In D. O. Cowgill and L. D. Holmes (Eds.), *Aging and Modernization.* New York: Appleton-Century-Crofts, 1972.

Plath, D. W. "Cares of Career, and Careers of Caretaking." *Journal of Nervous and Mental Disease,* 1973, *157* (5), 346-357.

Polanyi, M. *Personal Knowledge: Towards a Post-Critical Philosophy.* Chicago: University of Chicago Press, 1958.

Redfield, R. *The Little Community and Peasant Society and Culture.* Chicago: University of Chicago Press, 1956.

Redfield, R., and Singer, M. B. *The Cultural Role of Cities.* In R. Sennet (Ed.), *Classic Essays on the Culture of Cities.* New York: Appleton-Century-Crofts, 1969. Originally published 1954.

Reich, C. A. *The Greening of America.* New York: Random House, 1970.

Rogers, C. "On Learning To Be Free." In S. Farber and R. Wilson (Eds.), *Conflict and Creativity.* New York: McGraw-Hill, 1963.

Rosow, I. *Social Integration of the Aged.* New York: Free Press, 1967.

Sapir, E. "Language and Environment." *American Anthropologist,* 1912, *14,* 226-242.

Sapir, E. "Culture, Genuine and Spurious." *The Dalhousie Review,* 1922, *2,* 165-178.

Schatzman, L., and Strauss, A. "Social Class and Modes of Communication." *American Journal of Sociology,* 1955, *60* (4), 329-338.

Schuetz, A. "The Stranger: An Essay in Social Psychology." In M. Stein, A. K. Vidich, and D. M. White (Eds.), *Identity and Anxiety.* New York: Free Press, 1960. Originally published 1944.

Seeley, J. R. "Social Science? Some Probative Problems." In M. Stein and A. Vidich (Eds.), *Sociology on Trial.* Englewood Cliffs, N.J.: Prentice-Hall, 1963.

Shanas, E., Townsend, P., Wedderburn, D., Friis, H., Milhøj, P., Stehouwer, S. *Old People in Three Industrial Societies.* Chicago: Aldine-Atherton, 1968.

Simmel, G. "The Number of Members as Determining the Sociological Form of the Group." A. W. Small, trans. *American Journal of Sociology,* 1902, *8,* 1-46, 158-196.

Simmel, G. "The Metropolis and Mental Life." In R. Sennet (Ed.), *Classic Essays on the Culture of Cities.* New York: Appleton-Century-Crofts, 1969. Originally published 1902-1903.

Simmel, G. "The Stranger." In K. H. Wolff (Ed.), *The Sociology of George Simmel.* Chicago: University of Chicago Press, 1950. Originally published 1908.

Simpson, G. E., and Yinger, J. M. *Racial and Cultural Minorities* (3rd Ed.). New York: Harper and Row, 1965.

Smith, B. *Americans from Japan.* Philadelphia: Lippincott, 1948.

Smith, R. J. "Kurusu, a Japanese Agricultural Community." In University of Michigan Center for Japanese Studies, *Occasional Papers.* Ann Arbor, 1956.

Sone, M. *Nisei Daughter.* Boston: Little, Brown, 1953.

Spence, D. L., and Lonner, T. D. "The Empty Nest: A Transition Within Motherhood." *The Family Coordinator,* 1971, *20* (4), 359-376.

Spindler, G. D. "Personality and Peyotism in Menomini Indian Acculturation." *Psychiatry,* 1952, *15,* 151-159.

Spindler, L. S. *Menomini Women and Culture Change. Memoirs of the American Anthropological Association,* 1962, No. 91.

Spiro, M. E. "Culture and Personality: The Natural History of a False Dichotomy." *Psychiatry*, 1951, *14*, 19-46.

Spradley, J. P. *You Owe Yourself a Drunk: An Ethnography of Urban Nomads*. Boston: Little, Brown, 1970.

Strauss, A. L. *Mirrors and Masks: The Search for Identity*. New York: Free Press, 1959.

Strong, E. K. *The Second Generation Japanese Problem*. Stanford, Calif.: Stanford University Press, 1934.

Tebbets, R. "Japanese-Americans: In a No-Man's Land Between Two Giants." *Hokubei Mainichi*, Jan. 7, 1974, p. 1.

ten Broek, J., Barnhart, E. N., Matson, F. W. *Prejudice, War and the Constitution*. Berkeley: University of California Press, 1954.

Thomas, D. S., and Nishimoto, R. *The Spoilage*. Berkeley: University of California Press, 1946.

Thompson, W. I. *At the Edge of History*. New York: Harper and Row, 1971.

Toffler, A. *Future Shock*. New York: Random House, 1970.

Tsurumi, K. *Social Change and the Individual: Japan Before and After Defeat in World War II*. Princeton, N.J.: Princeton University Press, 1970.

Turner, V. W. *The Ritual Process: Structure and Anti-Structure*. Chicago: Aldine, 1969.

Valentine, C. A. *Culture and Poverty: Critique and Counter-Proposals*. Chicago and London: University of Chicago Press, 1968.

Wallace, A. F. C. Comment on "Enculturation—A Reconsideration" by N. Shimahara. *Current Anthropology*, 1970, *11* (2), 152.

Washburn, S. L., and Harding, R. S. "Evolution and Primate Behavior." In F. O. Schmitt (Ed.), *The Neurosciences: Second Study Program*. New York: Rockefeller University Press, 1970.

Wilson, G., and Wilson, M. *The Analysis of Social Change*. Cambridge: Cambridge University Press, 1945.

Wittgenstein, L. *The Blue and Brown Books: Preliminary Studies for the Philosophical Investigations*. New York: Harper and Row, 1958.

Yamamoto, M. "Cultural Conflicts and Accommodations of

the First and Second Generation Japanese." *Social Process in Hawaii*, 1938, *4*, 40-48.

Youmans, G. "Some Perspectives on Disengagement Theory." *The Gerontologist*, 1969, *9* (4, Pt. 1), 254-258.

Index

Author Index

251

Subject Index

Respondents' pseudonyms are indicated by asterisks.